I0085110

Identification of Ancient Olive Oil Processing Methods Based on Olive Remains

Peter Warnock

BAR International Series 1635
2007

Published in 2016 by
BAR Publishing, Oxford

BAR International Series 1635

Identification of Ancient Olive Oil Processing Methods Based on Olive Remains

ISBN 978 1 4073 0049 8

© P Warnock and the Publisher 2007

The author's moral rights under the 1988 UK Copyright,
Designs and Patents Act are hereby expressly asserted.

All rights reserved. No part of this work may be copied, reproduced, stored,
sold, distributed, scanned, saved in any form of digital format or transmitted
in any form digitally, without the written permission of the Publisher.

BAR Publishing is the trading name of British Archaeological Reports (Oxford) Ltd.
British Archaeological Reports was first incorporated in 1974 to publish the BAR
Series, International and British. In 1992 Hadrian Books Ltd became part of the BAR
group. This volume was originally published by Archaeopress in conjunction with
British Archaeological Reports (Oxford) Ltd / Hadrian Books Ltd, the Series principal
publisher, in 2007. This present volume is published by BAR Publishing, 2016.

Printed in England

BAR
PUBLISHING

BAR titles are available from:

BAR Publishing
122 Banbury Rd, Oxford, OX2 7BP, UK
EMAIL   info@barpublishing.com
PHONE   +44 (0)1865 310431
FAX   +44 (0)1865 316916
www.barpublishing.com

CONTENTS

LIST OF TABLES

LIST OF FIGURES

ACKNOWLEDGMENTS

This has been a long journey, and I must thank a great many people for their assistance, support and patience. First of all, I would like to thank my committee members for their support and patience over these many years, Dr. Lisa Sattenspiel, Dr. Kathleen Slane, Dr. Ralph Rowlett, and Dr. Karl Reinhard. I would especially like to thank my advisor, Dr. Deborah Pearsall, for the support and great deal of patience in guiding me through this.

There are too many people to list in the Hashemite Kingdom of Jordan who contributed to this work, and I would extend my thanks to all of them for their hospitality and aid. I would especially thank a number of people from the Ministry of Agriculture; Nawaf Fandi, Sami Friahat, Ali Friahat, and most of all Kamal Nuimat and Ali Abu Zurayk.

The staff at the American Center of Oriental Research (ACOR) in Amman, Jordan, who put up with the smell of charring olives and other such nonsense while I was working on my ethnographic and experimental research there. Pierre and Patricia Bikai, Kathy Nimri, Abed Adawi and everyone else gave aid and assistance along with good-natured ribbing and kept me going.

Many friends and colleagues in Israel also helped during the ethnographic and experimental research; Sam Wolff, Rafi Frankel, David Eitam, and Etan Ayalon. And to the Israel Olive Oil Museum at Shemen Industries in Haifa, where I performed several of the experimental crushing methods. Ehud Galili, Jacob Sharvit and the rest of the people at the Nautical division of the Israel Antiquities Authority for their participation with the archaeological samples.

Thanks to Oded Borowski for his comments and suggestions, and to the many colleagues in the paleoethnobotanical community who offered information and suggestions.

Bob Visalli and Bill Grimm for their help with the photographs. Dr. Mark Ellersieck for his help with the statistics. Anthropology Dept. staff Gail Lawrence and Mary Porter for their support and taking care of all my paperwork all these years.

The Episcopal Home for permission to use photographs from the Matson Collection in my research.

Finally, to my family, for their constant support even if they didn't really understand what I was doing. Sister Peggy, brother Tobin and my mother, Phyllis Sikkinga, who wondered if I'd ever finish. Thanks.

CHAPTER 1

INTRODUCTION

1.1 Introduction

The thesis presented here is that it is possible to determine the method of olive oil processing based on recovered archaeological olive remains. This research focuses on the complex issue of olive oil processing and the resulting technological changes associated with the olive oil industry during this industry's expansion from a small scale domestic to large scale industrial technology during the Chalcolithic through Iron Ages (≈ 4,300–586 B.C.) in Syro-Palestine (Figure 1.1). The ultimate goal was to see if the level or type of olive oil technology used at sites can be determined based on their olive remains. However, before this could occur, a methodology for doing these studies needed to be organized. The methodological component included: 1) an ethnographic study investigating how traditional oil pressing and processing affect olive remains, and the incorporation of those remains into the archaeological record, and 2) experimental studies to determine how different processing methods might affect olive remains and their incorporation into the archaeological record. The results from the experimental and ethnographic studies were then applied to archaeological remains from a Late Neolithic site to determine the possible type of processing technology. The type of processing indicated by the comparison of the experimental to the archaeological remains, crushing in a small basin, matches the olive oil processing artifacts and features found at the site. The methods used in this study can be applied to other paleoethnobotanical remains and technologies.

1.2 Background

The importance of the olive and olive oil in antiquity may not be fully appreciated in modern times. *"Olea quae prima omnium arborum est"*: the olive is first among all the trees (Columella, *De Re Rustica: De Arboribus* 5.8.1). Since antiquity the olive and olive oil was one of the most versatile plant resources available to Mediterranean cultures. The olive was one of the most important food and commercial crops of the ancient Near East (Avitsur, 1994; Ayalon, 1994b; Frankel, 1994; Liphschitz *et al*, 1991; Romero, 1998; Singer, 1996; Zohary, 1986; Zohary and Hopf, 2000; Zohary and Spiegel-Roy, 1975). "In ancient times, olive fruit in Israel was a necessary commodity for man's survival" (Heltzer and Eitam, 1996:1). While the olive fruit was an ancient food staple and olive wood had its uses, it was olive oil that was the olive tree's main contribution to ancient life.

The olive and its oil not only played an important role in the dietary and economic history of the Mediterranean region, they were an integral part of culture, language, religion, literature, art, customs and folklore of the many

Pre-Pottery Neolithic A	*c.*	8500–7500 B.C.E.
Pre-Pottery Neolithic B		7500–6000 B.C.E.
Pottery Neolithic A		6000–5000 B.C.E.
Pottery Neolithic B		5000–4300 B.C.E.
Chalcolithic		4300–3300 B.C.E.
Early Bronze I		3300–3050 B.C.E.
Early Bronze II - III		3050–2300 B.C.E.
Early Bronze V / Middle Bronze I		2300–2000 B.C.E.
Middle Bronze IIA		2000–1800/1750 B.C.E.
Middle Bronze II B - C		1800/1750–1550 B.C.E.
Late Bronze I		1550–1400 B.C.E.
Late Bronze II A - B		1400–1200 B.C.E.
Iron IA		1200–1150 B.C.E.
Iron IB		1150–1000 B.C.E.
Iron IIA		1000–925 B.C.E.
Iron IIB		925–720 B.C.E.
Iron IIC		720–586 B.C.E.

FIGURE 1.1: ARCHAEOLOGICAL PERIODS OF SYRO-PALESTINE (NEOLITHIC UNTIL IRON AGE), FROM MAZAR (1990, PP. 30).

Mediterranean nations through the ages (Frankel, 1999). Pliny considered olive oil to be a necessity (*Natural History* 14.29.150). Olive oil was considerably more important to daily life in antiquity than petroleum is today (Rosenblum, 1996), indeed, it was the petroleum of antiquity and touched almost every aspect of ancient life in some manner (Klein, 1994; Mattingly, 1996; Rogers, 1995; Sandy, 1989; Toussaint-Samat, 1992). Olive oil was highly valued in antiquity for a wide variety of purposes. It was an important dietary commodity, a main lighting fuel source, used in religious ceremonies, uses in crafts and industry, and of primary commercial importance as a major component of perfumes, unguents, and body oils.

Olive oil was a major part of the ancient diet (Avitsur, 1994; Frankel, 1997; 1999; Heltzer and Eitam, 1996; Mattingly, 1996; Sandy, 1989; Tzedakis and Martlew, 1999), not only for eating, but also cooking and serving foods (J. Frankel, 1996; Klein, 1994). Olive oil was an important main source of fats and calories to the ancient diet (Forbes, 1965; Melena, 1983; Zisling, 2000), and sometimes was the only source of fats available: "Olive oil probably provided one-third the caloric content of a peasant (largely cereal-based) diet in such areas as Italy and Greece," (Tyree and Stefanoudaki, 1996:171). Olive oil is considered the best of the edible vegetable oils (Singer, 1996), and could be produced in greater quantities than other oils, such as linseed and sesame, used for similar purposes (Tyree and Stefanoudaki, 1996). Since many ancient peoples, especially the poor, subsisted solely on bread and oil, olive oil was considered more valuable than gold in times of drought, war and siege (Singer, 1996).

As the "petroleum" of antiquity, olive oil served as the main fuel source for illumination (Avitsur, 1994; Blitzer, 1993; J. Frankel, 1996; Frankel, 1997; 1999; Heltzer and Eitam, 1996; Klein, 1994; Mattingly, 1996; Melena, 1983; Sandy, 1989; Tyree and Stefanoudaki, 1996; Tzedakis and Martlew, 1999; Zisling, 2000). One reason for this was that "It also burned without producing a bad odor as animal fat or castor oil did," (Tyree and Stefanoudaki, 1996:171). Mattingly (1996) suggests that ancient Rome with a population of 1 million would need nearly 3 million liters of olive oil a year for lamp lighting alone. The "pure oil of crushed olives" was used as temple lamp fuel in ancient Israel (Stager and Wolff, 1981).

While olive oil had everyday importance in everyday life and the economy, it also had an important symbolic and ritualistic function (David, 2000; Dolamore, 1994; J. Frankel, 1996; Frankel, 1997; 1999; Heltzer and Eitam, 1996; Klein, 1994; Mattingly, 1996; Ridgeway, 1996; Sandy, 1989; Stager and Wolff, 1981; Vickery, 1936; Weinfeld, 1996; Zisling, 2000). Perfumed oils were used since early antiquity in the Near East for liturgical purposes (Brun, 2000). Olive oil played a part in many ceremonies: the Bible contains numerous references to ritual anointing of kings (1 Sam. 16:1-13, 2 Kings 9:1-3) and priests (Ex. 29:7, Ex. 30:30-31), lighting the eternal lamp (*ner tamid*) (Ex. 27:20), sanctifying stelae (Gn. 28:18, 35:14) and the holy tabernacle and its contents (Ex. 30:23-30, 40:9). Sacred oil was also used in purification ceremonies (Lv. 12-32), a use mentioned in Hittite sources (Frankel, 1997). Olive oil could be used as a charitable donation or as an offering (Gen. 28:18; 35:14; Ex. 29:40; Num. 28:5), and

SITE	PERIOD
Abu Hamid	Chalcolithic
Teleilat Ghassul	Chalcolithic
Tell esh Shuna North	Chalcolithic
Zeragun	Early Bronze I, II
Tell el-Hayyat	Early Bronze II, III
Tell el-Hayyat	Middle Bronze V
Abu Thawwab	Early Bronze I
Khirbet Iskander	Early Bronze
Bab dh-Dhra	Early Bronze II – IV
Numeria	Early Bronze III
Deir 'Alla	Late Bronze
Tell Irbid	Late Bronze/Early Iron
Deir 'Alla	Early Iron
Mazar	Early Iron
Deir 'Alla	8-5th century B.C.
Deir 'Alla	7-5th century B.C.
Mazar	6-4th century B.C.
Mughayir	5-4th century B.C.
Udruh	Nabatean
Udruh	Roman
Jerash	Roman to Umayyad

FIGURE 1.2: JORDANIAN SITES CONTAINING OLIVE STONE REMAINS (FROM NEEF, 1990).

if you couldn't get to a shrine you could send olive oil (J. Frankel, 1996). Ritual meal offerings were also made using olive oil (Dolamore, 1994; Weinfeld, 1996).

Olive oil also had uses in crafts and industry. It was used in painting (J. Frankel, 1996) and in the lubrication and preservation of tools and leather (Avitsur, 1994; Cato, *De Re Rustica* 97). Olive oil may have been used to preserve and waterproof water bag skins, oiling the skins to keep them supple and prevent cracking. Cato details a large number of uses for the "amurca," the oily waste water separated from the olive oil after pressing, from protecting sheep from scab to cleaning copper vessels (Cato, *De Re Rustica* 91-103; 128-130). Mycenaean tablets point to possible industrial uses of olive oil in tanning and textile processing (Melena, 1983). Haldane (1990) states that in the Late Bronze period ($\approx$ 1,550–1,200 B.C.) olive oil was used primarily in industries including manufacturing textiles. In textile processing olive oil may have been used in at least two stages: one as a detergent in finishing and fulling, and second, in the oiling of warp and weft threads in order to ease weaving, possibly in linen fabrics. The multitude of olive oil's uses made it a highly valued trade item. The oil was not the only product of olive oil pressing that had value. Wastes from olive oil pressing also had a number of uses, both the solid pressing waste ("*jift*" in Arabic, "*gefet*" in Hebrew) and the oily water ("*amurca*" or "*lees*") separated from the oil during pressing (Cato; Columella). Traditional uses of the *jift* will be covered in the ethnographic research chapter.

Olive oil also played an important role in health, sport and beauty in antiquity. One of olive oil's major uses in antiquity was as the main ingredient and base in body care products such as medicinal ointments and unguents, soaps, bath oil, skin oil and moisturizers, and especially perfumes and cosmetics (Brun, 2000; J. Frankel, 1996; Frankel, 1999; Heltzer and Eitam, 1996; Klein, 1994; Mattingly, 1996; Melena, 1983; Sandy, 1989; Tyree and Stefanoudaki, 1996; Tzedakis and Martlew, 1999; Zisling, 2000).

The use of olive oil as a base for perfumes and unguents is well noted in Mesopotamia, Egypt and Hittite references (Brun, 2000; Frankel, 1997; 1999) and in the Bible (Ps. 113:2, 141:5, Eccl. 9:8, Mi. 6:15). Mycenaean Greek Linear B tablets refer more frequently to wild olives than cultivated ones, and that oil from wild olives was preferred for perfumes (Melena, 1983). Olive oil-based perfumes were produced and used in Palestine as early as the 14th century B.C. (Brun, 2000). Access to Arabian aromatics and local products, like Judean balsam oil, helped keep Palestine a perfume producing region throughout its history (Brun, 2000). During the second millennium B.C. olive oil became the most common perfume base in Mesopotamia and Egypt, as it was more easily produced than the commonly used base oils, such as ben and sesame (Brun, 2000). Green olive oil, from earlier unripe olives, seems to be preferred for perfume, though the highest quality oil was recommended for use in perfumes. During

the Late Bronze period ($\approx$ 1,550–1,200 B.C.) olive oil was primarily used as a raw material in textile, soap, and perfume industries (Haldane, 1990). The greater use of olive oil as a perfume base coincides with advances in processing technology during this period, suggesting that the commercial perfume industry spurred on technological development. Large scale olive cultivation on Delos around the time of Athenian domination appears to be a response to a growing demand for olive oil for food, lamps and perfumes. Perfume use becomes quite common beginning in the sixth century (Brun, 2000), especially in Greece and later, in Rome. Common perfumes were produced on a large scale during the Roman period, using a base from green olives mixed with such plants as iris, saffron and rose. The common use of perfumed oil led to large scale manufacturing characterized by larger, distinct and complex equipment. Perfume shops located in city centers such as Delos, Paestum, Capua and even Rome during Hellenistic and Roman periods indicates the importance of perfumers in those societies. However, perfumers were held in low public esteem. Since the trade was highly profitable but required large investments of capital to purchase imported exotic aromatics, the trade was likely financed by leading citizens who operated through their freedmen (Brun, 2000). Pliny (*Natural History* 12.111-123) provides a price list of perfume ingredients, including the imported aromatics from the Orient (Arabia, India and Persia). Judean balsam oil was the most expensive, selling for up to 1,000 denarii per setier (a Roman liquid unit of approximately a half liter). Brun (2000) believes that perfume production proved lucrative for not only the perfume makers, but also for the owners of olive groves.

Throughout the ancient world and especially in Classical periods "it was regular practice for athletes or others who had indulged in energetic work, even women, to rub olive oil on their bodies and then scrape off the mixed oil, dirt and sweat with a scraper called a strigil" (Boardman, 1977:192) (also Dolamore, 1994; Frankel, 1999). People would then re-oil themselves, usually with a perfumed oil (Avitsur, 1994; Heltzer and Eitam, 1996). In reference to this practice Pliny says that "there are two liquids that are agreeable to the human body, wine inside and oil outside," (*Natural History* 14.29.150). Pliny also believed that olive oil had the ability to give warmth to the body and protect the body from cold (*Natural History* 15.5). Columella gives directions for processing olive oil for cosmetics, unguents and ointments (*De Re Rustica: De Arboribus* 12.54). In modern times, low-grade olive oil is used in the manufacture of cosmetics, shampoo and olive oil soap.

Determining the use of olives and olive oil from archaeological remains is both easy and difficult. Olive oil was used for so many things in antiquity, and since it is a liquid, identifying the end uses is very difficult, as liquids leave few physical remains. Often, containers identified with the transport and storage of oil are all that remain. A small vial containing the residue from an olive oil based perfume or oil would be easy to identify as a perfume or oil.

However, a large storage jar with olive oil residue found at a household site could represent a number of things, such as oil for cooking or lamp fuel. Assumptions can be made based on associated artifacts and features. Oil storage jars found in association with a building containing materials for the perfume industry likely represent olive oil used in making perfume. Containers with olive oil residues found in association with holy places would suggest the oil was used in religious ceremonies, though other possibilities exist. Residue analysis can be used to identify containers used in the storage of oil and lamps for the use of oil as a fuel. Olive oil used as a base for perfumes, unguents and oils could be identified by residue analyses as well. Pollen analysis might be able to identify oil used as food by finding olive pollen in dietary remains (coprolites, skeletal stomach contents). However, determining the use of olive oil in antiquity from archaeological remains remains quite difficult.

If we can identify technological changes in the olive oil industry during the domestication and increasing importance of this commodity, we may be able to determine where, how and when these changes occurred. Older techniques were probably not replaced but rather supplemented by newer technology in the change from small scale domestic to large scale industrial processing. Being able to identify which technologies were in use will be important in determining which activities were practiced at archaeological sites. Because the olive oil industry became an integral part of trade in early Palestine, this study can also help us understand the transition and expansion from domestic production to the "industrial" processing and establishment of major pressing centers. For the purposes of this research, domestic production is defined as the production of olive oil for personal or family consumption, with little or no excess. Industrial production is the processing of olive oil with a primary purpose of trade, or where production is controlled by a central authority which takes a portion of locally produced oil as tribute or tax and the collected oil is then used for trade or tribute.

1.3 Literature Review

Despite the olive's importance in antiquity it is much less studied than other major crops such as the grains. Zohary and Hopf (2000) spend two chapters (109 pages) on the grains and legumes but only 6 pages on the olive. Much more research has been done on the domestication of the grasses (for instance, the large bodies of research by Hillman and Harlan) than on the olive (next to no research on origins of cultivation). Olive remains are mentioned in some excavation reports (for instance: Ford and Miller, 1978; Galili et al, 1989; Hoffman, 1982; Smith, 1998; Stewart, 1984; Stirling and Lazreg, 2001; Stager, 1985; van der Veen and van Zeist, 1982; van Zeist and Bottema, 1983; van Zeist, 1994; van Zeist, 1994; Vitto, 1986), but many excavation reports lack botanical analyses. Publication of reports is another problem (Warnock, 1998), limiting

access to information on remains. The literature review for this research included journals containing site reports for the primary region of interest (Syro-Palestine), including but not limited to: the *American Journal of Archaeology* (*AJA*), the *Annual of the Palestine Exploration Fund*, the *Bulletin of the American Schools of Oriental Research* (*BASOR*), *Levant*, the *Israel Exploration Journal* and *Mitekufat Haeven, Journal of the Israel Prehistoric Society*. Annuals and monographs included the *Annual of the American Schools of Oriental Research* series and the *Qedem* series of monographs put out by the Institute of Archaeology of the Hebrew University of Jerusalem. Two recent issues (Vol. 63(1), March 2000 and 63(2), June 2000) of *Near Eastern Archaeology* (*NEA*) were devoted to Ethnoarchaeology and were helpful towards that topic and Chapter 3.

Recently, a number of books dealing with olive oil and pressing in antiquity have been published (Ayalon (ed.), 1994; Eitam and Heltzer (eds.), 1996; Frankel, 1999; Hadjisavvas, 1992). These texts were vital resources of both information and further source material. The internet as well has provided new sources of information, including access to an olive oil resources group (OliveOil@ yahoogroups.com) providing world-wide contacts and a great diversity of information.

Figure 1.2 presents a list of sites in Jordan reporting olive stone remains. Some sites only list the presence/absence of remains, while others list number of stones (for some, the number of stones is estimated from olive stone fragments). The number of stones found varies from site to site, and abundance of stones within the number of samples taken also varies from site to site (10 out of 11 samples at Teleilat Ghassul versus 9 out of 46 from Early Iron Age Deir 'Alla). Manner of deposition and preservation are necessary for determining the use of the olives which were preserved. The reasons for determining use, manner of deposition and preservation will become clear as the uses of olive pressing wastes are discussed in Chapter 3.

1.4 Significance of Research

This study represents a new step in the analysis of botanical remains in Syro-Palestine. The importance of this project is that it combines several areas of research in a manner not previously done on a crop such as the olive: First, most other studies have focused on grains (such as Hillman, 1973; Hillman, 1984; and Samuel, 1993). Second, the primary interest of most other botanical studies involves the domestication of early food plants (see Miller, 1991; Miller, 1995; and Zohary and Hopf, 2000). Three) Tree crops in general are understudied. Four) While archaeological evidence of grain frequently preserves vegetative parts, in tree crops such as the olive, usually only the seeds are preserved archaeologically. The olive has a large pit (stone) and is unique among tree crops in that the fruit is not eaten raw (Borowski, 1987), but must be processed before use (though very ripe fruit may be infrequently eaten). Other than environmental studies such as Bottema and Woldring (1995) which attempt to identify olive cultivation, what limited research done on olive oil production has been confined to investigations of processing installations (see Frankel, 1999). Research on agricultural installations has not usually been included in mainstream modern Near Eastern archaeological research, even though historical accounts discuss and describe the history and technology of such devices.

Results from the ethnographic and experimental studies were used to determine which techniques and processes are associated with domestic versus industrial production, how each of these two types of production affected how their by-products were used and where they were used, and the effects of scale of production. This is important in understanding how olive remains enter the archaeological record. This study uses the unique approach of looking at technological change from the viewpoint of the material processed, the olive itself.

Understanding the changes that occurred in the development of the ancient olive oil industry and in the olive oil processing technology has important implications in comprehending the ancient economies, trade and trade networks in the region and broadens our knowledge of the ancient economy, social structure, geopolitical relationships and many other aspects (Heltzer and Eitam, 1996). It is hypothesized that the change from household production and use of olive oil to expanded industrial production was important in the establishment of localized "states" in Palestine, based in part on the trade of olive oil (Gitin, 1989; Kelm and Mazar, 1995; Mazar, 1990). At Kommos on Crete, Blitzer (1993) believes that small scale olive processing in the Middle Minoan period ($\approx$ 2,200–1,500 B.C.), possibly for family or settlement use, was replaced by centralized large scale production in the Late Minoan period ($\approx$ 1,500–1,000 B.C.) for export. The results of this study can be used to analyze olive remains to help determine oil processing technology and methodology, which will help answer the afore mentioned hypothesis, adding important information to our knowledge of archaeological sites and cultures.

The methods used in this study can be applied widely to other archaeological and paleoethnobotanical problems. Combining ethnographic, experimental and archaeological studies allows us to investigate and research more complex questions and problems. This type of research also provides a more multidimensional picture to such problems.

1.5 Research Design

1.5.1 Ethnographic

Although the ultimate goal of this research was to study archaeological olive remains and technological change, the first step in doing so was to research the methodology necessary to look at those remains. Several previous

methods were combined and applied to this particular problem. The first component of the methodology involved ethnographic studies investigating how processing and post-processing usage affects the olive stones and the incorporation of olive processing remains into the archaeological record. The ethnographic studies focused on observation, participation, and questioning informants and workers (Alexiades, 1996; Bernard, 1994; Cotton, 1996; Donnan and Clewlow, 1974; Gould, 1978; Gubrium and Hostein, 1997; Martin, 1995; Spradley, 1979). This method worked well during previous background research in Jordan, and language was not a handicap. The Jordanian and Israeli contacts who assisted me all spoke English and acted as interpreters when necessary. While on two separate USIA fellowships (1991–1992, and 1992) which provided a stimulus for this project and provided preliminary research on this topic, and also while in Jordan working on excavations (1993, 1994), I made contact with four farmers, several people in the Jordanian Ministry of Agriculture and Ministry of Forestry (K. Nuimat, N. Fandi, S. Friahat, A. Friahat, A. Zurayk), and several people whose families have olive groves although they themselves do not. These people formed an important core for the ethnographic research, providing me not only with information but with the contacts and leads from which the research evolved and expanded.

The ethnographic component focused on traditional olive oil processing practices, such as using olive pressing waste (*jift*) for fuel, fertilizer, and animal feed. These traditional technologies are found in more remote rural locations, primarily those in olive producing areas of Jordan and Israel. People contacted in these settings were observed and questioned, especially concerning domestic preparation of oil and ancestral traditions. Figure 1.3 shows the northern area of Jordan, Palestine and Israel where most of the ethnographic work was performed. Also shown is Tafila, in the southern area of Jordan, where additional ethnographic work was performed. The archaeological sites of Tel Miqne/Ekron and Kfar Samir are also marked.

The waste from olive oil processing is used in a number of different ways. It may be simply discarded and find its way into the archaeological record. In this discard process it may be deposited in a midden or other refuse pit, and possibly burned or charred. This seems highly unlikely however, because of the waste's multitude of uses. Sometimes the solid olive oil processing waste (*jift*) is treated with chemicals to obtain an additional pressing of lower quality oil, used mainly in soap and shampoo. The primary use of the *jift*, however, is as a fuel, for instance; in bread, pottery, glass (A. Fischer, *pers. comm.*) kilns, and in the soap industry (K. Yassine, *pers. comm.*). The range of fuel uses moves between domestic to commercial. *Jift* is used in household tabuns or ovens for cooking and small stoves heating individual rooms. The residual oil content of the waste provides a high, hot fire. A modern use of olive pressing wastes is for commercially sold charcoal, which is a preferred charcoal for use with water pipes.

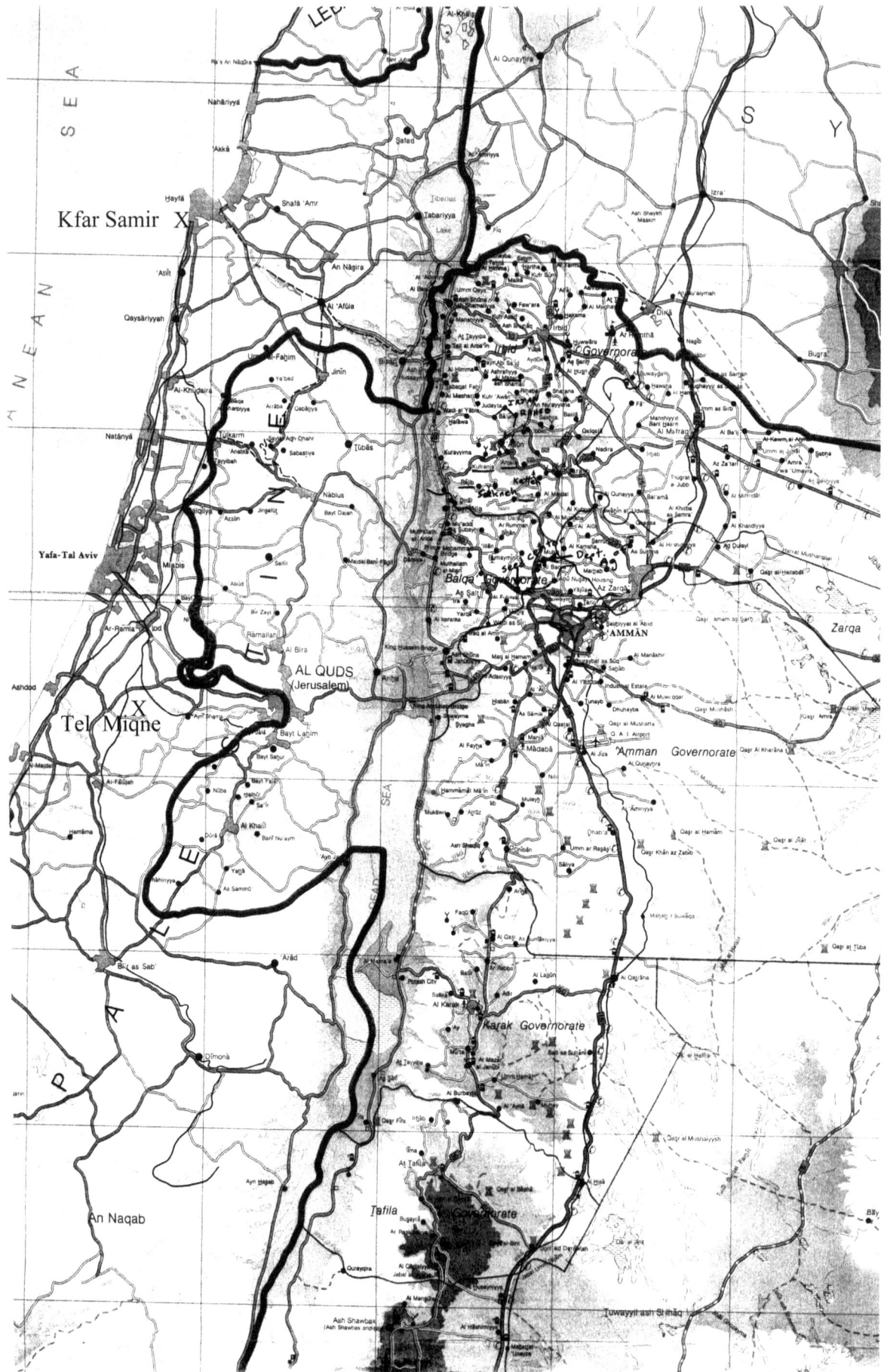

FIGURE 1.3: AREA OF RESEARCH

The *jift*, uncharred or as ash, may be used as fertilizer for fields or individual plants. In particular the waste is often spread in olive orchards or around individual trees. Infrequently, the *jift* may be fed to animals, which may further process the remains, and the pits excreted by the animals. Such animal waste may be incorporated into the archaeological record, or it could be processed further in the form of fuel. Animal dung is a common fuel source for a number of cultural groups in the region, as it was in antiquity (Miller and Smart, 1984). All of these processes provide different mechanisms for the incorporation of olive remains into the archaeological record.

Throughout the olive harvesting season in the fall and winter of 1996-97 I participated in and observed olive harvesting, pressing, and the use of olive pressing wastes. Participants in these activities were interviewed concerning the use of pressing wastes and the effects the various activities had on the olives and olive stones. I participated in olive picking with members of a major contact's family, and observed other olive harvesting. Farmers were questioned concerning picking and uses of pressing wastes in olive orchards. Traditional olive oil mills were visited and observed. Mill owners and workers were questioned about processing methods and possible modification of the olive stones, and about pressing waste use. Mill clients were questioned about other traditional practices and pressing waste uses. Markets in Jordan were investigated for modern end-use products of olive pressing wastes. Samples were taken from different stages of the various activities. This included but was not limited to; harvested olives, crushed but not pressed olives, freshly pressed *jift*, ash from hearths and tabuns, fertilizer and olive grove soils. The samples were processed and analyzed in a manner consistent with that applied to the experimental remains. Additional information on the use of olives, such as preserving olives for eating, was also gathered at this time.

1.5.2 Experimental

Step two of the methodology used experimental studies to determine how various processing methods might affect olive remains and their incorporation into the archaeological record (see Hillman, 1973; Hillman, 1984; Miller and Smart, 1984; and Samuel, 1993). Olive remains occur archaeologically in the form of seeds or pits called "stones." Olive oil processing is primarily a three-step process. In the first step, the olives are crushed to better facilitate the release of the olive's juices, then in the second step the crushed olives are pressed to express the liquid. The third step involves the separation of the watery "amurca" or "lees" (the non-oil component of the olive's liquid content) from the olive oil (usually the riper the olive the higher the oil content). There are a number of traditional or ancient processing technologies; milling/grinding, manual pressing/stomping, and extraction with boiling water (Avitsur, 1994; Ayalon, 1994a; Eitam, 1993; Frankel, 1987; Frankel, 1994; Mattingly, 1988a). After

some trial and error, I focused on the stage of processing which affects the olive stone, the first or crushing step. The experiments included: stomping with feet (1 version), grinding in a mortar and pestle, large and small (3 versions), grinding on a flat surface with a pestle (1 version), crushing on a flat surface with a roller (1 version), and crushing in basins with rollers (2 versions). I also obtained olive remains from traditional stone rotary presses and a modern commercial press for comparative purposes.

Some of the experimental processing remains were used in secondary experiments. Subsamples were taken from several sets of remains and tested to see how secondary use, such as a kiln fuel, may affect the remains. Some of the experimental processed remains were burned and charred in an open hearth and a small kiln. Samples of similar secondary usage were obtained from processing and secondary use activity sites during the ethnographic component.

Israeli archaeologists (E. Ayalon, D. Eitam, R. Frankel, S. Wolff) all expressed a willingness to assist me with my research and experiments. They discussed the research, showed me archaeological sites, and provided information concerning ancient and traditional practices. The Israel Olive Oil Museum at Shemen Industries in Haifa allowed me to use several Bronze and Iron Age artifacts in my olive crushing experiments, and similar artifacts were viewed at the Eretz Israel Museum in Tel Aviv. Other experiments were performed at the American Center of Oriental Research (ACOR) in Amman, Jordan, with help from its staff. Olives were purchased for the ACOR experiments from farmers selling olives outside modern commercial mill near Ajlun. Olives at the Israel Olive Oil Museum were purchased from the museum.

1.5.3 Analysis and Development of Test Expectations

Prior to experimentation I hypothesized that the various processing methods should alter olive remains differently. Treading or stomping by foot would probably do little or no damage to the remains. I did not believe that the amount of pressure applied in this method would break the stones, and that the crushing force would somewhat dissipated as well. Pounding with a mortar and pestle or using a small roller would result in highly fragmented and crushed remains. I believed that the direct crushing force of a pestle would easily fracture the olive stone. Rollers were expected to break the stones, but into larger fragments than those in mortar and pestle crushing. Crushing done with one or two horizontal stone wheels rotating in a fixed circular path over a stone base or platform (milling) would fall into a mid-range of alteration. I expected that the two extreme forms of alteration (either little or no, and large amounts of change) to be associated more with small scale domestic (foot treading, mortar and pestle) rather than large scale industrial (milling) processing. Large scale industrial processing, using milling to increase the oil yields, would then be evidenced by the mid-range level of alteration.

Relative abundance of olive remains at a site would also indicate type of processing technology. Small-scale domestic processing should be evidenced by small numbers of remains relative to other botanical remains (Miller, 1988). Large-scale industrial processing will produce greater amounts of waste, consequently producing more remains relative to other botanical types. The pressing waste or *jift* from both types of processing could be used as a fuel source, large-scale production's wastes possibly going to support other industries. Use of the *jift* as a fuel presents a problem, however, due to the tendency to the *jift* to burn to ash when burned.

The remains from the experimental and ethnographic research were analyzed to document the effects from each type of processing and use. Studying the remain's breakage patterns allowed me to compare and contrast the various experimental and ethnographically studied processing methods. The olive stones were separated from the processed material and passed through a series of geological screens. The volume and weight of the fragments passing through each stage of screening was recorded. The resulting data was then statistically analyzed (Snedecor and Cochran, 1989) to determine if the various processing methods could be separated from one another. Based on the observed and statistical analyses, it is possible to identify basic methods of olive oil processing.

Once the patterns for the various pressing methods and techniques were identified, the information was used to analyze olive remains from an archaeological site in Syro-Palestine and to determine the level of olive oil technology at this site.

1.5.4 *Study of Archaeological Remains*

After completion of the ethnographic and experimental studies, the results were applied to archaeological olive remains from Kfar Samir, a submerged Late Neolithic/Chalcolithic site off the Carmel coast of Israel (Galili and Sharvit, 1994-5; Galili *et al*, 1997; Galili *et al*, 1989). Close attention was paid to information from the Kfar Samir site reports, noting references to olive processing equipment and the botanical reports. Identification of processing features provides important collaborative evidence in verifying the processing method used at the site. The archaeological remains studied were from primary deposits only, ensuring their validity for time period and possible use in antiquity. Comparison of the archaeological data to the data from the experimental processing techniques

allowed me to determine the level or type of processing technology at the Kfar Samir site. The ability to identify the olive oil processing method from the olive remains will aid in following technological change in the ancient olive oil industry over time and space.

1.6 Summary

I address the question of technological change in olive oil processing in antiquity. This research makes significant contributions to archaeology and paleoethnobotany of the Near East. The complex issue of olive oil processing, and the resulting technological advances associated with the olive oil industry during this industry's expansion from the Chalcolithic to the Iron Age ($\approx$ 4,300–1,000 B.C.) in Syro-Palestine is tied to the expansion of trade and state building for this period. My goal was to determine if unique technological methods of olive oil processing can be identified from the olive remains of each unique method. Developing the methodology (experimental, ethnographic) for these studies is the first step in this study. I then apply the results from the experimental and ethnographic studies to olive remains from an identified archaeological olive oil processing site. The resulting data from the experimental/ archaeological comparison show that it is possible to identify different processing methods based on the resulting olive stone fracture pattern ratios caused by those processing methods. Using this research as a basis, it will be possible to look at archaeological olive remains from Chalcolithic through Iron Age sites in Syro-Palestine to determine the type of processing technology. Determining processing technology will allow us to follow the flow of technological advancement over time and space. However, all this must be balanced by the information provided by the ethnographic research, which clearly shows the problems working with multi-use materials such as olive remains.

In the chapters which follow I discuss: Chapter 2 is a review of the history of the olive and olive oil. Chapter 3 covers the ethnographic research on traditional olive oil production and the use of olive pressing wastes. Chapter 4 contains the experimental testing of various processing methods and the statistical identification of the different methods. In Chapter 5 the analysis of the archaeological olive samples and their statistical comparison to the experimental results is covered. Chapter 6 reviews olive oil's relationship to trade and the establishment of city-states in Syro-Palestine. And finally, in Chapter 7, the conclusions from the research presented in this dissertation.

CHAPTER 2

ORIGINS AND EARLY HISTORY OF THE OLIVE

2.1 Introduction

Evidence suggests that the olive originated in the area of Syro-Palestine, also called the Levant. Many scholars also consider the region to be the location where olive oil production first occurred. The Levant or Syro-Palestine includes the hilly areas on either side of the northern Jordan Valley and on up into modern Syria and Lebanon. The Mediterranean Levant covers an area around 1,100 km long and approximately 350 km wide. The topography includes low ranges of coastal mountains, the Orontes (north) and Jordan (south) rift valley, the inland mountain ranges, and the eastward sloping plateau. The plateau is dissected by numerous wadis flowing either into the Jordan rift valley or east into the Syro-Arabian desert. Since the life history of the olive differs greatly from the majority of domesticated Old World plants (grains and legumes) found (and researched) in this region, background information about the olive and its cultivation will be covered in this chapter. This chapter presents the evidence for the olive tree originating in Syro-Palestine, arguments for the origins of early olive use in ancient Syro-Palestine, and problems in distinguishing wild from cultivated olives.

2.2 Olive Origins

The family Oleaceae contains about 600 species in 24 genera worldwide, and includes plants such as Ash (*Fraxinus*), Jasmine (*Jasminum*), Lilac (*Syringa*), and Olive (*Olea*). There are about 40 *Olea* species worldwide, ranging in distribution from Africa to S. Asia to New Zealand. The olive (*Olea europaea*) is the only Mediterranean species of the genus *Olea*, a relic of the Mediterranean's tropical mid-Tertiary flora, the only member of the genus surviving from that time period in the region (Simmonds, 1976). As such, Zohary (1982a) considers the olive an outsider because of that. The olive has changed little over time. The olive flourishes in a Mediterranean climate characterized by hot dry summers and cool slightly wet winters (Dolamore, 1994; Ridgeway, 1996), however, *Olea* has rather exacting climatic conditions. It cannot stand temperatures below 16 degrees Fahrenheit or an average winter temperature of 37 degrees Fahrenheit, though it can survive freezing temperatures for short periods of time. The olive is more tolerant of heat and drought conditions and can withstand long periods without water, though this limits fruit production. *Olea* are rarely found above an altitude of

300 m and do not occur naturally in areas with less than 400 mm of rainfall (Zohary, 1982b).

The cultivated olive is the archetypal tree of Mediterranean lands (Mattingly, 1996), is characteristic of Mediterranean basin vegetation, and is often regarded as an indicator of the Mediterranean climate and the limits of Mediterranean vegetation (Hora, 1980; I.O.O.C., nd). The growth range of neither the wild or cultivated forms of *Olea* extends beyond the Mediterranean climate zone, because of this they are reproductively well separated from other members of the genus *Olea* (Runnels and Hansen, 1986). The olive is a common component of the Mediterranean maquis (dense shrubby underbrush) and forest (Feinbrun-Dothan, 1978).

Flora Palaestina (Feinbrum-Dothan, 1978) describes *Olea europaea* as: "Tree or shrub, 1.5-6 m. [in height] Leaves oblong to lanceolate, mucronulate, green on upper face, silvery with a dense scale cover on the lower. Flowers in small axillary panicles, entomophilous [insect pollinated] at first, then anemophilous [wind pollinated] at the end of anthesis. Corolla white to cream-colored. Drupe ellipsoid, truncate or tapering at the ends. Fl. May." New limbs sprout in no particular order, creating a dense cluster of branches. Dense clusters of suckers often grow up around the base of the tree. Most cultivated trees are pruned to facilitate easier fruit picking. Suckers and branches are also trimmed to aid in picking and to promote better fruiting.

Like the cherry, the olive is a pit or stone fruit. The olive stone is encased inside a fleshy fruit. There is a thick, almost leathery at times, skin (the epicarp) covering the fleshy pulp (mesocarp). Within is the hard stone (endocarp) encasing the true seed or kernel, the embryonic olive tree. The botanical term for this type of fleshy fruit encasing a stone derives its name from a Greek term for an overripe, wrinkled olive: Δρυππα, a "drupe" (Dolamore, 1994; Klein, 1994).

The olive, *Olea europaea*, has two named subspecies, the cultivated olive *Olea europaea* or *sativa*, and the wild *Olea europaea* subspecies or var. *oleaster* or *sylvestris* (Hora, 1980; Simmonds, 1976; Zohary and Hopf, 2000). The wild olive growing in the Mediterranean (*O. europaea* L. var. *oleaster*) is considered to be the wild progenitor of the cultivated olive (*O. europaea* var. *europaea*) (Besnard *et al*, 2000; Runnels and Hansen, 1986; Zohary, 1982a). Zohary and Hopf (2000) regard wild *Olea europaea* var.

oleaster as a truly wild. Renfrew (1973) and Simmonds (1976) both consider the wild olive (*Olea europaea* var. oleaster) to be an escaped rather than a truly wild variety or an ancestral form to the domesticate. Renfrew (1973) thinks *Olea europaea* var. europaea is derived from a wild *Olea* (*O. chrysophylla*) found throughout Asia and Africa. Simmonds' view (1976) is that the parents of the cultivated olive are not known, but were two different species. One was a "proto-*Oleo*" which is thought to be extinct. The other could be either an African form (*O. africana* (possibly Renfrew's *O. chrysophylla*)) found from southern Africa to the Sudan, or another form (*O. ferruginea*) native to Iran through the Himalayas. The cultivated type originates in the mountains of the eastern Mediterranean: the Taurus, Amanus, and Lebanese ranges as far south as the Upper Galilee (Simmonds, 1976). Simmonds supports this hybrid origin idea by citing the diversity of stone types found in archaeological sites in Syria (Byblos) dating to the 4th millennium BC (Chalcolithic: 4300–3300 BC), which are similar to the African species *O. africana*. Problems in determining wild versus cultivated type based on stone size will be discussed later. The various *Olea* species in the Mediterranean basin are a complex mix of genetically connected wild forms, cultivated clones and escaped cultivars. Recent genetic studies show that the olive originated and was cultivated in the Mediterranean basin (Besnard *et al*, 1998; Besnard *et al*, 2001), with a major center of origin in the Near East (Besnard and Berville, 2000). A majority of scholars believe that the olive's origin lies within the area of the Levant and most likely Syro-Palestine (Hadjisavvas, 1992; Kislev, 1996; Neef, 1990; Zohary and Hopf, 2000).

Cultivation of the olive spread west from the eastern Mediterranean, from the late Chalcolithic or Early Bronze Age onwards (Hadjisavvas, 1992; Liphschitz, 1996; Mattingly, 1996), establishing a secondary center of diversity in the Aegean, and possibly a tertiary center in Italy/Tunisia. Seagoing Phoenician traders are thought to have spread the knowledge of olive cultivation and processing (Eitam, 2000; Dolamore, 1994). Greene (1996) discusses the spread of viticulture west to North Africa by the Phoenicians; it is likely that the olive and olive oil processing spread along with it. Wolff (1996) points out that most scholars agree that the skills required for olive cultivation probably were carried along with olive plants themselves to North Africa by the Phoenicians or Greeks. Zohary and Hopf (2000) mention hundreds of recognized distinct varieties and suggest that different parts of the Mediterranean basin are characterized by specific local forms. For instance, the Aegean center is characterized by large-fruited types which rarely occur in eastern Mediterranean populations (Simmonds, 1976). Although the olive occurs naturally in Greece, it is possible that the technology and skills for cultivation and oil processing came from the Levant; the Greeks gave the olive a Greek name "*elaia*," rather than an imported Hebrew word for olive, "*zeit*" or "*zayit*," and evidence for cultivation appears later in Greece than for the Levant (Runnels and Hansen,

1986; Zohary and Hopf, 2000). Terral (2000) proposes using wood anatomy to distinguish between mature and immature olive wood, and uses wood type (mature vs. immature) as evidence supporting the evolution of olive cultivation in prehistoric France and Spain.

There are now hundreds of cultivated olive varieties comprised of mixtures of clones, many often localized in geographic distribution (Hora, 1980; I.O.O.C., nd). Maintaining the preferred genotype is only possible through vegetative propagation, due to interbreeding problems in sexual reproduction (Liphschitz *et al*, 1991). Cultivated olives are propagated by cuttings, often from suckers or shoots produced by a tree or stump (Besnard *et al*, 2000; I.O.O.C., nd). Early Old Testament texts show that the Levant's ancient inhabitants knew of the olive's vegetative reproductive capacity (Borowski, 1987) and probably used shoots or suckers to plant orchards. Cuttings are often grafted or budded onto the stumps of old trees or wild branches. Wild olives are self-incompatible (must be pollinated from another olive plant) and reproduce entirely from seed, thus they show a wide degree of genetic variation. Most seedlings raised from cultivars resemble wild forms and are usually useless in terms of fruit quality, having low percentages of oil. Such wild-looking progeny are called "feral" and are found throughout the modern Mediterranean basin (Forbes and Foxhall, 1978). Because seed propagation is impractical in oleoculture, cloning is necessary. However, wild forms showing superior qualities may have caught the attention of early cultivators and were probably picked up as new clones. Wild olives are frequently used as stock material for grafting. The hardy wild stems are planted in orchards as stock for grafting cultivated scions (the upper portion which will eventually produce branches and fruit) (Zohary and Hopf, 2000).

In numerous areas around the Mediterranean wild olives occur in areas untouched by cultivation. Unlike most other crops studied, such as the cereals, the olive leaves little clear archaeobotanical evidence which allows cultivars to be distinguished from wild ancestors (Kislev, 1996). Wild plants usually have spiny branches, and smaller fruits containing less oil. However, the stones are not considerably smaller in cultivated olives, though on average wild olives are smaller than domesticated olives (Zohary and Spiegel-Roy, 1975). Determining wild from cultivated is further complicated by the long history of human occupation in the region and subsequent human-olive interaction. There are also numerous "feral" trees (Kislev, 1996): trees considered be wild olives that are possibly abandoned or escaped cultivars from the ebb and flow of human history. Wild and feral types, escapees from grafting stocks, and spontaneous seedlings occur in disturbed areas, in areas of abandoned cultivation, and on the outskirts of cultivated fields (Zohary and Spiegel-Roy, 1975). Feral trees may revert to and exhibit wild characteristics, such as spinescent lower branches and smaller fruits (Zohary and Hopf, 2000). Determining the number of generations the plants have been growing in the wild is difficult, adding to the complexity of determining wild and/or feral to cultivated (Kislev, 1996). The wild and feral forms are fully interfertile with the cultivated varieties and may interbreed with them through sporadic spontaneous hybridization. This spontaneous genetic exchange causes the morphological boundaries between wild and cultivated olives to be blurred and makes distinguishing between the two difficult (Kislev, 1996; Liphschitz, 1996; Singer, 1996; Zohary and Spiegel-Roy, 1975). Some researchers (Forbes and Foxhall, 1978) believe that there are no longer any "true" wild olives due to the admixture of "domesticated" olive genes through pollination over the centuries. Liphschitz *et al* (1991) and Zohary and Spiegel-Roy (1975) believe that wild and cultivated olives are loosely genetically interconnected and comprise a single wild and cultivated species complex.

Determining wild from cultivated olives based on stone size is problematic due to the diversity found in stones of both wild and cultivated olives. The stones overlap considerably in size and show a great deal of variation even within a single tree (Liphschitz *et al*, 1991; Zohary and Hopf, 2000; Zohary and Spiegel-Roy, 1975). Selection of a larger mesocarp (the fleshy oil containing part of the olive fruit) does not necessarily go along with selection for a change in stone size. According to Liphschitz *et al* (1991) cultivated olives differ from their wild relatives in their larger fruit and higher oil content, both from the development of the fleshy oil-containing mesocarp. The increase in stone size is less pronounced. Olives under cultivation manifest considerable variation in the size, shape and oil content of their fruits (Zohary and Hopf, 2000). Runnels and Hansen (1986) point out that it is not possible to distinguish between wild or domesticated olive stones. While on average wild olives are smaller than cultivated olives (Zohary and Spiegel-Roy, 1975), the amount of overlap in the range of measurements is much too great to rely on for separating the two in the archaeological record (also see Renfrew, 1973). Charring, the most likely means of preserving the olive stones at terrestrial sites, may distort stone size, making determining wild from cultivated problematic (Wright, 2003). Even wild or feral trees produce the occasional large stone, making identification of large stones as evidence of cultivation problematic. The morphological similarities between wild and cultivated olives makes distinguishing between them almost impossible (Liphschitz, 1996). The difficulty in determining wild from cultivated based on stone size basically eliminates one method frequently used to determine wild from cultivated in other botanical remains (such as legumes and grasses, see Zohary and Hopf, 2000).

A factor of major influence on olive history and evolution is the olive's longevity, as trees may live 1,500 years or longer and are among the oldest trees in Europe and the Near East. The olive's longevity is mythical, yet real (Romero, 1998). Some groves in Israel are thought to be more than a thousand years old (Zohary, 1982a). Legend

FIGURE 2.1: OLD OLIVE TREE WITH HOLLOW CENTER, KETTEH, JORDAN

has it that the olive trees in the Garden of Gethsemane in Jerusalem, the olive tree of Plato, and trees on the island of Jerba are 2,000 years old (Dolamore, 1994), while other trees have been scientifically proven to date back more than seventeen centuries (Romero, 1998). Due to the olive's growth patterns, it is nearly impossible to date them using conventional methods such as tree rings and dendrochronology. The main trunk or the core may rot away but the "tree" continues to thrive through the shoots growing up from the roots at the base of the tree (Figure 2.1). This ability to sprout new branches from its rootstock means that the actual life span of an olive may be unlimited (Dolamore, 1994; Romero, 1998; Singer, 1996). Some currently growing ancient olive groves may represent even earlier orchards which have continued to thrive, providing information on socio-economic and agricultural conditions prevailing thousands of years ago (Singer, 1996). As the trees age, they frequently lose the center of the tree trunk, though ancient olive trees may bear fruit even after the trunk is hollow (Liphschitz, 1996; Singer, 1996). Ancient trees with their hollow centers filled in with stones are a common site in centuries old olive groves (Frankel, 1994; personal observation) (Figure 2.2) and this practice is mentioned in the Tosephta (Shevi'it 1:10). Many ancient groves in Jordan, still producing harvested fruit, are identified as "Romani" due to local beliefs that they were planted by the Romans (personal experience; Pilcer, 1996) ("romi": Singer, 1996). The variety "Nabali" is one of the oldest in Jordan, and is sometimes called "Roman," attesting to ancient origin (Ayoub, 2001). Residents of Harta, Jordan (north of Irbid) believe their olive trees are unique and that the Romans introduced the variety to the area (Batsell-Fuller, 1986). As time goes by, fast growing varieties are outnumbering the old "Romani" trees (Rafi Bataeneh, Chief of Eastern Section, Irbid Agricultural Directorate), which also disappear to human expansion and construction (Rosenblum, 1996; personal observation).

FIGURE 2.2: OLD OLIVE TREE WITH HOLLOW CENTER FILLED
WITH STONES

According to Shboul and Bataeneh (Dr. Nour Aldeen Shboul, Director, Irbid Agricultural Directorate; Rafi Bataeneh, Chief of Eastern Section, Irbid Agricultural Directorate), the older olive varieties in Jordan, including those the locals call "Romani," and considered native to area give the best oil (20-30% oil out of the oil/water mixture pressed from the olive fruit), while newer varieties imported from Spain, Italy, and Turkey only give 10-20%. However, the newer varieties are getting planted more often and have become predominant since they are easier to propagate. These new varieties have about an 80% efficiency in propagation. The older and better oil producing local varieties are difficult to propagate, with only around 20% success in propagation: they have a low shooting rate in grafting attempts. The newer olive varieties with larger fruit are usually used for pickling/ food, rather than oil, while the small-fruited older varieties are used more for oil pressing. One ethnographic contact stated a preference for the small-fruited older varieties of olives for oil.

The olive is a relatively slow growing tree and may require several decades to reach maturity and full productivity, although production may start 4-6 years after planting (Dolamore, 1994; Ridgeway, 1996; Zohary and Hopf, 2000). Rather than destroying the entire tree when it becomes unproductive, the branches are all trimmed back

instead (Singer, 1996): "To revive a long-forgotten tree, you must whack away to within an inch of its life" (Rosenblum, 1996:8). The tree sends out new shoots and branches and becomes productive again in a few years. The Levantine landscape is dotted with many ancient short, squat olive trees. Occasional cutting back of branches also prevents the trees from becoming too tall, making harvesting olives easier.

Olive production fluctuates from year to year. Often productivity is cyclical, with a tree producing many olives one year and few olives the next. This may be due to a number of factors such as pollination, variety of tree, location and rainfall. Some contacts in Jordan mentioned that productivity fluctuated, but not the entire olive crop, just individual trees or orchards. Since the entire olive crop does not have a poor year, I do not believe that this would affect olive oil production. I believe people in antiquity would identify and accommodate such fluctuations in production, as they do in the present.

The Levant is suggested as the area of origin for the olive and its subsequent cultivation by humans (Borowski, 1987; Dolamore, 1994; Heltzer, 1993; Liphschitz, 1996; Liphschitz et al, 1991; Singer, 1996; Tannahill, 1988; Zohary and Hopf, 2000; Zohary and Spiegel-Roy, 1975). Liphschitz et al (1991) reexamined an earlier study by Stager (1985) which discussed botanical material from Levantine archaeological sites. Liphschitz et al (1991) stated that it was difficult to determine whether olive cultivation was initiated in the Chalcolithic or Early Bronze Age. A number of sources (Liphschitz, 1996; Stager, 1985; Zohary and Hopf, 2000; Zohary and Spiegel-Roy, 1975) suggest that olive cultivation begins in the Chalcolithic. The process possibly began slightly earlier, probably in the Late Neolithic, based on more recent information (Eitam, 1987; Heltzer, 1993; Galili et al, 1989; Galili et al, 1997; Galili and Sharvit, 1994-5). Intentional cultivation as a subsistence strategy in the early Neolithic was a major advancement from the Epipaleolithic (Bar-Yosef and Meadow, 1995).

Mazar (1990) suggests that intensive olive cultivation, mainly in the plains and river valleys, began in the Chalcolithic and became a source of Levantine wealth in later periods. Support for a developing agriculture is based on food remains from settled sites such as Teleilat Ghassul, where the environment is not suitable for olives unless they were irrigated (as is now done in the Jordan valley) (Zohary and Spiegel-Roy, 1975). However, Borowski (1987) and Liphschitz et al (1991) think that cultivation began in the Early and Middle Bronze ages. Mazar (1990) also has olive trees appearing as a major crop in the hill country of Palestine at this time, which coincides with increasing settlement of the region. He suggests that much of the oil produced was for export and it is only during the Middle and Late Bronze Ages that olive cultivation expands out of the Levant.

In the studies of ancient Near Eastern settlement patterns, olive cultivation is often associated with sedentary lifestyles (the establishment of settled sites) and agricultural practices. Olive cultivation, because of the labor and time commitment necessary before a return on the investment occurs, may indicate labor intensive agriculture. This is especially true for areas where the olive would not be naturally found, and needed special care such as irrigation. Liphschitz et al (1991) think that because olives begin to set fruit only after several years, the presence of olives suggest organized settlements with permanent residents. They tie the olive to population increases and greater demands for food in the Early Bronze Age Levant (c. 3300–2300 BC). Prior to organized settlements, wild olive stands would have been sufficient for limited or smaller populations. However, Liphschitz et al (1991) believe that once an area's population began to increase, olive cultivation would be the only means of supplying the necessary amounts of olive oil. This would be especially true for settlements outside the olive's natural range.

A major problem with the idea of using olive cultivation as an indicator for sedentism is when was the olive actually cultivated? While the Late Neolithic and Chalcolithic periods in Syro-Palestine contain proof of olive use through seed remains (Epstein, 1993; Galili and Sharvit, 1994–5), it does not necessarily mean that olives were being cultivated. We do know that by the Late Neolithic and Chalcolithic periods the olive is definitely known. Kislev (1994–1995) suggests that the development of olive oil extraction methods lead to the olive's exploitation and that oil processing preceded domestication by several centuries.

Bar-Yosef and Meadow (1995:50) point out that "most hunter-gatherer diets in middle latitudes ... are based on vegetal resources." They also suggest that early Neolithic farmers utilized a varied array of subsistence strategies, which included the cultivation of olive trees. Further, ground stone tools first appearing in the Upper Paleolithic (beginning around 40,000 BP) and continuing into the Natufian (beginning around 13,000 BP) and suggestive of plant food processing are found in many sites in the Mediterranean climatic region. Since some ground stone tools were used for pounding and crushing, it is possible that some of these tools were used in processing olives for oil. Since it is suggested that wild stands were sufficient to fill the needs of early humans prior to the Chalcolithic and Bronze ages (Liphschitz et al, 1991; Zohary and Hopf, 2000), some interaction between the so-called "wild" olives and humans had to be taking place. This agrees with Rindos' coevolution theory (Rindos 1980, 1984; Watson, 1995) where a plant (in this case the olive) is first seen in a non-agricultural setting, or with Hillman and Davies' (1992) "nondomestication cultivation" (Watson, 1995). An increase in finds of olive remains may reflect a growing

interest in the protection and possible care of the tree ("incidental domestication"). Watson (1995) urges that while Hillman and Davies' model is important their work centers on one grain (einkorn wheat) and domestication of fruit trees "must be considered." A problem with Rindos's model is that this process of genetic change occurs in "malleable species" (Pearsall, 1995), species where genetic change can occur easily. Due to time and propagation factors involved in olive cultivation, I question whether the olive can be considered a "malleable species." Overall, the suggested evolution of olive cultivation fits fairly well with the theories (Hillman and Davies, Rindos, Watson) suggested above.

Finding olive remains at sites outside its natural range could reflect human dispersal. The presence of the plant outside its normal range, as in areas requiring irrigation (as suggested by Teleilat Ghassul and other sites), may point to a change from "incidental domestication" to intentional cultivation. At what point selection for a fleshier oil-bearing mesocarp begins to take place is unknown. However, with specialized domestication, morphological changes often appear, though this is difficult to see in the olive due to the slow evolutionary process caused by the olive's slow growth and long life.

Not all olives may have been used for their fruit. Liphschitz et al (1991) suggest that there are dual purpose varieties, with the carbonized stones and charred wood of pruned twigs representing use as firewood. It is entirely possible that the remains of olives from early Mediterranean sites represents the remnants of wood used for fuel, especially pruned branches. An investigation of wood types (charcoal) and a correlation between olive wood and seeds might clear up this question. Cutting down the whole tree was unlikely, due to its economic importance. Any tree not producing fruit, except the olive or fig, could be cut down according to Jewish law (Mishnah Kila'im 6, 5).

As Zohary and Hopf (2000) state, carbonized stones and charred wood (possibly prunings used as firewood) constitute the bulk of olive remains in archaeological excavations. These carbonized remains present several problems. First, as Liphschitz et al (1991) point out, carbonization may alter the size or shape of remains. This becomes an important factor since some investigations attempt to determine wild versus cultivar by the size of the stone. As shown by the results of a seed carbonization study (Wilson, 1983), dimensional changes in seeds vary significantly according to the heating environment, for instance, making the original seed size difficult to determine. However, as there are no studies of carbonization effects on olive stones, it remains a subject for further research. Second, do the remains represent plants collected for fuel, or do the remains represent waste left over from oil pressing and used as a fuel afterwards? An increase and decline of environmental olive pollen at Sagalassos, Anatolia, was used to suggest social, economic and political factors such as political disorder, olive cultivation and site abandonment

(Bottema and Woldring, 1995). Runnels and Hansen (1986) state that palynological evidence can be used to determine cultivation. They note that the pollen of wild olives can be distinguished from cultivated olives using morphological differences in the exine or outer coat of the pollen grain, however, most studies only take identification to genus. Liphschitz *et al* (1991) both agree and disagree. They think that pollen analysis shows it is not possible to identify the different types of olive with light microscopy, though it is possible with SEM (Scanning Electron Microscopy) at magnifications over 2000X. However, they suggest that at only very high SEM magnification (over 4200X) are even slight differences seen, and only by surface texture and not by size. Therefore identification of olive pollen from archaeological sites to subspecies using light microscopy is problematic.

Using olive wood to determine cultivation is also problematic. Analyses of wild and cultivated olive woods show no differences between them (Runnels and Hansen, 1986; Liphschitz *et al*, 1991). And, one cannot be sure what the olive wood was used for: artifacts, construction, fuel, or fodder instead of prunings for increased fruit yields. Thus olive wood finds do not necessarily mean olive cultivation was taking place. However, timber is usually a reliable indicator of the local vegetation. Olive wood finds could indicate the presence of olive in the area, but could not be used to determine if the wood represents wild or cultivated. Another possibility is that the wood represents trees no longer useful as olive producers which are being used secondarily for fuel or construction material. The relative proportions of olive versus other local woods in archaeological remains may indicate the relative abundance of olive in the natural vegetation during different periods. Higher percentages of olive wood at sites may indicate an increase in olive cultivation, and increases in the frequency of olive wood in the archaeological record may indicate the presence of organized olive orchards (Liphschitz *et al*, 1991).

Identification of olive oil production areas through associated features is possible. Oil presses and crushing features, mills or basins, especially in large numbers as at the Iron Age site of Miqne in Israel can be definite indicators of oil processing (Eitam, 1996; Gitin, 1989; Gitin, 1996). Some types of installations are more closely linked to olive oil production than others which may have multiple uses, such as presses used for both wine and oil. This problem of multiple feature use occurs throughout the Mediterranean basin where olive oil is produced (Anderson-Stojanovic´, 1997; Foxhall, *pers. comm.*; Frankel, *pers. comm.*). Frankel (*pers. comm.*) believes that since olives were cultivated and pressed prior to the introduction of grapes into Palestine in antiquity, presses

and crushing platforms (possibly for treading olives) would then be adapted from olive to grape/wine use. Frankel (*pers. comm.*) doesn't believe that grapes are native to Syro-Palestine but are from further north, Turkey and the Caucuses in origin. Renfrew (1973) and Zohary and Hopf (2000) point to evidence of grapes beginning in the Early Bronze Age (around 3,000 B.C.). According to Frankel (*pers. comm.*), therefore any pressing installations before the Early Bronze Age have to be for olive oil rather than wine. In some cases olive and wine presses are nearly the same (Foxhall, *pers. comm.*; Sandy, 1989), and the Hebrew word for press,"*Gat*," could mean either olive or wine press or both (Frankel, *pers. comm.*) (the word "Gethsemane," as in "The Garden of Gethsemane," is a Greek altered Hebrew phrase (*Gat Shemanim*) meaning oil vat). Thus the presses mentioned in James, Leonard and others in McGovern *et al* (1996) could also be oil presses and the treading basins mentioned in Greene in the same volume may also be for olives. Herr (1997) suggests that many private houses in the Iron IIC show signs of small scale "cottage industries" such as olive oil processing alternating with textile dying. Identification of olive oil processing is complicated by features or artifacts which are not easily identified as such in archaeological sites, for instance, a roller or pounding stone used on a flat surface or the flat surface itself. Since the features and artifacts which may have been used in olive oil processing can be difficult to identify, and may in some cases be somewhat mobile (rollers or pestles carried from area to area, site to site), identifying olive oil production based on recovered olive remains offers an option in determining this important industry.

2.3   Summary

The olive, unlike other major domesticates of the Old World Near East (grasses and legumes), is long lived and asexually propagated. And it is the fleshy covering of the fruit, not the seed itself, that is utilized. Evidence supports an origin and evolution of the olive in the area of Syro-Palestine, which would further support that this region is also the area of the olive's first use and cultivation. Due to the centuries of olive cultivation in the region and their close morphological characteristics, it is difficult to identify wild from feral from cultivated olives. Determining olive type is complicated by the fact that it is impossible to distinguish stones or wood of the wild, feral and cultivated olives. Being able to identify wild from cultivated would help determine when intensive olive oil production began, using the olive stones alone. Since it is not possible to use the stones to determine wild from cultivated, determining the production method based on the stone fragments, or, using the stones to determine if production is occurring, is the next best thing.

CHAPTER 3

ETHNOGRAPHIC RESEARCH

3.1 Introduction

The first component of my research is the ethnographic fieldwork. The goals of this portion of the research are to: 1) follow the steps of traditional olive oil processing, from picking through to the disposal of the pressing wastes, 2) identify traditional olive oil processing methods, especially small-scale domestic methods, 3) identify post-processing usage of olive stones and pressing wastes, and finally, 4) determine the final disposition of the olive processing remains, in whatever form, in order to identify how those remains get incorporated into the archaeological record. The ethnographic research investigates traditional olive oil processing from the olive picking to the final disposal of the remains, and includes associated activities concerning the olive and olive oil such as eating olives and taste preferences. The ethnographic research brings to light a number of practices previously undocumented or seldom noted. This ethnographic research documents traditional olive practices at a time when traditional methods are fast disappearing and the older generations with the knowledge of old ways and traditions are dying off.

While several of the methods and uses presented here represent a mere fraction of the olives or methodologies used, detailed discussion about them is important. Identifying the various processing methods and the uses of processing wastes contributes to understanding the mechanisms for incorporating olive remains into the archaeological record. For instance, olive pressing waste (*jift*) is used in a number of different ways, especially as a fuel source. Of special interest to this study was the high proportion of responses noting *jift*'s tendency to be totally consumed, leaving nothing but ash. Understanding the processes that affect olive remains before and during incorporation of those remains into the archeological record not only allow us to better interpret olive finds, this understanding and information can be applied to other archaeological remains as well.

This chapter will cover: the area where the fieldwork was researched, olive picking, pre-crushing activities, olive oil processing, uses of pressing wastes, the ultimate disposal of olive pressing wastes, eating olives, and cultural aspects of the olive. For all of the research presented here, including discussion of both small and large scale olive oil production, olive oil production and olive pickling occurs

only when olives are ripe and being picked. Olives do not hold very long without processing before going rotten.

3.2 Methodology

The ethnographic fieldwork follows standard ethnobotanical field methods, based on ethnographic and ethnoarchaeological methodology and studies (Alexiades, 1996; Bernard, 1994; Cotton, 1996; Donnan and Clewlow, 1974; Gould, 1978; Gubrium and Hostein, 1997; London, 2000; Martin, 1995; Matthews *et al*, 2000; Spradley, 1979; Zuckerman, 2000), in particular, employing "participant observation" methods. Fieldwork strategies include direct or participant observation (Alexiades, 1996; Bernard, 1994; Martin, 1995), open-ended and semi-structured interviews (Alexiades, 1996; Bernard, 1994; Cotton, 1996; Martin, 1995), and focus interviews (Martin, 1995). Stanislawski's (1974:15) definition of ethnoarchaeology: "participant observation study of the form, manufacture, distribution, meaning, and use of artifacts, and their function, or institutional setting and social group correlations among non-industrial peoples," is appropriate. My research on olive oil pressing parallels that done on pottery (Hole, 1979; Ochsenschlager,1974), animal husbandry (Geraty and LaBianca, 1985; LaBianca, 1984), agriculture (Fuller, 1986; Palmer, 1998a; 1998b), and grains (Hillman, 1973; 1984; Hillman and Davies, 1992; Musselman and Al-Mouslem, 2001).

Throughout the olive harvesting season in the fall and winter of 1996-97 I participated in and observed olive harvesting, olive oil pressing, olive pressing waste (*jift*) use, and sampled the various remains resulting from those activities. These samples include but are not limited to; harvested olives, crushed but not pressed olives, freshly pressed olive oil processing waste (*jift*), ash from hearths and tabuns, fertilizer and olive grove soils. While the research concentrates on traditional activities, I also investigate and sample modern methods. Traditional methods of olive oil processing are found in the more remote rural locations, primarily those in the olive producing areas of Jordan, Palestine and Israel. People contacted in these areas were observed and interviewed, especially concerning domestic preparation of oil and ancestral traditions.

The participant observation method worked well during previous background research in Jordan. I conducted interviews in English; the Jordanian and Israeli contacts who assisted me all spoke English and acted as interpreters when necessary. Two separate USIA fellowships at the American Center of Oriental Research (ACOR) in Amman, Jordan (1991-1992, and 1992) provided a stimulus for this project and contributed to the preliminary research on this topic. During the fellowships and while excavating in Jordan (1993, 1994, and 1996) I made contact with farmers, people in the Jordanian Ministry of Agriculture and Ministry of Forestry, and several people whose families have olive groves. These people formed an important nucleus for the ethnographic research, providing me not only with information but also the contacts and leads from which the research evolved and expanded.

I had a core group of three contacts who aided me with the majority of contacts, interviews and also provided me with transportation. One of these contacts is Jordan's top olive specialist. An additional group of eight contacts assisted on other interviews and travel. This group of eleven contacts served much like what Hammersley and Atkinson (1983) describe as "gatekeepers" and "sponsors;" opening the way to other contacts. This method of beginning with one contact who recommends another, who in turn recommends another, and so on is referred to in Bernard (1994) as "snowball sampling." This method of information gathering was quite effective in obtaining names of people to see, villages to investigate and traditional olive oil mills to visit. For instance, stopping at one village or mill I might be told of where to find another mill in that village or a nearby village and the names of people to contact or talk to.

Nineteen contacts, including two of the three core contacts, were college educated and worked in areas related to the olive and olive oil production (Jordanian Ministry of Agriculture, Jordanian Ministry of Forestry, Jordan's National Centre for Agricultural Research and Technology Transer (NCARTT), or the Department of Nutrition and Food Technology at the University of Jordan). These contacts provided specific information on olive oil history, culture, processing and use. These same contacts also contributed to the wealth of traditional ethnographic information. Most of these contacts were selected on the basis of their knowledge and reputation (Martin, 1995). Over one hundred and twenty-five people were interviewed, though the exact number is impossible to determine due to the fluid situations encountered at some interview locations. Many interviews (21) were conducted at olive oil presses and mills, where people were constantly entering and leaving. While I would be interviewing the press owners, workers and press clients, some people would leave the interview while others entering the press would enter into the interview. Not all people present would make statements, some would only nod their heads or agree with statements other people made. Similar experiences occurred when I interviewed people in a small village square, at an old mill stone set up in the center of the square. Fifteen

interviews were conducted at traditional mills or with their owners (three mills were not in operation at the time of the interview), and six modern oil mills were visited. National and regional offices of the Jordanian Ministry of Agriculture were called on, where I met with both administrative personnel and field agents. An agriculture experimental research station, two agricultural stations, three Ministry of Forestry stations and a tree nursery were also visited.

I obtained additional contacts and information via the internet, most through an olive oil discussion list (OliveOil@yahoo.com). Other members on the list include growers, processors, people associated with olive oil production equipment, and academics. List members are from throughout the world, including: Australia, Greece, Italy, Jordan, Spain, Syria, and Turkey.

3.3 Field Research And Observations

The ethnographic research focuses primarily on those aspects of traditional olive oil processing that apply to the main goal of my research; to investigate those processes which affect the olive remains and their incorporation into the archaeological record. In order to determine which aspects of processing affected the olives, it was important to cover the entire process of olive oil production, from the very beginning to the last possible end use of pressing wastes. The beginning is the point at which humans begin to manipulate the fruit: i.e., picking the olives. From there, the research includes all aspects of processing the olives into oil, and after that, the uses of pressing wastes. Throughout the course of the fieldwork, contacts also supplied information that, while not directly related to the focus of research, is none-the-less important ethnographic information on the olive tradition in the Near East. This information includes: eating olives, taste preferences, economic and social implications, and folk stories about the olive and olive oil.

3.3.1 Area of Research

Irrigation now permits the growth of olives just about everywhere in Syro-Palestine. Areas with the longest tradition of olive cultivation lie in northern Jordan, especially in the hilly areas around Jerash, continuing north past Ajlun to Irbid (see Figure 1.3). In Israel and Palestine the areas include places such as Hebron, the Galilee, and the Carmel coast. The majority of the fieldwork was done in and around the Jerash to Irbid region of northwestern Jordan, and the Carmel coast/Galilee region of northern Israel. Fuller's (1986) study was also conducted in the region, at Harta, north of Irbid. The Irbid agricultural directorate alone accounts for 26% of the olive producing area of Jordan (Shboul, *pers. comm.*; Bataeneh, *pers. comm.*), producing around 7,000 tons of oil per year, just under half of Jordan's total olive oil production. I traveled as well to the Tafila region of south-central western Jordan, a secondary olive producing area.

3.3.2 Olive Picking

The process of making olive oil begins in the olive orchards. From October through January, when the olives ripen in Jordan, harvesting takes place. Some contacts believe that olives left on the tree until November/December have a higher oil content, sometimes almost double the amount of oil. Other contacts think that the percentage of oil decreases as it gets colder: the oil in the olive in December is less than in November, while olives in January have the least oil of all. In the West Bank town of Salfeet, a committee of local growers set strict rules concerning harvesting, including a provision that in order for the olives to be fully mature, none can be harvested before November 1st (Martin, 2001).

The method for picking olives has not change much over the centuries. The methods employed by the family with whom I picked are virtually the same as those practiced at the turn of the century. The same methods are demonstrated in the photos of the Matson Collection (Library of Congress, Episcopal Home), a collection of photographs showing life in Syro-Palestine taken in the late 1800s to mid 1930s. Children were first set to work picking up all the fallen olives on the ground around a tree (Figure 3.1). Once the ground had been picked clean, large tarps or blankets were spread on the ground around the tree (Figure 3.2). The olives would then be picked from the tree and dropped to collect on the tarp. To reach the fruit higher up the tree small ladders would be used, mainly around the outside of the tree. Some of the younger pickers would climb up into the trees and stand on branches or the main tree trunk while picking (Figure 3.3). After a tree had been stripped of its fruit, the olives would be collected in the tarps, the larger twigs, sticks and leaves sorted out, and the olives then bagged in large sacks. Children would pick up any leftovers or missed fruit. Once a significant number of bags (I was not told how many) were picked to warrant pressing, they would be taken to the mill. Rosenblum (1996) mentions having an experience similar to mine on his Palestinian olive picking trip. Pickers would often sing special songs during the olive picking (Ayoub, 2001), a practice I observed while picking.

The proper method of picking olives was to "milk" the branches. You peel, pick or strip the olives off the branches similar to a person milking a cow (or more commonly in the Near East, a goat) and let the olives drop onto the tarp (Figure 3.4). "Milking" the fruit off the branches is the best way to pick, as it protects the olives from bruising which triggers acidity (Rosenblum, 1996). Shaking the branches to let the really ripe olives drop was allowed, as long as the shaking wasn't hard enough to break the branches. According to White (1970) olive picking requires skill and care. Careless picking removes the bark and damages the tree. One should pick the lower branches by hand. Those upper branches that could not be reached by ladder could be beaten with a stick, preferably a reed and not a pole so not to damage the tree and branches (White, 1970). Amiry and Tamari (1989) mention shaking or beating the olives off the tree, while Sandy (1989) mentions beating with sticks as a harvesting method. Hand picking is preferred (Ayoub, 2001; Davis, 1996; Dolamore, 1994; Forbes, 1965; Klein, 1994; Knickerbocker, 1997; Ridgeway, 1996; Zisling, 2000). Strict rules set by the local growers committee in the West

a

b

FIGURE 3.1: OLIVE PICKING HAS CHANGED LITTLE OVER THE YEARS
a) PICKING OLIVES OFF THE GROUND (MATSON COLLECTION B224;
© MATSON COLLECTION AND THE EPISCOPAL HOME)
b) CHILDREN PICKING OLIVES OFF THE GROUND IN 1996, NEAR IRBID

FIGURE 3.2: TARP LAID UNDER OLIVE TREE TO COLLECT OLIVES AS THEY ARE PICKED OFF THE TREE, NEAR IRBID

a

b

FIGURE 3.3: USING LADDERS AND STANDING ON BRANCHES TO PICK OUT OF REACH OLIVES a) MATSON COLLECTION B222 (© MATSON COLLECTION AND THE EPISCOPAL HOME) b) 1996, NEAR IRBID

FIGURE 3.4: YOUNG GIRL "MILKING" THE TREE
(MATSON COLLECTION B223;
© MATSON COLLECTION AND THE EPISCOPAL HOME)

Pilcher (1996) states that "You can always tell when a family is picking the olives off its own trees by the gentle treatment the tree receives. The olives are removed by hand in a method called "milking" that ensures that the tree remains undamaged for the coming seasons." Pilcher promised the pickers he hired to pick his olives (for half the crop) that he'd invite them back in coming seasons if they picked this way instead of beating the trees. "Palestinians, like the Israelis and the French, are Milkers. Many Spaniards, Italians, and Greeks are whackers. It is a question of economy. Milkers run their fingers quickly down a branch ... " Beating the branches is faster and allows crews to harvest tall trees without a ladder, though the method does break branches (Rosenblum, 1996:56). Beating the tree with sticks to shake down the fruit damages the tree and reduces the next year's yield (Hibler, 2003). In Rosenblum's book, the people doing the hand picking were usually "family" groups or traditionalists, while "whackers" tended to be hired workers, something my experiences agree with. One contact told me that people she talked with concerning picking techniques said all the knowledge supposedly came from "Palestine."

There are a number of other harvesting methods, such as using special rakes, goat's horn finger attachments, and mechanical shakers to remove the fruit from the trees (Dolamore, 1994; I.O.O.C., nd; Knickerbocker, 1997; Ridgeway, 1996; Rosenblum, 1996; Zisling, 2000). Some of these methods, especially the mechanical shakers, are used mainly in larger commercial orchards. While the mechanical shakers are the fastest method, the method also harms the trees. The traditional small family holdings and most small-estate fancy oil producers continue to use hand harvesting.

I was told by one contact that Jordan was getting more requests for exported oil, since Jordan is one of the few remaining places not using chemicals to induce fruit dropage to speed up harvesting. No one I interviewed mentions or reports using chemicals to induce olives to abscise from the trees. I was told that abscission chemicals were not used in Jordan (Bataeneh, *pers. comm.*). When these chemicals were tested in Irbid they damaged the trees. The trees lost their leaves as well as the fruit, and, some olives remained on the trees, which then required hand picking. Since many of the groves are small family-run groves and there is plenty of cheap labor available in Jordan, chemicals aren't necessary.

This first step in the olive oil process, picking the olives, does not lead to any modification of the olive stones. Efforts are taken not to damage the fruit during picking. The stone is protected by the full flesh of the fruit. The various methods of picking may, however, affect the tree. For instance, beating the tree can break branches and twigs which can affect olive production in later seasons. Overall, the various picking methods do not affect the olive fruit or stone.

Bank town of Salfeet require that olives must be hand picked rather than knocked out of trees with a stick so no tree limbs are broken (Martin, 2001). Many of the quality, extra-virgin oils listed by Ridgeway (1996) specifically say they are picked by hand. Shaking branches for those out of reach or striking branches with pliant twigs so as not to harm olives may be allowed (Forbes, 1965). Occasionally, both in Jordan and Israel, I did see people beating the trees with long thin sticks. A contact from the Tafielah area said that people sometimes beat trees with sticks when picking. While I was picking a couple of the young women did take small branches and beat the tree with them. They were quickly yelled at by my contact (I heard the word *harahm*: forbidden). According to the International Olive Oil Council (I.O.O.C.) harvesting by beating the tree damages the tree (also: Davis, 1996; Zisling, 2000). My contact's father gave him this advice, "Never beat the tree, always pick, drop the olives to the cloth set on ground around the tree. Milk the tree, don't take leaves in your hand." This advice is very old: Pliny states that care must be exercised in knocking the fruit from the tree so as not to injure the tree or disturb the bud of next year's crop (*Natural History* 15.3.11), and a Moroccan proverb declares (with the olive tree speaking): "Caress me, don't beat me, If you want my fruits another time." (Rosenblum, 1996:203).

3.3.3 Pre-Crushing Preparations

After picking, the olives are taken to the mills, where they undergo the three-step process (crushing, pressing, separation of oil and lees) of being turned into olive oil. It is recommended that the sooner the olives are crushed and pressed after picking the better, though Dolamore (1994) suggests that a short period of storage allows fermentation to begin, helping to release more oil. If olives are stored too long they ferment and generate heat, which may taint the flavor of the oil. Immediate pressing also limits the possibility of insects and decay affecting the oil (I.O.O.C., nd), which people in antiquity recognized as well (Cato, *De Re Rustica* 3.4; 64.1; Columella, *De Re Rustica: De Arboribus* 12.52.3; Pliny, *Natural History* 15.4.14). As one contact put it: it is best if the olives go straight "from the tree to the stone." At modern oil mills this is usually the case, however, at the old traditional mills people frequently pre-process the olives. At many of the old traditional mills people talked about how they would prepare the olives prior to crushing and pressing. Preparation usually involved; 1) drying the olives prior to crushing, 2) boiling the olives before crushing, 3) smoking the olives before crushing, or 4) any combination of the first three in no particular order.

In one village a mill owner said that the olives go straight from the tree to the modern press, but that dried olives were taken to the old presses, though some contacts said dried olives were done at modern presses as well. The olives are spread on rooftops, courtyards, and in rooms to dry (Figure 3.5). The olives dry for several days to a week though no more than three days according to Sandy (1989). Drying is done to allow the olives to ripen further (Wolff, 1976), to reduce the acidity (Amiry and Tamari, 1989), or to reduce the water content of the fruit before pressing (Avitsur, 1994; Ridgeway, 1996; Sandy, 1989). Drying does have the drawback in that it may induce rotting in the olives, causing bad tasting oil (Avitsur, 1994; Ridgeway, 1996). One contact said that you have to dry the olives in open areas, free to the wind and sun, for if they are closed up the olives will heat up and get a bad smell. Baussan and Chibois (2000) also note the practice of drying prior to pressing occurring at one of the oldest mills on the island of Corsica. A contact from the internet group mentioned receiving a copy of a circa 1895 lithograph showing olive oil production in southern Italy, and the caption mentioned storing the olives until they were matured, *i.e.*, turned a brownish black.

Boiling the olives prior to pressing is another common traditional pre-processing practice. Boiling makes the flesh come off the olive stone, making pressing easier (Al-Rub, 1992). Each farmer boils his own olives at home, then takes them to the mill for processing. "We boil the olives and spread it on the roofs of the houses till it hardens. Then we press it," from an old woman in the village of Tibneh (Khammash, 1995:59). After boiling the olives are dried, then processed, however, in some locations the olives are dried first, then boiled. I had two contacts argue over which the proper method was: boil first, then dry, or dry first, then boil. Boiled or dried olives produce a darker, brown, oil (Zureiq, *pers. comm.*; Koch, *pers. comm.*). According to one source olive oil made from boiled and dried olives is better than oil just from dried olives. A group of contacts in the far north of Jordan made the remark that "People in the north are smarter than those in the south," referring to the practice of boiling the olives before pressing, suggesting that this is done only in the north but not in south. One contact from the olive oil internet group mentioned the practice of boiling olives occurring in northern Cyprus, but that the resulting oil is not to everyone's taste.

Another pre-processing practice mentioned by several contacts was roasting or smoking the olives before processing. The olives are smoked or roasted over low fires, using a "dry heat" (Takruri, *pers. comm.*). Not only does roasting the olives give them a smoky taste, but it makes them softer and easier to press. Takruri (*pers. comm.*) believes that roasting also cuts down on emulsions that give the oil a bitter taste. There was one mention of a mid-processing practice similar to the previous procedure. One contact said that sometime in the past, about 45 years ago, after crushing the olives the women would roast the mash and then press it for oil. He said that this is best tasting oil of all.

The practice of drying (Avitsur, 1994) and boiling the olives prior to processing is disappearing, according to several contacts, due in part to more olives being grown. Drying and boiling olives are time consuming practices difficult to continue with increasing volumes of olives. Also, as younger generations are brought up on the taste of modern, mass produced olive oil, the taste preferences for traditionally-made oil is disappearing as well. As Baussan and Chibois (2000:50) point

FIGURE 3.5: OLIVES DRYING IN A ROOM PRIOR TO PROCESSING, NEAR IRBID

out, the flavor of the oil (in their case, from dried olives) "does not appeal to the contemporary palate, and it's value is historical." These forms of pre-processing have no apparent affect on the olive stone.

3.3.4 Processing Methods

Once the olives are picked and any pre-processing procedures out of the way, the olives are taken to the oil mill, where they are crushed, pressed and the oil separated from the lees/amurca (water portion of the fruit). Many people combine these three steps of processing olives to oil and refer to the entire process as "pressing." In traditional olive oil processing there are a wide variety of methods and procedures, depending in part on the amount of oil desired or availability of processing equipment. At modern mills olives are processed all together regardless of type or variety (black/green, large/small) (Frankel, *pers. comm.*). At traditional mills people pay more attention to ensure that the olives pressed together are uniform in type and variety. Using the same type and variety of olives helps give traditional oils distinct flavors.

Processing is one of two stages, the other being post-pressing usage, which may cause major alterations to the olive stone. While some methods might have a major impact on the stone, others may have little effect. Processing methods identified during this stage of the research were then used in my olive crushing experiments. I will use the term "crushing" to mean the pre-pressing modification of the fruit, basically the breaking of the fruit to enhance the release of the oil, while "pressing" is defined as the act of putting pressure or other means to express the oil from the fruit. Before describing the different processing methods, I will give a detailed comparison between traditional and modern mill operations. This comparison is followed by descriptions of a variety of traditional olive oil processing methods.

3.3.4.1a Traditional Press Operation
A 73 year old press owner from Kfur Sum described a traditional olive oil processing operation. His press presses 1000 "*mud*" (15 kilos) of olives every 24 hours (1,500 kilos = 1 ½ metric tons). Picked olives are dried in open areas, exposed to the wind and sun. If the olives are kept in closed areas they heat up and begin to smell bad. While the olives are drying a reservation is made at the press (Figure 3.6). At the agreed upon time the olives are brought in for pressing. The olives are put in a machine that blows away the leaves and then the olives are washed in hot, not boiling, water. The cleaned olives are put into the mill (a two stone style mill) and crushed (Figure 3.7). The crushed olives are put into a bin. From the bin the olive "mash" is packed into baskets (Figure 3.8). Some baskets have a "lip" holding the mash in or on the basket (Figure 3.9). Another style of basket has a hole in the middle of the basket, this style of basket fits around a central spike (Figure 3.10). As the baskets are filled they are stacked for pressing. After 4 full baskets are stacked, one empty basket is placed in the stack, followed by a steel disc weighing about 10 kilos. More full baskets follow the steel disc. Once the stack reaches the appropriate height for the press, the stack is put into the press. This contact's mill had two hydraulic presses: one large press with a capacity of approximately 45 baskets and 16 metal discs and able to press 20 "mud"; and one smaller press holding approximately ten fewer baskets. The presses are pressed upwards hydraulically on a pedestal. The presses exert a maximum pressure of around 500 psi. The presses used in the traditional mills are upright hydraulic presses (Figure 3.11), which have only recently replaced upright screw presses. The old screw presses exerted a downward pressure, the opposite of the hydraulic presses. As the olive mash is pressed the oil squeezed from the mash runs out of the baskets. The oil collects in small wells near the press, from which it is pumped into containers on the roof. During the cold of winter hot water pipes run from a stove

FIGURE 3.6: OIL MILL AT EL MAZAR, NEAR IRBID

21

FIGURE 3.7: CRUSHING OLIVES WITH A 2-STONE MILL, EL MAZAR

a

c

b

FIGURE 3.8a-b: "PACKING" BASKETS WITH OLIVE MASH, SAMOUA
FIGURE 3.8c: PUTTING CRUSHED OLIVES INTO BASKET-CONTAINERS FOR PRESSING (MATSON COLLECTION 3968; © MATSON COLLECTION AND THE EPISCOPAL HOME)

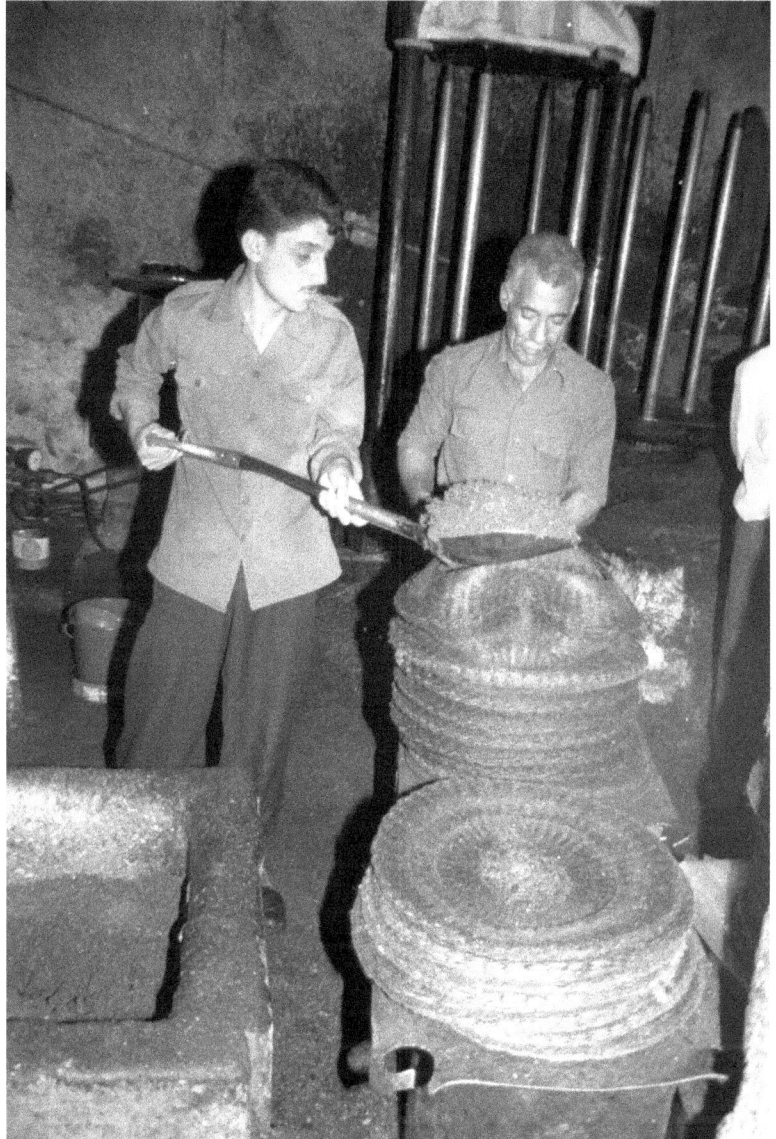

FIGURE 3.9: PUTTING OLIVE MASH INTO BASKET
WITH POCKET, EL MAZAR

a

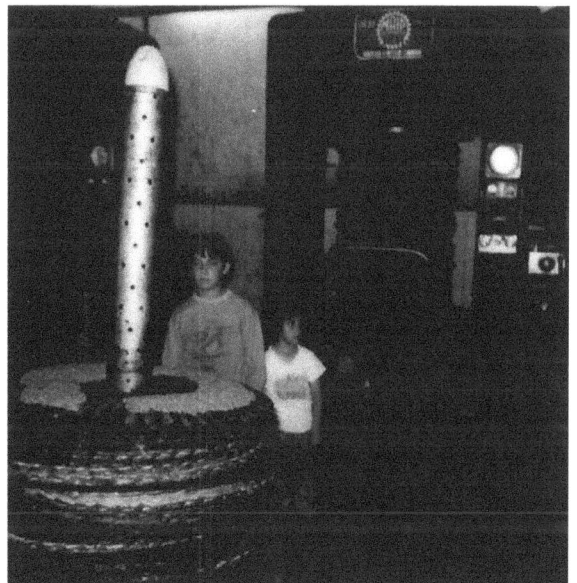

b

FIGURE 3.10a-b: OLIVE MASH ON BASKETS WITH HOLE IN CENTER TO FIT OVER SPIKE, TOBNEH

FIGURE 3.11a: UPRIGHT HYDRAULIC PRESS, TOBNEH. LAYERS OF MASH-FILLED BASKETS ARE SEPARATED WITH METAL PLATES

FIGURE 3.11b: UPRIGHT HYDRAULIC PRESS, EL MAZAR. LAYERS OF MASH-FILLED BASKETS ARE SEPARATED WITH METAL PLATES. A STREAM OF PRESSED OIL IS RUNNING INTO THE CONTAINER AT THE BOTTOM.

to the roof circulating hot water to prevent the oil from freezing. Sometimes a little hot water is added to the oil itself. All the hot water used at this press is heated by a *jift*-fueled stove, utilizing the waste product, the *jift*, from the pressing process. The water and oil is separated at a later date. Out of 100 kilos of oil, the mill owner gets ten. After pressing, the baskets are taken from the press and the squeezed pulp and stones removed (Figure 3.12).

At another press, the owners had dispensed with the traditional crusher four years previously and now use modern machinery to clean and crush the olives. This mill continues to use a hydraulic press rather than a centrifuge system (see Figure 3.10). At this mill they stack the olive mash laden baskets in sets of ten baskets followed by a metal plate. This pattern (ten baskets + one metal plate) continues until there are twelve sets totaling 120 baskets. The arrangement in the number of mash-filled baskets in a group separated by a metal disk varies from press to press, location to location. For instance, at a site in Greece it was five or six mash filled baskets followed by a plate (Knickerbocker, 1997).

3.3.4.1b Modern Olive Oil Processing

There are several modern methods of olive oil processing (Dolamore, 1994; I.O.O.C., n.d.; Knickerbocker, 1997). At modern olive oil mills in Jordan, the processing procedure is set up in "lines," with the processing machinery all in a row. Modern mills in Jordan are usually described based on the number of "lines" the mill operates. At the modern oil mills the olives are dumped into a bin (Figure 3.13) from which the olives are conveyed to a cleaner that washes the olives and removes leaves, twigs and other debris (Figure 3.14). The olives are then sent into a crusher that grinds the olives, stone and all, into a fine mash. The crushed mass is then transferred to a long "vat" or trough containing a corkscrew auger (Figure 3.15). The auger helps to homogenize the mash. If the mash is too thick, water may be added to it. The mash then goes into a large centrifuge that spins out the liquid content of the mash (Figure 3.16). The liquid is piped to a separator, which also filters the oil (Figure 3.17). From the separator the oil is dispensed into containers (Figure 3.18), which are then weighed.

Samples were taken for comparative purposes at a one line modern mill on the outskirts of Irbid, Jordan. A sample was taken from the augered vat, prior to the centrifugation step, providing an olive mash sample from modern equipment. Samples of *jift* and olive oil were also obtained at this mill.

3.3.4.2 Crushing Methods

As previously mentioned, the first step in processing olives to produce olive oil is to crush the fruit to facilitate releasing the oil from the fruit's cells. Crushing the olives ruptures the oil-containing cells of the mesocarp within the fruit and allows the release of the oil from those cells. The sharp fragments of broken stones helps facilitate the release

a

b

FIGURE 3.12a: REMOVING PRESSED BASKETS FROM PRESS, EL MAZAR
FIGURE 3.12b: EMPTYING PRESSED OLIVE MASH (*JIFT*) FROM BASKETS, EL MAZAR

of oil from the pulp by puncturing the oil-containing cells (Mattingly, 1996). Traditional methods of crushing olive fruit vary greatly and are somewhat dependant on the quantity of olives being crushed and/or the volume of oil desired. Some of these methods are still in use, though like many traditional practices fading away, while others are noted from historical and/or other sources. These methods

include: treading or stomping, using a hand quern or mill, using a mortar and pestle, and finally, using millstones, including large cylindrical rollers.

3.3.4.2.1 Treading
The most basic of these methods may be simply treading or stomping the olives to crush them, similar to treading

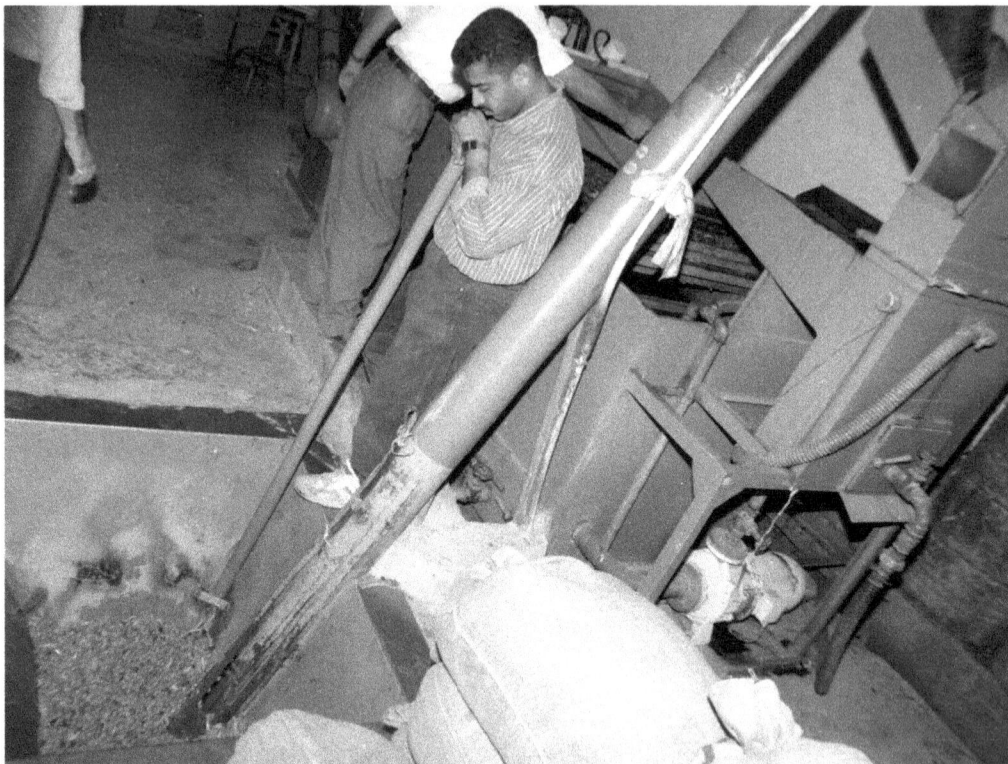

FIGURE 3.13: OLIVES AT THE BEGINNING OF THE MODERN MILL PROCESS, IRBID

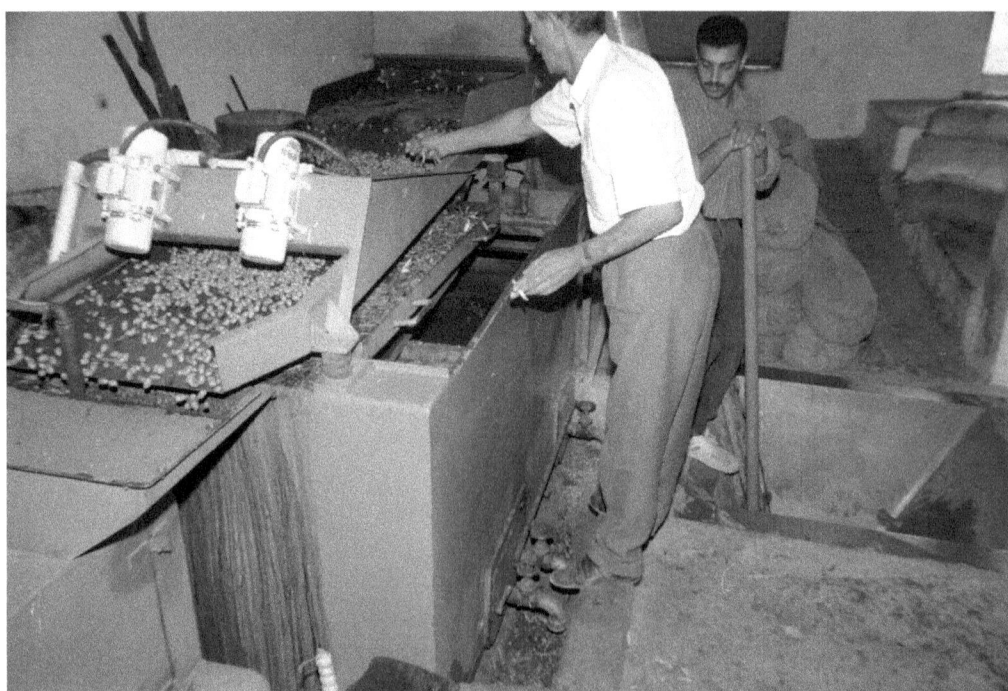

FIGURE 3.14: CLEANED OLIVES HEADING TO CRUSHER, MODERN MILL, IRBID

a

b

FIGURE 3.15a-b: CRUSHING OLIVES,
MODERN MILL, EL MAZAR
a) TROUGH FOR CRUSHING OLIVES
b) CORK-SCREW AUGUR IN CRUSHING
TROUGH

FIGURE 3.16: CENTRIFUGE AT
MODERN MILL, IRBID

FIGURE 3.17: SEPARATOR: SEPARATING WATER AND OIL, FILTERING OIL, IRBID

FIGURE 3.18: FILLING CONTAINERS WITH PROCESSED OIL, IRBID

grapes to produce wine. Treading is one of the more primitive methods of crushing (Brun, 2000; Chabour, 2004; Dolamore, 1994; Eitam, 2000; Frankel, 1994; 1999; Toussaint-Samar, 1992), and could until recently still be observed (Gal and Frankel, 1993). It is thought that the three stages of production (crushing, pressing and separation) could all be carried out in one simple installation (Dalman, 1935; R. Frankel, 1996; Gal and Frankel, 1993). A typical treading installation consists of stone-cut depressions with two levels. The top level is a large shallow crushing platform. This upper crushing platform would drain into a lower collection vat (Figure 3.19, 3.20) (Frankel, 1999; Gal and Frankel, 1993; Zisling, 2000). Such installations are quite similar to simple wine-presses. The olives or grapes are crushed on the upper surface and the expressed liquids (oil or wine) seep or are pressed out to drain into the lower basin. There are often two holes on each side of

the pressing/tramping area (Frankel, 1999; *pers. comm.*). The holes are for either; (1) poles with rope slung between them for the people tramping the fruit to hang on to while tramping, or (2) for hanging a tension or torsion bag press. This pressing method will be discussed later (see section 3.3.4.4.2).

Although Foxhall (*pers. comm.*) believes that references to treading are a misinterpretation, there is fairly strong evidence to support the technique. Treading the olives is done wearing wooden sandals (Brun, 2000; Eitam, 2000; Frankel 1987; Gal and Frankel 1993; Tzedakis and Martlew, 1999). This may be what is referred to by Micah in the Bible, when he says "Thou shalt tread the olives," (Micah 6:15). According to Frankel (1987) there is also some discussion about treading olives in the Hebrew Mishnah. R. Frankel (1996; 1997) points

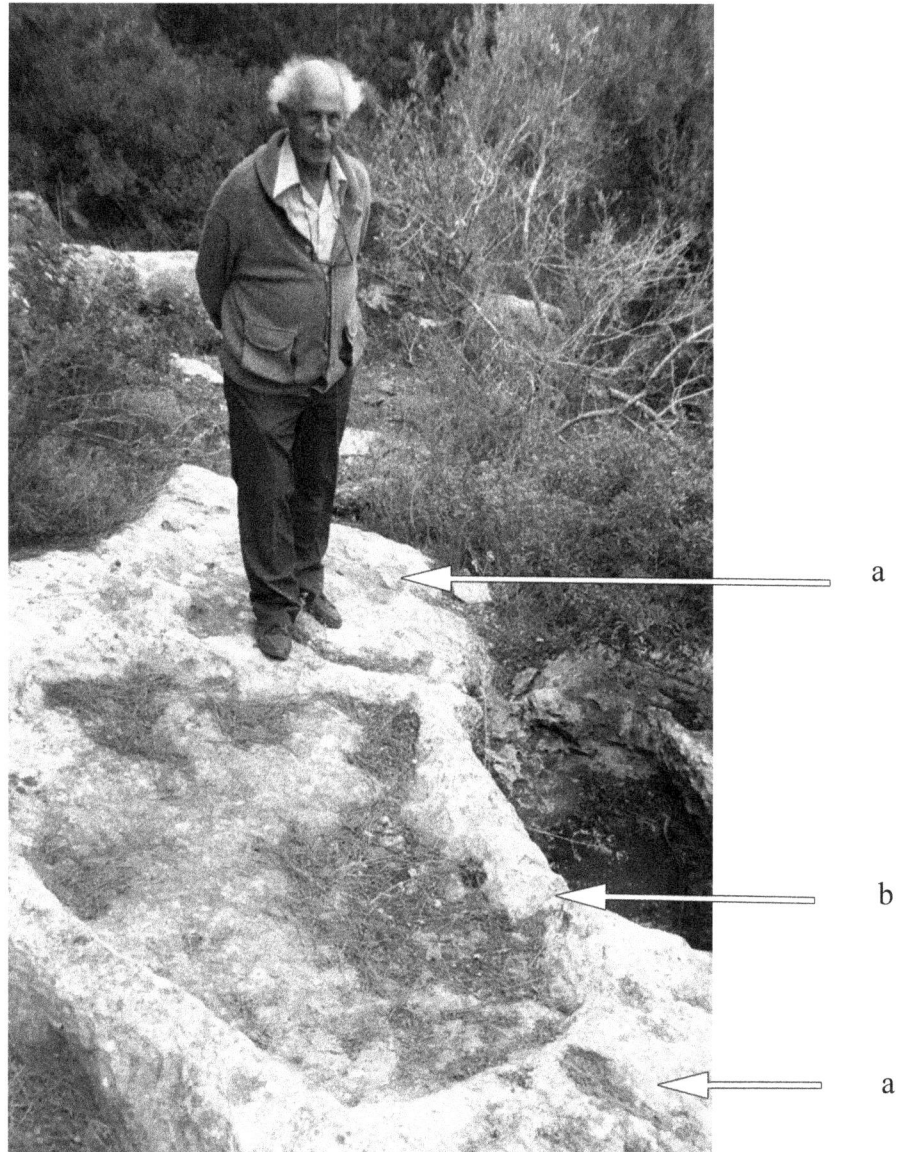

FIGURE 3.19: FOOT-TREADING CRUSHING PLATFORM, BEIT HA'EMEK, ISRAEL
a) HOLES FOR POLES AND POSSIBLE BAG PRESS OR BALANCE ROPE
b) SLOT DRAINING FROM UPPER PRESS BASIN TO LOWER COLLECTING BASIN

out that the Latin word *trapetum*, a style of Roman mill, is derived from the Greek word for treading. This derivation raises the question of why the derivation is not from the Greek word for crushing? Also, one of the crushing devices described by Columella (*De Re Rustica* 12.56.6) is called a *solea*, the sole of a shoe. Liddell and Scott (1968), in their Greek-English dictionary, list the word κρούπεζαι for "*high wooden shoes*, used in Boeotia for treading olives." These may be the Greek shoes, sandals or clogs mentioned in Amouretti (1986) for treading olives. They also list the word τράπέω, to "*tread grapes*." The displays at the Olive Oil Museum in Haifa include a drawing of a woman wearing wood sandals treading olives in a basin.

Wearing wooden sandals to crush olives by stomping is documented for North Africa (Amouretti and Comet, 1992). It is a method preferred by women and done on a circular platform. This technique produces low amounts but gives highly prized oil. The practice of using treading to produce a special oil is supported by Tyree (*pers. comm.*) who recounts that "talking to someone in Izmir, Turkey, whose mother, now in her 70s, remembers stamping on olives in sacks to obtain an oil made without crushing the pit – for specialty, holiday gifts." Frankel (*pers. comm.*) says that while not actually documented, old people have mentioned treading olives. When the Croatian city of Dubrovnik was under siege by the Serbians (during the break up of the former Yugoslav Republic) "some farmers went back to the old method that a few rural families still use today: they put the olives in stone tubs, add very hot water, and walk on them with specially made wooden shoes" (Rosenblum, 1996:262). Since Croatia is just up the coast from northern Greece, the practice may be the modern day equivalent to ancient Greek references to special olive stomping shoes/sandals. Frankel (1999) refers to treading olives in a sack from a source at Santa Lucia Di Mercurio-Corsica in recent times.

According to Litchfield (1984), a person grinding olives in a hand quern worked the fresh-ground olive paste by

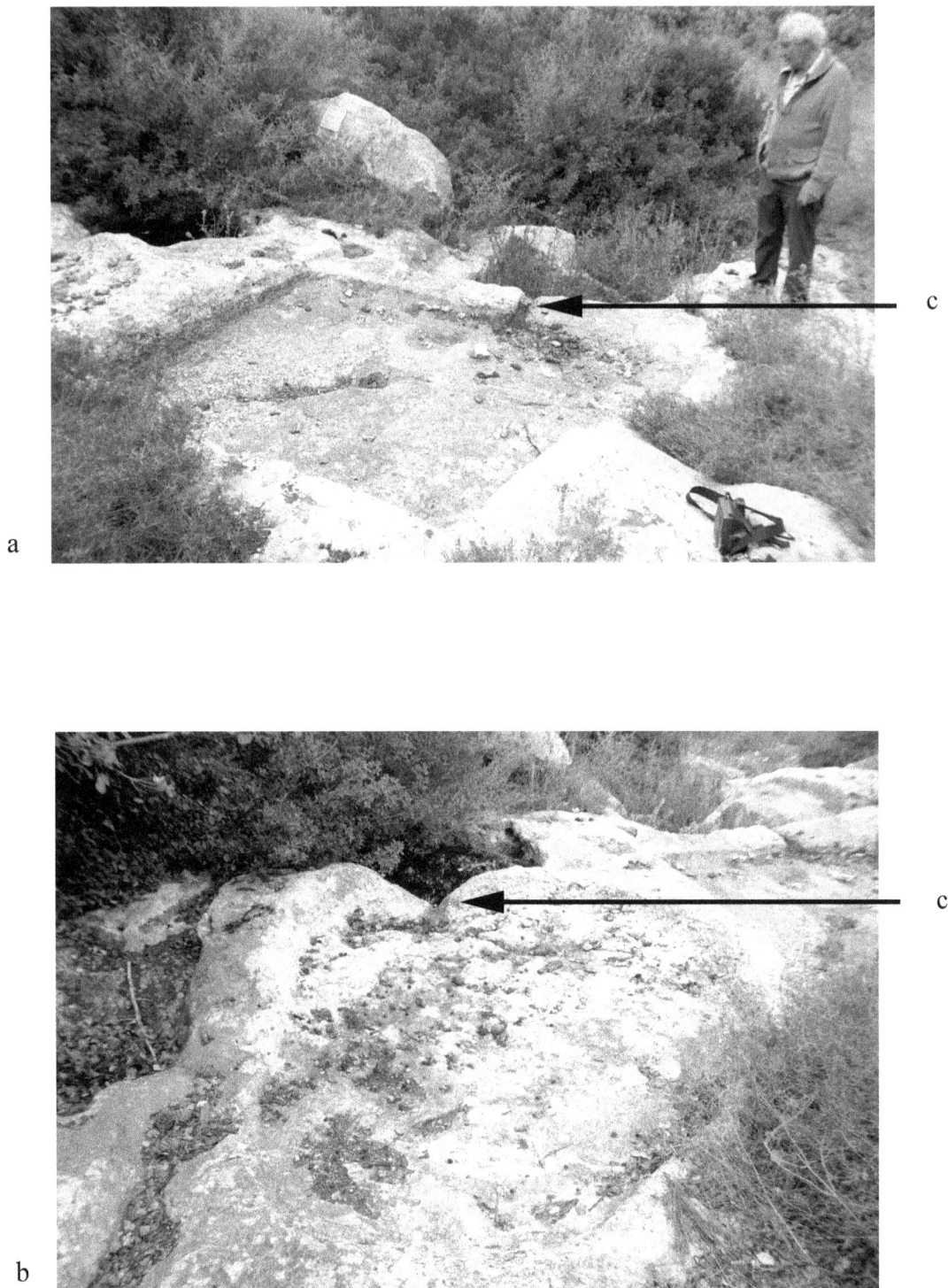

FIGURE 3.20a-b: CRUSHING PLATFORM WITH DRAIN NOTCH LEADING TO COLLECTING BASIN, BEIT HA'EMEK, ISRAEL
c: NOTCH

trampling it with her bare feet (Figure 3.21). Whether or not this could be the remnant of a previous treading method prior to use or introduction of the hand quern for olive crushing is open for debate.

Since grapes ripen and are harvested and pressed before olives, crushing/pressing installations could be used for processing both; wine first, then olive oil (Foxhall, *pers. comm.*; Frankel, 1999; *pers. comm.*; Wolff, 1976), a view

supported by the biblical verse: "the vats will overflow with new wine and oil" (Joel 2:24). Also, rural poor people in modern Greece use the same press for wine and olive oil (Wolff, 1976). Frankel (1999) believes that these types of installations are mistakenly translated as "wine press" in the Bible.

Since the grape vine did not occur in Israel till the Early Bronze Age (around 3,000 B.C.) (Frankel, 1994; Zohary

FIGURE 3.21: WOMAN MIXING OLIVE MASH WITH FOOT
(LITCHFIELD)

FIGURE 3.22: HAND QUERN

FIGURE 3.23a: "GRINDING AT THE MILL, JERUSALEM"
(STEREOVIEW PHOTO, COSMOPOLITAN SERIES NO. 548)

and Hopf, 2000; Zohary, 1986; Zohary and Spiegel-Roy, 1975), installations predating this time period are evidence that the platforms are for olive (Frankel, 1994).

3.3.4.2.2 Hand Quern

The use of the horizontal olive hand-mill (quern) has been overlooked in previous discussions of olive oil production devices (Frankel, 1999). I interviewed an elderly Bedouin woman now settled in Madaba, Jordan, an area not traditionally known as an olive producing area. The woman talked about the women of the household and associated extended family making olive oil in the household, using a hand quern (Figure 3.22). The small rotary hand querns in Jordan are typically made of basalt. The two disc shaped stones are flat-sided on the grinding surfaces, while the other surfaces may be flat or convex, though the bottom surface of the lower stone is usually flattened. The peg around which the top stone rotates is smaller than the hole in the upper stone, which allows the top stone to move in an elliptical pattern over the bottom stone. The hole also needs to be big enough to let the raw material (grain, lentils, olives, etc.) enter (Figure 3.23a-b). The elliptical pattern moves the top stone off the lower one around the

edge so that the ground material can exit out the side as the stones rotate. In addition to my observations, the only other literary reference of employing this technique to crush olives is by Litchfield (1984:341) for Tunisia:

While traveling near El Djem, Tunisia in December 1981, I encountered a farmer's wife who used a rotary hand quern to extract olive oil from olives... The process I observed consisted of three steps: grinding, working, and decantation. The initial grinding step was carried out with the stone rotary hand quern placed upon a large sheet of plastic. Whole black olives were fed into the center cavity of the top stone and ground (both pulp and pits) to a paste which fell from the sides of the quern onto

FIGURE 3.23b: USING QUERN TO GRIND FLOUR (LITCHFIELD)

a

b

FIGURE 3.24: a) GRINDING OLIVES WITH HANDQUERN (LITCHFIELD)
b) HAND QUERN OPENED AFTER GRINDING OLIVES

the sheet of plastic [Figure 3.24]. The pigment from the olives quickly blackened the quern, the plastic, and the hands of the operator. When sufficient paste had been collected, it was placed in a large crock. Water was added, and the mixture was worked with the foot for several minutes [Figure 3.21]. The crock was then filled with hot water, stirred, and left to stand overnight. The oil separated out as the upper layer and was skimmed off with a distinctive shallow metal ladle. The remaining paste and liquid were fed to goats and camels.

There is one case of photographic documentation showing the quern method in use. A photograph in the Matson Collection (no. 563) is labeled "Oil Press" and shows a large quern being turned by a camel (Figure 3.25). Frankel (1999) notes an unusual type of horizontal olive mill found in North Africa and Spain (his type T37). He believes that this type of mill is similar to the donkey-powered rotary grain grinding mill and is probably the *mola olearius* referred to by Columella. The Matson photograph is probably of this type of mill being used in Palestine in the late 1800s or early 1900s.

Litchfield (1984) also mentions that the hand quern is preferred for making small amounts of oil for immediate family needs. An added benefit to using the quern is the cost, since a mill is not paid for making the oil. The use of the quern grinding technique was reported to me by Dr. Musa Numan Ahmad of the University of Jordan, and M. Adawi, the chief cook at the American Center of Oriental Research in Amman, Jordan. Dr. Ahmad mentioned that olives ground in rotary querns were usually pitted, unlike Litchfield's example. The Bedouin woman mentioned previously did not grind the olives, stone and all. Instead, the women of the household pitted the olives prior to grinding them in the quern. They would utilize the cleaned olive stones later.

Roman writers (Cato and Columella) recommended not crushing the olive stone because doing so would impart a bad flavor to the oil. These references led modern authors (Forbes, 1965; Cotton, 1979; White, 1984) to believe that the Greeks and Romans pitted the olives prior to crushing. Tyree and Stefanoudaki (1996) do not believe this practice occurred, at least not for the large volume mills. Documentation of this activity in antiquity might actually be referring to small scale processing instead, or for specialty oils. According to Avitsur (1994), producers of the very finest olive oil used to pit the olives prior to crushing.

3.3.4.2.3 Mortar and Pestles and other Pounding Methods
One of the more common methods of crushing olives for oil production involves merely picking up a stone and beating the olives with it, a practice which likely evolved into the use of mortars and pestles. The amount of oil produced is typically for a single serving or meal.

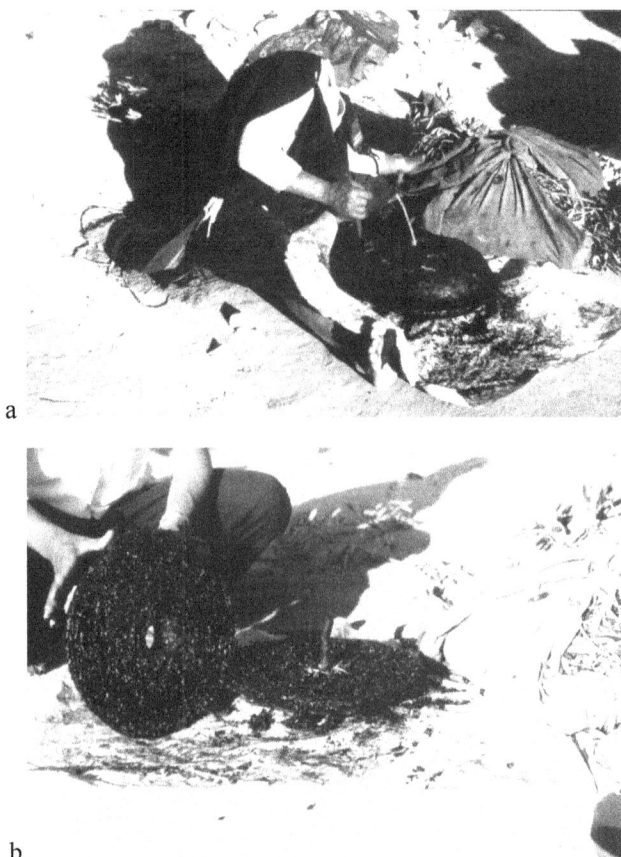

FIGURE 3.25: CAMEL TURNING LARGE QUERN-STYLE
"OIL-PRESS" (MATSON COLLECTION NO. 563; © MATSON
COLLECTION AND THE EPISCOPAL HOME)

The small amount of oil produced using a mortar is also sufficient for use as a base in making small amounts of perfume, and the mortar could be used to grind and mix the other perfume ingredients (Brun, 2000). A number of contacts in rural Jordan, when describing the making of small amounts of oil, mention putting a small pile of olives on a flat surface and crushing them with a stone. Similar ethnographic evidence from the Mesara region in South-Central Crete had "simple processing practices in the region included crushing olives in the field by beating and rolling them on a stone slab with a water worn cobble or boulder," (Blitzer, 1993:171). One contact states that his mother crushes olives with a stone in a basin. He further said that if it is only a small quantity of olives, they are pressed at home the old way, otherwise they would be taken to a modern mill. At the traditional mill at Al Mazar an elderly woman said they would first roast the olives, then beat them with a stone, and finally press the mash with their hands. She also told a story about a man from Palestine who showed up one day and while demonstrating a pressing method, crushed the olives the same way. In northern Israel a contact spoke of using a wood hammer and stone bowl to crush olives. Frankel (*pers. comm.*) does not believe this method was extensively used. However,

when the Croatian city of Dubrovnik was under siege by the Serbians (during the break up of the former Yugoslav Republic), people made oil by beating olive filled burlap bags with hammers (Rosenblum, 1996). Chabour (2004) mentions the use of spiked bronze clubs as rudimentary processing tools. Avitsur (1994) refers to first warming the olives slightly and then crushing them between a hand-held stone and a flat rock. Contacts in Kufranja, Jordan, said that in the home, for a small amount of oil, one crushes the olives with a rock. There are also Mishnaic references (Frankel, 1994; 1997:210; *pers. comm.*) to olive oil made exclusively for the Temple in Jerusalem, prepared by pounding olives in mortars.

An improvement in this crushing method involves using a stone mortar or cup-shaped depression and stone pestle (Avitsur, 1994; Brun, 2000; Tyree and Stefanoudaki, 1996; Tzedakis and Martlew, 1999). The use of mortars and pestles for olive oil spans from antiquity to the present. Large numbers of mortars and basins probably used in olive oil extraction have been found on Cyprus dating from the Neolithic to Early Bronze periods (Hadjisavvas, 1992). At Middle Minoan (≈ 2,200–1,500 B.C.) Kommos on Crete, the large number of stone mortars, bases, hand tools and olive remains suggested a methodological procedure for processing olives (Blitzer, 1993). There are also numerous small depressions, Neolithic or Chalcolithic, in Israel (Eitam, *pers. comm.*). Eitam (1993) experimented with a number of such rock cut installations, which were presumably mortars and basins for olive oil crushing, to determine the volume of oil such installations could produce. The Early Bronze Age site of Beth Yerah in Israel has numerous mortars in its olive pressing "factory" (Esse, 1991), and there are a number of sites from Iron Age Israel with a variety of crushing features, including mortars (Gal and Frankel, 1993). Moving forward on the time line, Amouretti and Comet (1992) mention the use of mortars and pestles for oil processing in 19th century Syria.

In my interviews, one contact spoke of an olive crushing method that has not been noted elsewhere, and might loosely fit into the crushing by pounding category. He mentions a method where horses pull stones behind them over a flat surface to crush the olives, which are then pressed in the regular way (an upright screw or hydraulic press). This procedure is very similar to a traditional threshing process, where wood sleds with stones (usually pieces of basalt or flint) imbedded in their bottom surface are dragged over harvested grain to separate the grain from the stalks (Figure 3.26). I have found no other evidence of this method.

3.3.4.3 Milling Methods
While mortars and pestles were adequate for crushing small amounts of olives, larger volumes of fruit necessitate a different crushing method. Milling olives by crushing them with cylindrical stones increases the volume of olives that could be crushed. Such methods are necessary for increased oil production, especially if large quantities of

FIGURE 3.26: "THE THRESHING FLOOR OF NAZARETH, PALESTINE"
THE BOTTOM OF THE SLED WOULD BE STUDDED WITH STONE NODULES.
(KEYSTONE VIEW COMPANY NO 497-(11071))

FIGURE 3.27: "CRUSHING OLIVES WITH FRAGMENT OF ANCIENT OLIVE. AT BEIT
JIBRIN." (MATSON COLLECTION NO. 3967; © MATSON COLLECTION AND THE
EPISCOPAL HOME)

oil were to be produced for export. Milling includes simple rollers and complex mills. Most of the traditional mills I visited use two large revolving millstones. I did visit one operational single millstone mill and saw three other single millstone mills. Contacts mentioned other mills of that style which I did not visit.

3.3.4.3.1 Rollers

"The simplest method of crushing olives in antiquity, and still in use in Greece and other parts of the Mediterranean in the recent past, is to spread the fruit out on a hard surface and roll a large cylindrical stone over it," (Forbes and Foxhall, 1978:39). Frankel (1997) also believes that the earliest crushing method used stone rollers. Rollers can be used on flat surfaces or in shallow depressions, which may be caused by the continued use of a large roller on a flat surface over the same area (Figure 3.27). Such depressions may have eventually evolved into crushing basins specifically designed for use with rollers. I consider the utilization of a roller, either on a flat surface or contained within a basin, to be the precursor of the circular one or two stone rotary mill, a "proto-mill." A mill is defined as a machine for expelling juice from vegetable tissues by pressure or grinding (Webster's Dictionary, Seventh New Collegiate Edition, definition 5b).

Using a stone roller is also a faster method than using a mortar and pestle. Early rollers were probably elliptical stones (Eitam, 2000). Later rollers were stone cylinders about 50-60 cm (20-24 inch) long by 25-30 cm (10-12 inch) in diameter (Avitsur, 1994). The shape is similar to stones used as roof rollers, cylindrical stones used to pack, spread and smooth out plaster or clay flat-topped roofs (Avitsur, 1994; Ayalon, *pers. comm.*). According to Ayalon (*pers. comm.*) the stones for roof rollers tend to be long and thin while the rollers for crushing olives are short and fat, though some are shaped with pointed rather than squared off ends. A column drum fragment can be used as a roller (Tyree and Stefanoudaki, 1996) (see Figure 3.27), and Amouretti and Comet (1992) mention column drum rollers used in antiquity in Syria and North Africa, and in modern Spain.

In 1932, Avitsur (1994) witnessed the use of a roller by two women in the village of Khirbet 'Azzun (in modern Ra'anana, Israel). The women sat facing each other and pushed the roller back and forth over the olives between

FIGURE 3.28: "CRUSHING OLIVES" (MATSON COLLECTION NO. 562; © MATSON COLLECTION AND THE EPISCOPAL HOME)

a round block of stone rolled by two men seated across from each other. During my fieldwork, one contact asked his 90 year old mother how she made olive oil in the past, including when she was little and helping her mother. She told him that if there were not a lot of olives, two women sitting or kneeling on a big flat rock (the rock had a rough surface or bumps) would roll a large long cylindrical stone back and forth to crush the olives. The crushed olives would be put in a big wooden basin. Four other contacts mentioned crushing olives on a large flat surface by rolling a cylindrical stone back and forth. Two Matson Collection photographs (no. 3967, Figure 3.27 and no. 562, Figure 3.28) illustrate the use of stone rollers around the turn of the century.

Archaeological evidence of rollers and associated basins comes from Cyprus (Hadjisavvas, 1992) and Israel. In Iron Age Israel there are a number of sites with a variety of crushing features, either mortars or basins: "Early installations specially adapted for crushing the olives can be divided into two main types: round mortars for pounding and rectangular basins used with cylindrical stone rollers" (Gal and Frankel, 1993:133). However, the use of rollers and basins appears to dominate olive oil production at sites from the Bronze into the Iron Age (Eitam, 2000; Frankel, 1999). It is during this time period that commercial production of oil rapidly expanded. Tel Miqne (Ekron) is considered to be a major Iron Age olive oil production site (Gitin, 1989; 1996) and the olive oil industrial complex there used the larger push-roller and basin method of crushing (Figure 3.29, 3.30). Smaller basins using hand-pushed rollers have also been found (Figure 3.31), including at underwater sites off the Israeli coast near Haifa. The basins from the underwater sites

them (see Figure 3.28). Chabour (2004) mentions a similar approach where olives are put into a pit and crushed with

FIGURE 3.29: LARGER PUSH ROLLER BASIN FLANKED BY TWO BEAM PRESS COLLECTING VATS (IN BACKGROUND). BEAM PRESS WITH STONE WEIGHTS (MIDGROUND). SMALL HAND ROLLER BASIN (IN FOREGROUND). ISRAEL OLIVE OIL MUSEUM, SHEMEN INDUSTIRES HAIFA, ISRAEL

FIGURE 3.30: a) LARGE CRUSHING BASIN WITH PUSH ROLLERS AND PRESSES (ISRAEL OLIVE OIL MUSEUM, HAIFA, ISRAEL)
b) PUSH ROLLER CRUSHING BASIN AND PRESSING COMPLEX (ISRAEL MUSEUM, TEL AVIV, ISRAEL)

probably date to the Chalcolithic period (Galili *et al*, 1997) (Figure 3.32). Esse (1991) notes crushing basins at the Bronze Age sites of Ras Shamra and Ta'anach, while at Iron Age Timnah olive crushing was done in large basins with cylindrical rollers (Kelm and Mazar, 1995). Vickery (1936) mentions a trough found next to the remains of an olive press at Palaikastro in Greece, and suggests it may have been used for crushing olives.

As the olive oil industry developed, crushing basins evolved from the smaller basins using hand-pushed rollers to larger basins using push rollers. The major commercial oil producing sites, such as Miqne/Ekron, contain numerous examples of these larger basins.

3.3.4.3.2 Rotary Mills
A major step in the evolution in olive oil crushing is moving from a short, elongated roller to a tall, thin roller (Frankel, 1999). The crushing stone sits on a hard surface, usually stone, and rotates around a central axis. A main advantage of rotary versus reciprocal movement (as in the up and down motion of mortar and pestle or the back and

FIGURE 3.31: SMALL BASIN WITH HAND ROLLER, OLIVE OIL MUSEUM, HAIFA, ISRAEL

FIGURE 3.32: CRUSHING BASIN FROM KFAR SAMIR NEAR HAIFA, ISRAEL (GALILI)

forth motion of a roller in a basin) is that movement is in one direction only and thus can be performed continuously. Frankel (1999) believes that rotary mills were first used to crush olives, and later still for grinding flour. Grinding grain on a saddle quern used a reciprocal motion, while crushing olives using a mortar and pestle involved a partial rotary movement along with the vertical stroke. However, I did not find using any rotary motion helpful when using a mortar and pestle (see experimental chapter).

These rotary mills may have one or two crushing stones (Rosenblum, 1996), with the millstones usually made of basalt and the base of limestone or basalt. This type of mill first appears around the Hellenistic Period and soon becomes the predominant type of mill (Frankel, 1994; 1999), in use through to today. A notable type of this mill is the Roman concave millstone *trapetum*, such as that described in great detail by Cato (also Tyree and Stefanoudaki, 1996). Other Roman writers, such as Columella in *De Re Rustica: De Arboribus*, also go into detail concerning press installations and equipment.

During my research, I observed four single millstone mills. At one mill, the mill stone was said to have been brought from Hebron in the late 1930s/early 1940s. Another mill was moved from a farm to the farmer's house (Figure 3.33). This mill was said to be Roman ("Romani"), but is probably more modern (early Islamic period) (Frankel, *pers. comm.*). A third mill was worked until 1955 by the contact's grandfather, then temporarily abandoned. The contact now runs the mill for tourists (Figure 3.34). The mill stone at this site is unusual in that it is made of limestone rather than the usual basalt.

I observed eleven twin millstone mills (see Figure 3.8). At one site the millstones, obtained from Palestine, had the rarer limestone millstones (Figure 3.35). This mill was used at its present location for around 40 years, the

FIGURE 3.33: SINGLE MILLSTONE MILL, MOVED TO FARMER'S BACKYARD, INBEH, JORDAN

FIGURE 3.34: SINGLE MILLSTONE MILL, DONKEY IN BACKGROUND, TOURIST ATTRACTION, MI'ILYA, ISRAEL

FIGURE 3.35: TWIN MILLSTONE MILL WITH LIMESTONE MILLSTONES, MARHABA, JORDAN

contacts did not know how long it was used in Palestine. At another site, the press and stones were from Italy. Amiry and Tamari (1989) also mention a twin millstone operation in their typical Palestinian village.

The millstones were turned by animals or people (Dolamore, 1994; Eitam, *pers. comm.*). One contact's elderly mother told of a single millstone installation where three to five strong men turned the millstone. At the reconstructed Roman press at the Olive Oil Museum in Haifa, I turned a single millstone installation by myself with ease (Figure 3.36). A number of contacts mention using donkeys and horses, and one referred using cattle or oxen to turn the

stones. I did observe the use of a donkey in one instance (see Figure 3.34). The donkey-powered mill caters to the tourist trade and thus is not an actual "working" mill to which people bring olives for processing. The Matson Collection photograph of the large quern mill labeled "olive press" shows a camel providing the power (see Figure 3.25). All the traditional mills I visited, save the donkey-powered mill, use mechanical power to turn the millstones.

Some contacts believe the "old" or traditional crushing methods do not break the olive stone. Or, if the stone is broken, it is only broken in half or in large parts, the actual seed itself is unaffected. They believe that the bad taste of modern oil is due to the olive fruit, stone and all, being crushed and pressed. Several modern scholars, however, do not believe that breaking the pit has any impact on the flavor of the oil (Frankel, *pers. comm.*; Tyree and Stefanoudaki, 1996). According to Al-Rub (1992) the olive seed has limited affect on the flavor of the oil.

Rotary stone crushing mills have only recently, in the years after World War II, fallen out of use. The rotary stone mills continue in use in a number of small villages and locations throughout rural areas in Jordan and Israel. They are slowly being phased out by the quicker and more volume efficient modern centrifugal mills. As I traveled throughout Jordan, I found a number of these older traditional mills or their components ruined and abandoned, some only recently (Figure 3.37). It is difficult to determine the number of mill stones used in many of these. One abandoned press installation I visited is inside a cave. One contact said her family also knew of a press complex located in a large cavern in Palestine (prior to the family coming to Jordan). Borowski (*pers. comm.*) mentioned another near Lahav, in Kh. Zaaq.

a

b

FIGURE 3.36: a) ROMAN OLIVE OIL COMPLEX, OLIVE OIL MUSEUM, HAIFA, ISRAEL
b) ROMAN MILL AT COMPLEX

remains. This is taken up in Chapters 4 and 5.

3.3.4.4 Pressing Methods

After crushing the olives, the liquid content of the crushed fruit is extracted. As with the crushing technologies, there are a wide variety of methods for doing this, once again often dependant on the quantity of crushed fruit to be pressed and/or the amount of oil desired. Pressing methods run the gamut of techniques from simply using one's hands to the modern centrifuge. Some of the old methods are still in use, while others are known only from historical sources. Pressing methods include seepage and skimming, water "pressing," hand pressing, bag or torsion pressing, stones, beam presses, wedge presses, screw and hydraulic presses, and finally, the modern centrifuge.

3.3.4.4.1 Seepage, Skimming and Water Washing

These first methods of "pressing" do not actually require pressing to remove the olive oil. In the first practice, seepage, the oil is allowed to seep out of the crushed olive mash. One contact mentions that his mother, after crushing olives in a mortar and pestle, puts the olive mash in ceramic containers and let them sit for a short time. She then pours off the oil that naturally leaks out of the crushed olives. This oil is "the best tasting of all the oils." Frankel (*pers. comm.*) believes this method may also have been used in conjunction with large crushing platforms.

The second technique uses hot water to remove the oil from the crushed olives. In this process the crushed fruit is put into a container, whether it be a hole in the ground or a ceramic vessel, and heated (but not boiling) water is poured over the mash. The hot water helps separate the oil from the mash, and the oil then floats to the surface of the water where it is skimmed off and collected (Eitam, 1993; *pers. comm.*; Stager, 1983; Knickerbocker, 1997; Tzedakis and Martlew, 1999). This is probably the simplest method of removing the oil from the lees (Frankel, 1999). Several contacts mention this technique. Some said it was a method used prior to the last fifty/sixty years or by people two generations ago. In one account the crushed olives were placed in a large wooden basin. Boiling water was poured

The crushing or milling stage of olive oil processing may produce major alterations to the olive remains. Whether or not these changes occur and the degree to which they occur depends greatly on the method of processing. Some types of processing may have little or no affect on the olive stones, while other methods may produce major changes. I found no references to the effects of treading on olive stones, but it appears to be minimal. Using a hand quern may or may not affect the olive stones since there are two ways to process the olives. One method grinds the olives with the stones and another method pits the olives prior to grinding. The first method crushes the stones to fragments while the second leaves the stones whole and undamaged. Pounding olives with a stone or using a mortar and pestle breaks the stones. Crushing olives with large stone cylinders and mill wheels also fragments the stones. Identifying breakage patterns for each of the various crushing methods will enable us to determine the different methods from archaeological

a

b

FIGURE 3.37a-b: ABANDONED MILLSTONES AND BASES OUTSIDE IRBID, JORDAN

over the olives, which were then stirred. This caused the flesh to come off the olive fruit and the seeds to fall to the bottom of the basin. While still in the basin the loose flesh would then be squeezed for the oil, which was later scooped off the top of the water.

Vickery (1936:52) mentions a similar oil extraction method still used on Crete: "The fruit is first drenched in hot water, then crushed in a simple machine; then it is placed in settling vats." The oil floats to water's surface, the water is drained out of the vat at the bottom through a hole, leaving the oil in the vat. There are a variety of decantation methods, including: overflow decantation (an opening at the top allows the oil to flow out), underflow decantation (an opening at the bottom allows the water to flow out), and a combined overflow and underflow decantation (Frankel, 1999). Pithoi (large pottery storage vessels) found on Crete have small holes near the base. While Warren (1972) suggests that these pithoi originally contained wine which was decanted through the hole, it seems reasonable that such vessels could be used to separate olive oil and lees. Spouted tubs that may have been used for wine pressing or olive oil separation or both were found in the same area (Leonard, 1996).

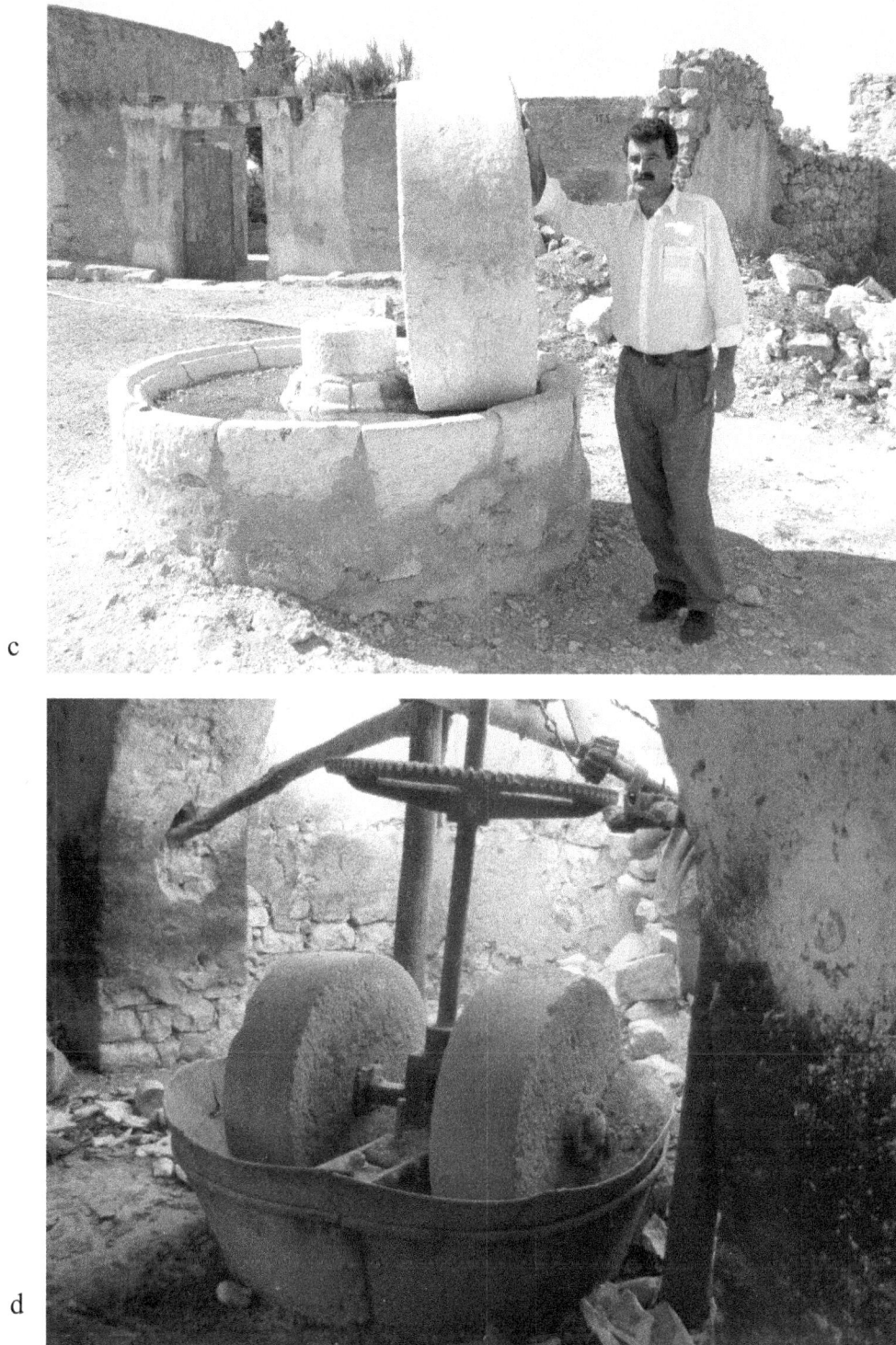

FIGURE 3.37c: OLD MILL SET UP AS A ROADSIDE ATTRACTION, KUFR ELMA, JORDAN
d: ABANDONED MILL COMPLEX, TALIFAH, JORDAN

There are a number of minor variations to these pressing and separation methods. Several contacts mentioned mixing or stirring the mash by hand to help release the oil, after adding the hot water. Litchfield (1984) describes an example were the mixture was stirred by foot (see Figure 3.21). After standing overnight, the oil separates out as an upper layer which is skimmed off with a distinctive shallow metal ladle. One contact mentions using the hand to dip or skim up the oil that has risen to the top of the water, then wiping the hand on the edge of a bowl or jar to scrape off and collect the oil. Ethnographic studies from the Mesara region of South-Central Crete has oil being skimmed from a basin by hand (Blitzer, 1993). Hadjisavvas (1992) believes that a family's consumption needs could have been easily satisfied by crushing, heating and skimming from open vessels. Oil extracted in this manner would not

41

produce the characteristic pressing installations, especially those associated with industrial production.

A number of people also said that this method was useful when doing only small, household pressings. The olive oil produced in this manner is probably the "washed oil" mentioned in religious texts, such as the Samaria ostraca (Eitam, 1993; Frankel, 1997; Stager, 1983). The method may have produced only the "best" oil (Eitam, 1993).

3.3.4.4.2 Hand and Torsion Methods

The most common method of extracting the oil from the olive fruit is by applying some form of pressure to the crushed fruit. The simplest method of actually "pressing" the oil by force is to squeeze the mash in one's hands over a bowl or container. Several contacts in my study described this method, as does Avitsur (1994).

One contact told of a Palestinian who demonstrated the way his family made small amounts of olive oil. The olives were roasted then beaten with a stone. The olive mash was then put in a *kaffiyia* (the traditional Arab head wrap). The *kaffiyia* was twisted, squeezing out the oil. Another contact mentioned hearing about this method. This torsion-bag method is also recorded in Corsica, Italy and Turkey at various points in history (Amouretti and Comet, 1992). The olives are put in a long bag or sack, which is then stomped on to crush the olives. The bag is then hung in a torsion rack and twisted to express the oil (Amouretti and Comet, 1992; Serpico and White, 2000; Tzedakis and Martlew, 1999). This method is simple and easy to use.

Frankel (1999; *pers. comm.*) believes the torsion or bag pressing method was an early pressing technique. This technique is illustrated a number of times in Egyptian art (James, 1996, Lesko, 1996; Murray, 1999) (Figure 3-38), and was used to press grapes in ancient Egypt (Brun, 2000). This manner of olive oil processing may not be significantly different from that described for wine making by James (1996) and Murray (2000). James (1996) identifies hieroglyphs from the reign of Den, 4th king of the First Dynasty (*c.* 3000 B.C.) as oil-presses rather than wine presses. The oil-press hieroglyph is represented by what looks like a bag stretched between two poles. Perfumers in ancient Egypt used cloth torsion presses (Brun, 2000; Vogelsang-Eastwood, 2000), and since olive oil was a significant component of the perfume industry torsion pressing technology could have easily been adapted for olive oil pressing. Forbes (1965) also mentions the Egyptian "wringing the cloth." This consists of filling a cloth with grapes or other ingredients, and then folding the cloth in such a way that both of the two ends on each side of the cloth fold around a stick. The two sticks are then twisted in opposing directions, thus expressing the liquid contents. Variations on the technique include hanging the bag from a pole at one end and twisting it at the other, or hanging the bag between two sticks and then twisting it (as in Figure 3.38) (Murray, 2000).

Frankel (*pers. comm.*) believes this last method was used in connection with broad crushing platforms. One such platform has two holes at either end of the platform (see Figure 3.19). Frankel (*pers. comm.*) suggests the holes are for either a torsion press mechanism, or for a rope that people could hang on to while treading. Using a rope to steady one self while stomping fruit is also shown in Egyptian tomb paintings (James, 1996; Lesko, 1996).

3.3.4.4.3 Pressing with Weights: Stones and Beam Presses

Other than applying pressure to the crushed olives by torsion, by far the most common methods of pressing olives involves some sort of press installation, from very simple stones to complicated metal machines. According

FIGURE 3.38: EGYPTIAN PAINTING SHOWING TORSION OR BAG PRESS. FROM AMMOURETTI AND COMET 1992, P.74

to Brun (2000) perfumed oil producers pressed olives in fabric sacks. The sacks were possibly bags from torsion pressing being utilized for a different pressing method. In most of the following methods, the crushed olives are usually put in some type of container to keep the mash together, allowing it to be economically pressed without extruding out and escaping. The majority of published sources and contacts interviewed during my research refer to these containers as baskets, though Frankel (1999) refers to them as "frails." These containers are commonly called *guffe/quffet* in Arabic, *eqel* in Hebrew (Avitsur, 1994) and *fiscus* in Latin (Frankel, 1999). The word *guffe* refers to any container in general; baskets made from old automobile tires and used in archaeological excavations are also called *guffe*. None of the contacts interviewed during the fieldwork have a special name for the baskets, other than *guffe*. The baskets used in olive oil pressing are not really baskets but rather large fiber discs. Some are solely flat discs (see Figure 3.9a, b; Figure 3.10), while others have a wide lip or "pocket" around the edge (see Figure 3.9c, d). Some baskets have a hole in the middle to accommodate a central stacking rod for the press (see Figure 3.10), others have no such hole and merely sit on top of each other.

The disc material is traditionally fibers such as hemp or esparto grass, though modern discs may be made of nylon (Avitsur, 1994; Dolamore, 1994; Frankel, 1999; Knickerbocker, 1997; Ridgeway, 1996; Rosenblum, 1996; Toussaint-Samar, 1992). One contact mentioned "luffa" for disc material. Avitsur (1994) says the baskets in Syro-Palestine were originally made from date palm fibers (a material also mentioned by Frankel, 1999), but later were made in Nablus (Schechem) from coconut fibers or nylon. He also mentions that goat hair baskets were used on occasion. Although these discs are used primarily with beam, screw or hydraulic presses, they may have been used in simple weight pressing as well. The remains of baskets mixed with olive pressing residues have been found in pits at the Neolithic/Chalcolithic site of Kfar Samir, just off the Mediterranean coast near Haifa (Galili and Sharvit, 1994-5; Galili *et al*, 1997).

A number of contacts mention the simplest form of this style of pressing: using large, heavy stones to press the olive mash (also Avitsur, 1994). One contact talked about putting the crushed olives in woven bags, possibly burlap, made in Aleppo, Syria and then squeezing the bags with large stones. Another contact told of putting the olives in baskets or bags and then pressing by hand with a large piece of wood. Behind a modern olive oil mill in Ketteh, Jordan, are the remains of an ancient press installation. The installation is cut into the

bedrock and consists of a larger basin or depression and two smaller basins or bowls. Roller-crushed olives (not in bags or baskets) would be put into the large basin and a piece of wood or board placed on them, followed by a heavy rock or several rocks. The expressed liquid would drain out through a hole at the bottom of the larger basin into the first of the two smaller settling basins/collecting bowls. While in this first, smaller, basin the oil and water (lees) would separate. The oil, rising to the top of the stone-cut bowl, would then flow through a small channel into the second, collecting basin.

Other stone presses include a small stone pressing platform, usually with a groove or channel for the oil (Eitam, *pers. comm.*; Frankel, 1994; Hadjisavvas, 1992) (Figure 3.39). The size of some of these small press beds suggests portability. There is variability in design, some stones having the channel ending in a collecting cup while others apparently drained off the edge into a container. Crushed olive mash in small cloth bags would be pressed on these small press beds using heavy stones for weights (Eitam, *pers. comm.*) (Figure 3.39b), though, as both Hadjisavvas

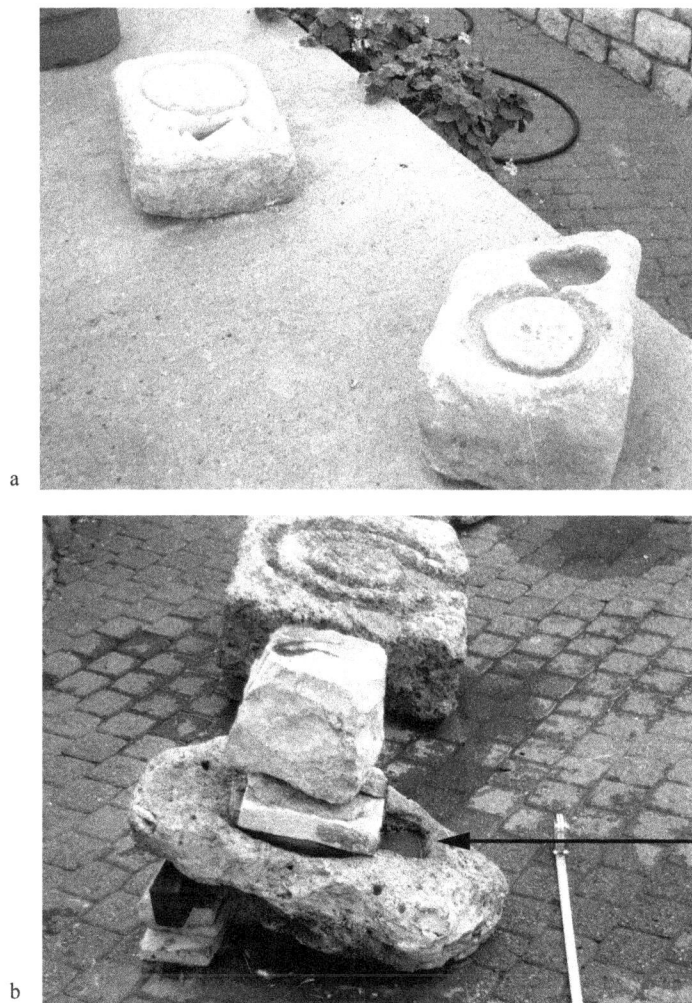

a

b

FIGURE 3.39a: SMALL PORTABLE OLIVE OIL PRESS BEDS, OLIVE OIL MUSEUM, HAIFA, ISRAEL

b: PORTABLE PRESS IN USE, NOTE LIQUID FILLING CUP, OLIVE OIL MUSEUM

a

b

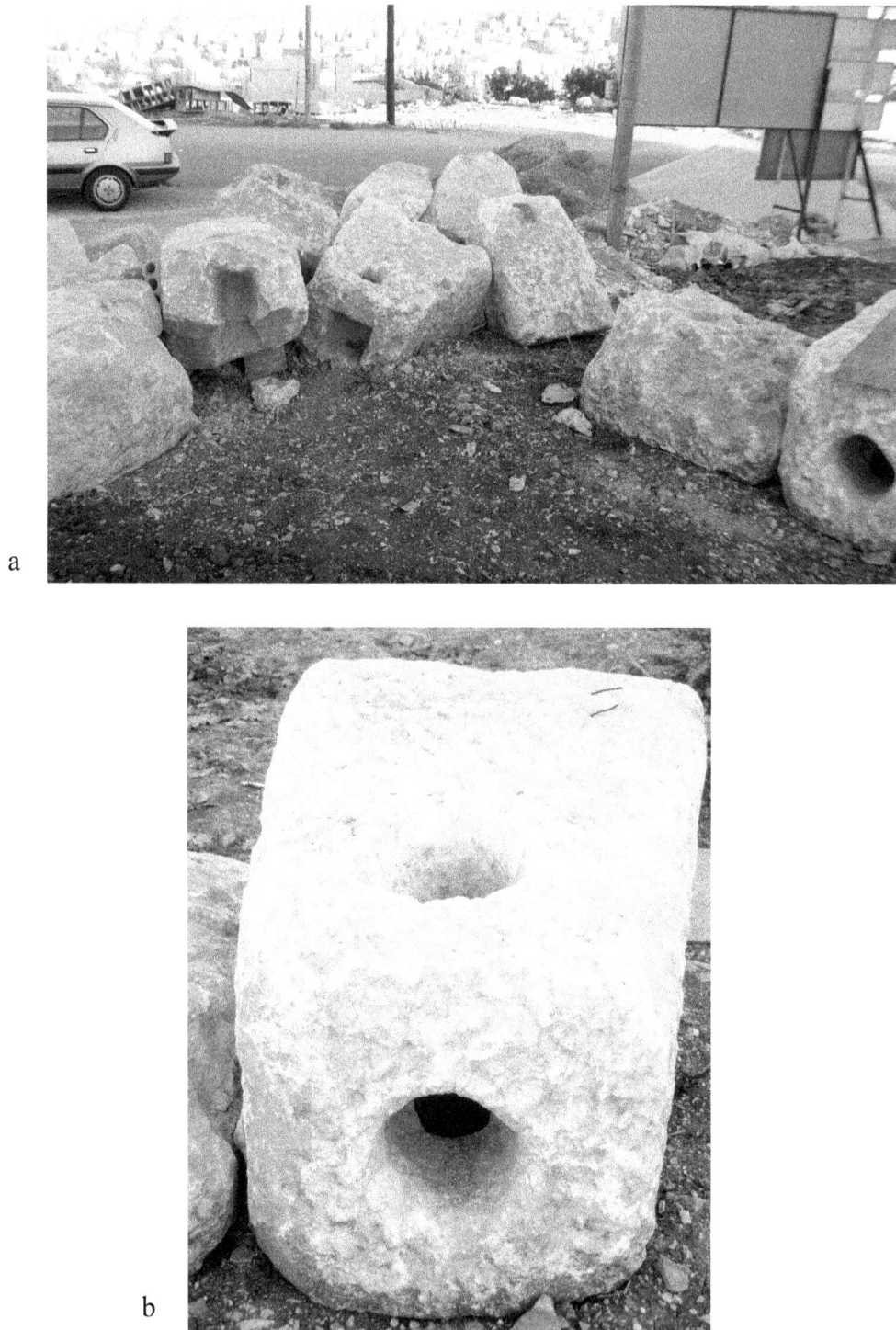

FIGURE 3.40a-b: STONE OLIVE OIL BEAM PRESSING WEIGHTS FOUND DURING HOUSE CONSTRUCTION, AMMAN, JORDAN

(1992) and I have observed, some may have been used with beam presses.

There are Mishnaic references (Frankel, 1994; 1997; *pers. comm.*) to olive oil made exclusively for the Temple. This oil was prepared by pounding olives in mortars and expressing the oil using the weight of stones. In the village of Mashhad in the Galilee, oil produced this way is called *zeit a-frish* in Arabic, which means "crushed oil" (Frankel, 1994), another olive oil designation referred

to in texts. "Crushed oil" only means oil pressed by the weight of heavy stones, "*shemen katit*" in Hebrew (Eitam, 1993; Stager, 1983). Eitam believes that this is the method frequently used with small rock-cut depressions.

Stone weights are also an important feature of beam presses, where a wood beam is used to compress a stack of olive mash filled baskets (Amouretti and Comet, 1992; Dolamore, 1994; Frankel, 1994; see authors in Eitam and Heltzer, 1996). These stone weights become more complex over time (Eitam, *pers. comm.*). Earlier weights were rough stones with a hole drilled through them for a rope, the more stones hung from the end of the beams meant more weight (see Figure 3.29). Later weights were huge carved blocks or cylinders attached by complex systems of ropes, levers and pulleys to the beams (Figure 3.40). During pressing, the ropes would be tightened until the weights lifted from the ground. As pressing continued, the ropes could be tightened again and again. Several contacts mentioned this form of pressing. A seventy-seven year old contact said this was the way it was done when he was younger: "You would put a rope through a hole in the stone and keep tightening the rope until the stone lifted off the ground." It is likely that various pressing forms were in concurrent use; for instance, Matson Collection photographs show the simpler style still in use in the late 1800s/early 1900s (Matson Collection photographs no. 3969 and 3970).

3.3.4.4.4 Wedge, Screw and Hydraulic Presses

The wedge press was an early upright press where pressure was applied by forcing wedges, usually wooden, into a frame. The frame sat above a stone press bed onto which baskets of crushed olives sat. Wood boards were laid into the frame on top of the baskets. Wood wedges were then pounded between the boards to exert pressure on the baskets, expressing the oil. Paintings depicting wedge presses were found in the House of the Vettii in Pompei and the Casa dei Cervi in Herculaneum (Museum of Naples) (Brun, 2000).

A major innovation in pressing technology was the Roman screw press (Dolamore, 1994) (Figure 3.41). This technology was known in the first century B.C. (Vitruvius, *De Architectura* 6.6.3; Pliny, *Natural History* 18.317), though according to Pliny screw presses which exerted pressure directly on the olive pulp only became widespread a century later. The use of a large wood screw is quicker and more efficient than using ropes and levers to weigh down the wood beam in the beam press installation. The screw, attached to heavy stones or to bedrock and to the end of the beam, could be easily tightened and loosened. Using a screw increased productivity. This eventually led to the development of the upright screw press, where the beam was dispensed with and the screw put direct pressure on the stack of olive mash filled baskets. The wood or stone frameworks (Figure 3.42) of such upright screw presses eventually gave way to metal (Figure 3.43). Many contacts mention using such upright metal screw presses. One contact still uses an old screw press that his grandfather bought and worked, though the contact now operates the mill and press as a tourist attraction.

The screw press is eventually replaced by upright hydraulic presses. This is the type of press equipment in use at all the traditional mills I visited (see Figure 3.11). The hydraulic press is much faster than the screw press. Other than the method of applying pressure (hydraulic vs manpower), the only difference is that most screw presses press from top to bottom (that is, the pressure is applied from above)

FIGURE 3.41: ROMAN SCREW PRESS USING A WOOD SCREW ATTACHED TO A BEAM PRESS, OLIVE OIL MUSEUM, HAIFA, ISRAEL

while the hydraulic presses usually apply pressure from the bottom upwards. The hydraulic press is being replaced, along with the traditional crushing methods used prior to pressing, by the modern centrifugal mills. One mill in Jordan does use a hybrid system of modern crushing and traditional (hydraulic press) pressing (Warnock, personal observation; also see, Avitsur, 1994) (see Figure 3.10a).

There is little evidence to suggest that the pressing step in olive oil processing affects the olive remains. Pressing might cause some stones which had already cracked to separate into multiple fragments, but appears not to cause breakage itself. None of the contacts interviewed thought so, nor did several scholars (Ayalon, *pers. comm.*; Eitam, *pers. comm.*; Frankel, *pers. comm.*). Thus, the changes to the olive remains likely occur either at the crushing stage or in post processing usages.

3.3.5 Use of Pressing Wastes

Identifying and studying the various uses of the processing wastes is important as these uses directly affect what is recovered archaeologically. There are few references to the use of olive processing wastes, both liquid (lees, amurca)

a

FIGURE 3.42a: ROMAN OLIVE OIL COMPLEX WITH ROLLER MILL CRUSHING BASIN AND STONE FRAMEWORK FOR SCREW PRESS, AMMAN, JORDAN

FIGURE 3.42b: ROMAN SCREW PRESS
FROM FRANKEL 1994, P.69

FIGURE 3.43: METAL SCREW PRESS, OLIVE OIL MUSEUM, HAIFA, ISRAEL

and solid (*jift*). What few references there are deal primarily with the solid wastes (*jift*), few uses of the lees/amurca are mentioned. However, here I am more concerned with the uses of the *jift* as it contains the stone remains usually found in archaeological contexts. While identifying different processing methods provides information on how olive remains are altered, identification does not show how the remains are incorporated into the archaeological record.

Observations of how the solid olive pressing waste, the pulp and stones leftover from pressing, are both used and disposed of is important in interpreting archaeological olive remains. Post-pressing uses of the pressing waste or *jift*, can further alter the olive remains, and the final disposition of the remains or residue may also depend upon the uses to which it is put. All of these uses affect how the remains are incorporated into the archaeological record, how the remains are discovered in that same archaeological record, and the ultimate analyses and interpretation of these remains. Understanding the uses and disposal of the *jift* has an important bearing on how researchers interpret olive finds from archaeological sites. Understanding the reasons behind the use of *jift* for particular applications may also provide insight into the economic role of agricultural by-products. Knowledge provided by such insight may also be applied to archaeological models to understand the importance of agricultural wastes.

This section will describe the use of olive oil processing wastes, concentrating mainly on the use of the solid waste (*jift*). *Jift* is used for commercial and domestic fuels, for making jewelry and cosmetics, as animal feed, for fertilizer, in making soap, and in construction. The *jift* from oil mills is sometimes sold to companies that do a second oil "pressing" using chemical extraction methods. The oil produced by this method is an inedible, low grade oil used in olive oil soap and cosmetics. No alteration of the stones takes place, and the *jift* is sold, usually for fuel or to charcoal companies.

3.3.5.1 Fuel

Above all other uses, the primary application of olive pressing wastes is as fuel, for both domestic and commercial usage. Almost every contact interviewed mentioned the use of *jift* as a fuel, a use also cited by many researchers (Amouretti and Comet, 1992; Avitsur, 1994; Burgess, 1999; I.O.O.C., n.d.; Foxhall, 1998; 1995; Goor, 1966; Mason and ᶜAmr, 1993, 1995; Matson, 1966; Mattingly, 1996; The Olive Oil Source, 2001; Roldán *et al*, 2000; Rosenblum, 1996; Rye, 1981; Sethom, 1964; Tzedakis and Martlew, 1999; van Zeist, 1994). One contact said that the only use for *jift* in the old days was for fire. The use of *jift* as fuel seems reasonable, given the limited availability of fuel resources in the region.

While wood was probably the premier fuel source for the ancient world, limited supplies in some regions necessitated the use of alternative or supplementary fuels. Many areas around the Mediterranean basin where olives are grown and pressed do not contain abundant supplies of natural fuels. Wood is scarce. According to Smith (in press), "Other fuels than wood, often termed 'traditional fuels', were necessary for cooking, pottery production and other activities requiring a heat source. Crop processing residues, by-products of food production and animal dung are not waste, but valuable sources of fuel." A number of traditional fuels, including animal dung (Anderson and Ertug-Yaras, 1998; Bottema, 1984; Madella, *pers.*

comm.; Miller, 1984; Miller and Smart, 1984) and *jift*, are used throughout the Near East. Contacts at the Ramtha Agricultural Experiment station told me that when or where energy resources are limited (referring to the lack of woody resources in Jordan) alternative fuel sources such as *jift* and dung are greatly relied upon. The use of wine pressing wastes as fuel has also been suggested (Buxo, 1996; Mangafa and Kotsakis, 1996; Murray, 1999). Rye (1981) points out the advantage of agricultural wastes over wood as fuel is that agricultural wastes are replenished annually, whereas wood supplies can be easily depleted and exhausted. Agricultural waste fuels are also cheap and abundant when available. For fuel-starved areas around the Mediterranean basin, *jift* was and is a valuable fuel.

The composition of *jift* makes it an ideal fuel: "the dried, crushed pits of pressed olives (*jift*), when burned, proved ideal as a long-lasting source of heat" (Doumani, 1995:33). *Jift* gives off a high amount of heat, approximately 9,200 BTU (British Thermal Units) per pound compared to wood (≈ 5,000 BTU per pound) or even coal (between ≈ 9,500 and 14,000 BTU per pound depending on type of coal) (propane ≈ 22,000 BTU per pound; natural gas ≈ 24,000 per pound; heating oil ≈ 19,000 BTU per pound) (www.oit.doe.gov/nice3/factsheets/trivalley.pdf; home.att.net/~hvac/fuels.htm; www.pomaceoil.com/plantoperations.english.html). The hard, woody stones supply the main fuel source and the crushed fruit pulp retains some of its oil, providing a fuel source that generates a high BTU. This combination results in a fuel that gives a steady, high temperature and has a long burning time. These burning characteristics also result in the total consumption of *jift* fuel: *jift* burns almost entirely to an ash free of large inclusions. The use of *jift* as a fuel offers advantages over customary fuels such as wood; *jift* is available in volume, gives good heat, and leaves little residue. This last is advantageous, since cleaning out a firebox can be time-consuming and can slow or halt the fire's intended activity.

Ethnographic research around the Mediterranean basin has established that *jift* is used as fuel, both domestically and industrially (Foxhall, 1995; Goor, 1966; Melkawi, 1995; Sethom, 1964; Warnock, personal observation). It is unlikely that ancient peoples ignored this valuable resource. Principle sources of fuel in the ancient Near East were agricultural and industrial wastes, including *jift* (Foxhall, 1998; Matson, 1966; Rye, 1981; www.terradimare.com/imperiaolio/st_cucina-g.htm). *Jift* was not the only waste component used as a fuel. Cato mentions soaking wood in the oily amurca. Such wood burned "well" but without a lot of smoke or odor (*De Re Rustica*, 130).

The use of pressing wastes as fuel is relevant to both ethnographic and archaeological research. Ethnographic studies (mentioned above) support paleoethnobotanical evidence for the use of alternative fuels. These ethnographic studies also provide evidence for the management and movement of materials within and between sites. The use of alternative fuels, such as *jift*, especially for industrial

FIGURE 3.44: BRAZIERS (KANON) FOR SALE IN THE ASH SHUNA MARKET, JORDAN

purposes, required organized agricultural practices, where agricultural residues were collected (possibly sold), and transported to use locations (Smith, 1998). The use of alternative fuels means that fuel-gathering was integrated into agricultural production (Smith, 1998). Foxhall (1998:39) notes that there are complex "links between animal husbandry and agricultural by-products within the lowland Mediterranean agricultural systems of the ancient Greek and Roman world." These links include fuel production.

The use of *jift* as fuel is one explanation for the absence or relative scarcity of olive remains at archaeological sites. The alteration of the olive remains due to fuel use affects its incorporation into the archaeological record. How the remains are incorporated, where they are incorporated, and why the remains show up in a particular location are explained by patterns of *jift* use.

3.3.5.1.1 Domestic Fuel Use

For people in olive producing areas, *jift* fuel has a number of advantages, not the least of which is that it is cheap and abundant. *Jift* as a fuel has multiple uses and is burned in most household situations needing a fire. The main domestic uses of *jift* are for cooking year-round and heating in the winter (Al-Omari and Al-Azraie, 1995; Okla and Azraie, 1994; Olives Australia Newsletter, 1997; Omari & Azraie, 1994; Kafafi; *pers. comm.*; Sarpaki, 1999; Tarawneh, *pers. comm.*; Tzedakis and Martlew, 1999). "Large amounts of *jift* were consumed every winter as fuel for braziers" (Doumani, 1995:33). This use followed immigrants to new areas of olive cultivation, such as Australia, where Greek immigrants used *jift* as stove fuel (Karavis, *pers. comm.*). Almost every contact in my study mentions the use of *jift* as a fuel, and there is general agreement in how it was prepared and used, with some minor variations.

Sometimes the *jift* is used with other fuels, such as dung, straw and sticks (Eitam, *pers. comm.*; Yassine, *pers. comm.*). Mixing *jift* with charcoal makes both last longer. While some people in my research said they prefer *jift* by itself and do not mix it with anything else, others talked about blending it with other fuels. An elderly woman mentioned mixing *jift* with dung for cooking bread and said she saw her mother and grandmother doing it also. Another woman said that in the old days, if people were moving around (i.e., a semi-nomadic pastoralist) and near an oil press, they would mix the *jift* with straw.

The loose *jift* from traditional presses is usually given free of charge to those who want it, only one press owner said he charges people for it. People pressing olives have first right to the *jift*. At the larger operations and modern mills, the *jift* is usually sold to companies which extract the residual oil through chemical processing (Avitsur, 1994; Bataeneh, *pers. comm.*; I.O.O.C., n.d.; Rosenblum, 1996). One contact said he received 7 Jordanian Dinars (JD) (about $10 U.S.) per ton of *jift* (in 1997). The oil produced from chemical "pressing" is an inedible, low quality oil usually used in soaps and cosmetics. As traditional mills fall out of use, so does the use of *jift* as a fuel; people switch to modern gas or electric heaters and stoves.

When *jift* is used as a cooking fuel, it is commonly used loose. Most contacts mentioned using *jift* as a cooking fuel for open grills or braziers and in the traditional bread ovens, or *tabuns* (Amiry and Tamari, 1989; Avitsur, 1994). The burning *jift* gives off a "good," even heat. *Jift* is used as fuel in *kanons*, the open grills or braziers (without the grill on top) used for heat, cooking meat kabobs, and as a traditional means of heating coffee pots (Figure 3.44; also 4.7). Matson (1966) mentions the incompletely burned *jift*

FIGURE 3.45: CERAMIC TABUN, TRADITIONAL BREAD OVEN (ON SIDE, NOT IN USE), TAFILAH, JORDAN

from kilns being used in Greece to fuel small braziers for winter heat. One contact said that *jift* is also used as fuel to cook *kanafie*, a favorite cheese pastry sold in bakeries and sweet shops. The pan containing the *kanafie* is raised above the fire rather than in or right on it, since *jift* gives off a hot fire and cooking the *kanafie* requires only a little heat.

The standard *tabun*, or traditional bread oven, is a large ceramic ring or dome with a circular opening at the top (Figure 3.45). Since people make their bread in the early morning the *tabun* is heated at night so that the *tabun* is hot and ready to use by morning. A fire is made inside and outside the *tabun*. Then the fire is covered. A limited oxygen supply means the fire would not burn quickly but produces a slow, controlled, even-heating fire. In the morning, the *tabun* is uncovered and opened, and the bread dough is stuck to the inside surface of the heated *tabun* (see Figure 3.46a). The top hole is capped and the entire *tabun* is then re-covered by hot coals and ash, which bakes the bread (Figure 3.46b, 3.47). When the bread is done, the coals and ash are brushed aside, the lid lifted, and the bread removed.

Another contact uses a stove fired by *jift* and wood to bake bread (Figure 3.48). This stove, a large metal rectangular box on legs, has a revolving circular tray that spins in and out of the oven. The bread is put on the tray's surface outside the oven and rotated into the cooking area. Other contacts interviewed in the area said they use the same type of stove. This stove design may be a regional characteristic, rather than the norm, as I only

FIGURE 3.46a-b: TABUN IN USE. CIRCULAR METAL LID RESTING BEHIND TABUN. TAFILAH, JORDAN

a

b

FIGURE 3.47a: COOK HOUSE WITH
COVERED TABUN INSIDE
b: CLOSE-UP OF COVERED TABUN,
TAFILAH, JORDAN

FIGURE 3.48: METAL BREAD OVEN WITH
ROTATING CIRCULAR TRAY. SHOWN BEING
LOADED WITH *JIFT* FUEL. MI'ILYA, ISRAEL.

a

b

FIGURE 3.49a-b: MAKING *JIFT* BALLS FOR FUEL, EL MAZAR, JORDAN
a: NOTE THE PILE OF *JIFT* IN THE FOREGROUND

this mill and modern centrifugal mills was dry and crumbly, and did not leave an oily residue on my hands. The Tobneh *jift* was said to be only good for cooking since it was too dry and could not be made into balls. People had tried adding water to this *jift* so it would stick together better, but that did not work. However, others using *jift* from a modern press said that sometimes one has to add water to the *jift* if it is a bit dry, but it packs up alright otherwise. One contact said he had heard of people mixing *jift* with diesel fuel to form balls.

The balls of *jift* are then dried, reducing the water content. During the olive pressing season, roofs, courtyards and other open areas are covered with drying balls of *jift* for the upcoming year's fuel supply (Figure 3.51). Once dried, the *jift* balls are stored protected from the weather. One contact showed me a small side storage room containing the last few *jift* balls from the previous season, while outside the new season's *jift* balls were drying.

The main use of the *jift* balls, according to most contacts, is for winter heat (also Martin, 2001). The balls are used in small stoves similar in principle to antique box stoves (Figure 3.52a), where the stove sits in the middle of the room radiating heat (Figure 3.52, 3.53). The chimney pipe extends to a hole in the roof. One contact and his wife were almost asphyxiated by carbon monoxide from a kerosene space heater. The next day they returned to using a traditional *jift* stove. They said it burns better and does not give off "bad gas" like gas or kerosene stoves (also Sarpaki, 1999). The *jift* burns "good," and stays hot for a long time in the stove. Six or seven balls lasts about three hours, with 50 balls average for one day and evening. Another contact said when using *jift* balls for heating, 4-5 kilos would last about 12 hours/all day long. One other contact would fill the stove 5-6 times with about 20 *jift* balls (these were a bit smaller – baseball sized) for one day's heating. This last contact said that they got the *jift* free, saving a great deal of money on fuel and heating costs.

These small stoves are dual purpose machines, doubling as an oven. To cook or bake bread one removes the stove top (which has two holes in it) and puts a curved top on it (like an inverted wok). Traditional Arab/Bedouin bread is baked on a curved surface/pan (*saj*) (Figure 3.54). The people said this "stove/oven" was a clean system for using in the home. There are very few fumes except those going up the chimney (Sarpaki, 1999), and the *jift* burns totally to ash leaving little residue. They believe this is an example of "modern people using an old resource" (i.e., the *jift*).

saw it in northern Israel/Palestine and not at all in Jordan. Dr. Slane (*pers. comm.*) suggests that the design probably descends from a British solid fuel stove.

For some cooking applications and for use as heating fuel, the loose *jift* is pressed into blocks or balls. The pressed *jift* forms a type of briquette, usually around 8 to 12 cm in diameter (Figure 3.49). While the whole family may contribute, it is usually only the women and children who participate in making the *jift* balls. *Jift* from the traditional presses is considered better for this purpose, since the pulp pieces are larger and retain more oil: *jift* from modern centrifugal mills is finer in fragment size, and drier with a much lower oil content. *Jift* from the Al Mazar (traditional) mill is soft and slightly sticky; it still has a slight oil content and packs well (Figure 3.50a). This *jift* left my hands feeling oily. The *jift* from the Tobneh (Tibneh) oil mill, which uses modern crushing and traditional (hydraulic) pressing, is considered by contacts to be inferior to traditionally processed *jift* as heating fuel (Figure 3.50b). *Jift* from

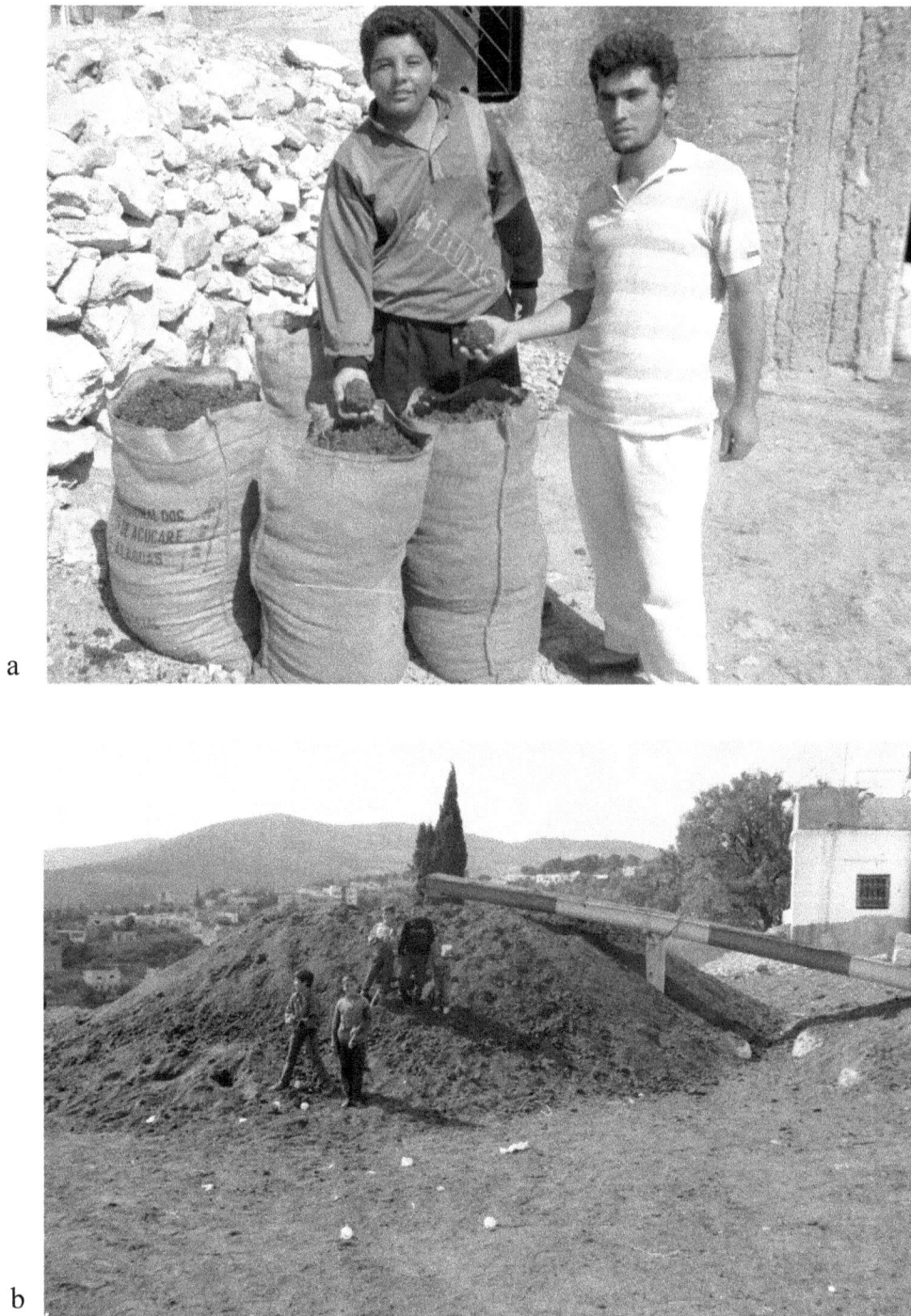

FIGURE 3.50a-b: *JIFT*
a: AL MAZAR, JORDAN, TRADITION MILL, *JIFT* SOFT AND STICKY, PACKS WELL
b: IRBID, JORDAN, MODERN MILL, *JIFT* DRIER, DOES NOT PACK AS WELL

In another use of *jift* as a fuel, a contact recounted that when she was a child, her family used *jift* to heat bath water. They had an upright water heater with a stove at the bottom and would buy paper bags of *jift* from shops in Amman. The bags were about 5-6 inches by about 3 inches; the *jift* looked like a "log" roll. To use it, one would split the top/side of the bag, and add a little bit of kerosene to help light it. Two bags were enough to heat all the water for baths. The *jift* gave a high, clean heat, and old *jift* burned better than new.

At the Roman site of Volubilis in Morocco, the house of a rich oil merchant has a press complex in the lower portion of the building. Rosenblum (1996) says the *jift* from this complex was used to heat the house's baths.

3.3.5.1.2 Commercial Fuel
While much of the *jift* from smaller traditional village mills is used by the local inhabitants for domestic purposes, at the larger processing complexes the *jift* serves other, sometimes large-scale, industries. In antiquity as

a

b

c

d

FIGURE 3.51: *JIFT* BALLS DRYING FOR STORAGE
a: AL MAZAR, JORDAN   b: QAFQAFA, JORDAN   c-d: AL MAZAR, JORDAN

FIGURE 3.52a: BOX STOVE *C.* 1800–1900
(COURTESY GOOD TIME STOVE CO.)

FIGURE 3.52b-c: *JIFT* STOVES, AL MAZAR, JORDAN

FIGURE 3.53: *JIFT* STOVE, QAFQAFA, JORDAN

well as the present, a number of industries use *jift* as a fuel for heating and firing. Some industries, such as olive soap making, are closely associated with the olive pressing process. As already mentioned, *jift* fuel offers advantages over fuels such as wood; *jift* is available in volume, is an excellent heat source, and leaves little residue. For industrial applications, this last characteristic is highly advantageous, since cleaning out a firebox is time-consuming and slows or halts production. Modern commercial uses of *jift* also include a burgeoning charcoal industry. Recent commercial enterprises in Jordan process *jift* into charcoal, which is then sold in stores and shops throughout the country.

In the following section the various industrial uses will be discussed, followed by information on *jift* charcoal manufacture and use.

3.3.5.1.2.1   Industrial Fuel

A number of industries world-wide utilize processing waste products as fuel (called "biomass"), often to power

a

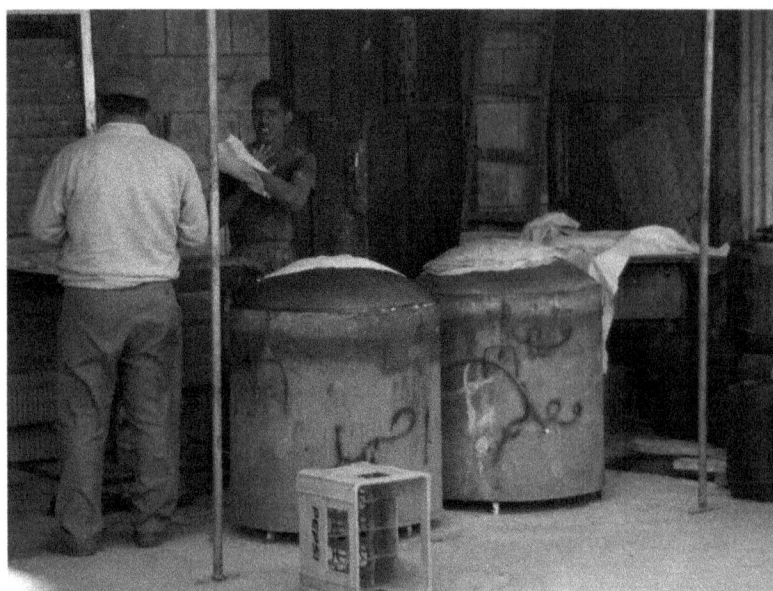

b

FIGURE 3.54a: CURVED PANS FOR BAKING TRADITIONAL BREAD, ASH SHUNA, JORDAN

b: BAKING BREAD ON CURVED PAN, ASH SHUNA, JORDAN

54

the very factories and processing plants that originally produced the waste products. The sugar industry uses the squeezed woody pulp of sugar cane (called "bagass") to fire boilers at sugar mills (www.travelgrenada.com/clarks.htm; http://jeffbarbee.com/old/people.htm; http://en.wikipedia.org/wiki/Sugar_cane), and the macadamia nut industry uses broken shells left after removing the kernel as boiler fuel for their plants and other industries (www.macadamiacastle.com.au/story/macamania.html; www.macadamiacr.com/ing/proceplant.html; http://maunaloa.com/quality.htm).

Similarly, *jift* from the oil mills may be used as fuel at the olive oil mills themselves, in factories, power plants, and for firing kilns. The *jift* from the second chemical "pressing" is sold to various industries, such as kiln fuel and charcoal manufacturing. Avitsur (1994) reports *jift* sold to bakeries as fuel, and used as factory fuel in the late 1800s/early 1900s. In the oil mills the *jift* is used to heat water used in the pressing process itself (Avitsur, 1994; Dolamore, 1994; Olives Australia Newletter, 1997; Rosenblum, 1996); Foxhall (1998) also thinks this was a use for Hellanistic/Roman *jift*. Heating water with *jift* at the mill is described in detail by one press owner and was mentioned earlier (for the detailed workings of a traditional mill) (also Kiritsakis, 1990). *Jift* is also used in the soap industry, usually as the fuel for cooking the large vats of soap (Avitsur, 1994; Al-Omari and Al-Azraie, 1995; Doumani, 1995; Loubani and Azraie, 1994; Okla and Azraie, 1994; Omari & Azraie, 1994; Bataeneh, *pers. comm.*; Yassine, *pers. comm.*).

Finally, contemporary use of olive pressing wastes as an energy producing fuel is on the rise (Ollero *et al*, 2002). Two proposed biomass-fired power plants in Spain will use pressing wastes as fuel (Australian Olive Grower, 1998; Australian Olive Grower, 1999; Burgess, 1999; Olive Oil Source, 2001). These power plants plan to use olive pressing wastes to generate energy and will be the largest power plants in Europe fired exclusively with biomass. A Turkish company is also looking into fueling a power station with olive wastes (Australian Olive Grower, 2000; Turkish Daily News, 2000). In Greece, biomass fuels involving olive pressing wastes are being used in a number of applications, including: heating greenhouses, heating buildings from individual or central boilers, and energy for agricultural industries (Hellenic Center for Investment (ELKE) Enews, 2005, www.elke.gr/newsletter/newsletter.asp?nid=394&id=424&lang=1).

Pottery making is a traditional industry extending from the Neolithic to the present that has high fuel demands. Modern potters around the Mediterranean basin continue to use *jift* as kiln fuel. Limited ethnographic studies in North Africa and Greece show that in areas of olive cultivation, *jift* is preferred over wood to fire pottery kilns (Smith, 2001), a finding that conforms to research by myself and others in Jordan (Melkawi, 1995; Mason and ᶜAmr, 1995). Lazreg (2001) mentions that olive oil pressing wastes are a great

fuel for firing pottery and similar industries, heating baths, and cooking. In Greece, the black sludge remaining after the second pressing of olives, called *pirini*, is considered by many potters to be the best fuel for firing the traditional pottery kilns. This is because the *pirini* gives good heat, reduces the length of the kiln firing time, and produces limited ash (Matson, 1972). *Pirini* is also used to fire bricks and roof tiles (Matson, 1966). In Tunisia, potters rely heavily on supplies of pressing waste (Sethom, 1964), called *grignons* (Peacock, 1982), which they buy from oil mills (Stirling, *pers. comm.*). In the pottery quarter of Fez, in Morocco, the makers of tesserae (*furmah*) for ceramic mosaics (*zillij*) use olive pressing waste (*faytour*) in bi-level, beehive shaped kilns. The olive waste is preferred because it burns at an "extraordinarily high temperature" (Werner, 2001). The use of olive stones as kiln fuel on Crete is also noted (Tzedakis and Martlew, 1999).

Melkawi's (1995) ethnoarchaeological research on traditional pottery making in Jordan includes detailed information on fuel preferences and use. I visited the same pottery factory Melkawi visited, in Zizia near the international airport, and corroborated her findings. The potters there use traditional methods, such as foot-spun throwing wheels, to produce unpainted pottery used in daily activities. The pottery is fired in brick beehive-shaped kilns. The Zizia potters have two seasons for firing. During the summer, the main firing season, the kilns are fired constantly. In the winter season the potters only fire about twice a week. The potters use wood and other materials to start the firing, but *jift* is the main fuel. The potters also use refuse as fuel (waste oil, manure, tires, plastic, junk). This particular factory has used *jift* as their main fuel since opening in the 1980s. The potters try to get as much *jift* as possible during the winter/fall pressing season and store it up, though they sometimes run out (thus the reason for refuse fuel use). The potters prefer *jift* as a fuel because it is cheap and easy to store. *Jift* also generates more heat in the kiln and is a slower burning fuel (long, steady burn and heating). Finally, the *jift* burns completely to ash, unlike wood or refuse, nothing is left. The ash left in the kiln is easy to clean out after firing. When firing is done and the kiln cools a bit, they rake out the ash and throw it into a ditch (wadi) behind the factory and cover it with dirt. A possible reason this ash is not utilized (for instance, as fertilizer) is due to the location of the industry. The kiln is in a remote location, far from orchards and other agricultural areas which might use the ash as fertilizer. Another explanation is since the potters mix the *jift* with refuse, farmers may prefer pure *jift* ash without unburnt refuse inclusions.

Evidence from antiquity supports the use of *jift* as a fuel in the pottery industry. For example, *jift* was used to fire pottery kilns in Roman Palestine (Vitto, 1986). Roman Leptiminus in Tunisia was a large scale producer of amphorae, coarse ware and 'African Red Slip' pottery (Smith, 1998). According to Smith (1998:193), production on that scale "would have required considerable amounts of high quality fuel." Smith goes on to suggest that pressing waste from olive oil production was transported to the kiln sites for use as fuel. Ash layers made up exclusively of intact carbonized olive stones and fine ash are thought to be spent fuel dumps from pottery kilns (Smith, 1998, 2001; Stirling and Lazreg, 2001). Among the finds at Leptiminus are 5 amphora of burned olive remains, which are a prime source of fuel (Stirling and Lazreg, 2001). Charred olive stones have been found at other Tunisian excavations (Ford and Miller, 1978; Hoffman, 1982; Stewart, 1984; van der Veen and van Zeist, 1982; van Zeist and Bottema, 1983, van Zeist, 1994). Van Zeist (1994) and Ford and Miller (1978) suggest the large numbers of carbonized olive stones found in ash lenses at Carthage may be evidence of the use of olive pressings as fuel. Finds of carbonized and unconsumed stones may be due to the high volume of pressing wastes used or to a reducing atmosphere which prevented the stones from being consumed. According to Adan-Bayewitz (1993), fuel for firing pottery at Kefar Hananya in the 1st century B.C. may have included *jift*, based on the discovery of olive oil installations there. In the Islamic period (Ummayed and Abbassid) at Jerash, pottery kilns have olive remains in them along with other possible fuels (wood) (Melkawi, 1995).

There appears to be a link between olive oil production and pottery production in antiquity. The main olive oil producing region of Tunisia was also a major pottery production center, at least up till the seventh century A.D. (Mattingly, 1988b). Other regions in the Roman world (Tripolitania – Libya, and Baetica – Spain) with large scale olive cultivation and oil production were also known for large scale pottery production (Mattingly, 1988b). Olive pressing wastes were likely used as fuel in these areas as well (Smith, 1998).

Literary sources also support the use of *jift* as kiln fuel. The Mishnah mentions the use of "olive-oil cakes" several times (Mishnah Shabbath 3.2; Tosefta Kelim Baba Kamma 3.13), including the use of *gepet* (pronounced geh-fet or jeh-fet, i.e. *jift*) as fuel for pottery kilns (Frankel, 1994).

The use of *jift* to fuel pottery kilns suggests its use in similar industries, such as the early glass industry (Fischer, *pers. comm.*). Glassblowers from Hebron, Palestine, who currently use motor oil as their primary fuel, say that 50-100 years ago olive waste was used as fuel in glass furnaces (Fischer, *pers. comm.*). Traditional kilns of the 1950s and 1960s in south Italy and Sicily included olive wastes as one of the fuels (Stern, 1999). Burned olive pits at Byzantine Sepphoris suggest that olive pressing waste was used as a fuel source, in addition to wood, in the glass furnaces (Fischer and McCray, 1999). Olive presses have been found at Sepphoris, as well as at other Byzantine glass-related sites such as Jalame and Beth She'arim, suggesting at least a regional use of *jift* in the glass industry (Fischer, *pers. comm.*), a hypothesis I would support.

Experiments in replicating a Nabataean pottery kiln found at the site of Zurrabah in the Petra area (Mason and cAmr, 1993; 1995) illustrate the advantages of *jift* as a kiln fuel. Initial experiments in firing using pine wood produced large amounts of ash and charcoal, which clogged the fire chamber and were difficult to remove (cleaning out the fire chamber). Subsequent firings using *jift* fuel produced only residues of ash, which were easy to clean out. Mason and cAmr (1993) also believe that as agricultural waste, *jift* would have been a more likely choice for kiln fuel than the scarcer and more precious woods. Using *jift* fuel the replicated kiln achieved high temperatures over a duration of four hours: "The pressings released a strong heat, burning with a yellow flame that breaks into a green/blue flame, and temperatures in excess of 800°C could be reached without much effort" (Mason and cAmr, 1995:635). Mason and cAmr felt that several factors support their argument for the use of *jift* fuel in the pottery kilns: there is archaeological evidence for the cultivation of olives in the Petra region from at least the first up to the sixth century A.D.; the (disturbed) remains of an ancient olive press can still be seen at Zurrabah near the kiln site (Zayadine, 1982); a large number of charred olive stones were found during the Zurrabah excavations (Zayadine 1982), and the tons of ash excavated from the pottery kilns contained almost no wood charcoal. Mason and cAmr (1995) concluded that *jift* was "almost certainty" used for fuel by the Zurrabah potters.

In using the *jift* as fuel, Mason and cAmr (1995) observed that as the *jift* aged it consolidated into dry lumps that burned well. Fresh *jift*, with a higher moisture content, required fairly hard compression to consolidate. Some *jift* was pressed into brick molds while other *jift* was simply rolled into balls (similar to those used for domestic fuel). After the pile of pressings was exposed to the heavy rains of 1991/92, the *jift* was easier to mold into blocks, but then the blocks required a very long drying period. Lumps of *jift* burned well, however, loose *jift* tended to cover unburnt fuel, preventing its combustion. Poking the fire was required to get air to the unburnt *jift*.

According to Smith (2001), ethnographic work would elucidate the preference of *jift* as kiln fuel. The explanations I have encountered in my research may all factor into the choice of *jift* as a fuel source: low or no cost, readily available in a fuel resource poor area, burns with no odor or smoke, and provides a good, high heat. One explanation, reported by practically every contact I consulted, including the Zizia potters, and mentioned in Mason and cAmr's studies (1993; 1995) stands out; *jift* as a fuel is consumed almost totally to ash. One older woman, referring to *jift* as a fuel, said that the "fire eats it," as it completely turns to ash. Another contact remarked that the *jift* turned to ash "like the ash of a cigarette" (very fine ash); numerous other contacts used the same expression. This phenomenon was also directly observed in experiments, as I discuss in Chapter 5. This is an important discovery, as it raises major questions concerning archaeological olive remains. If olive pressing wastes burn to ash, what do the olive remains found at archaeological sites actually represent?

However, the suggestion that all of the *jift* burns completely to ash may be flawed based on the archaeological reports cited above (i.e., Smith, 2001; Stirling and Lazreg, 2001; Van Zeist, 1994; Zayadine 1982). For instance, an improperly stoked fire will produce unburnt fuel. In ash samples collected from a tabun, I observed numerous inclusions, including some uncharred olive stones (Figure 3.55). Ethnographic studies show that in a "true fire" situation, fuel does not always burn completely (Miller and Smart, 1984:19). It may be that in small, highly controlled fires, such as the stoves used for home heat, practically all of the fuel is totally consumed. In larger fires, such as kilns, there is a greater chance for some unburned fuel to remain. The amount of uncharred or unashed fuel might be miniscule compared to the total amount of fuel used and the resulting ash. People may overlook or disregard the minute traces of unburnt fuel when discussing what remains when *jift* burns. Again, the archaeological reports offer some insight: charred olive remains are usually found associated with, or within, large ash lenses. This suggests that the olive remains are a minor, unconsumed remnant from a greater amount of totally ashed fuel. The size, duration, and how a fire is tended may have a great deal to do with what happens to the olive remains in the fire. A small, short duration, poorly tended fire may leave more unashed remains than would a large, long duration, well tended fire (the fire is stoked and stirred so all the fuel burns). Or, a small, long duration, well tended fire may leave fewer unashed remains than a large, long duration, poorly tended fire (which might leave a fair amount of unashed material). If the type of fire plays a role in determining what remains survive, the provenience, associated artifacts and features, and surrounding matrix will play an important role in interpreting the remains.

Finally, another suggested use of olive oil processing waste as a fuel source involves the production of methane. The organic components of the waste are broken down by methane producing bacteria, the resulting methane is used as fuel (Roldán *et al*, 2000).

3.3.5.1.2.2 Charcoal

A further commercial use of the *jift* is in the manufacture of charcoal (Olives Australia Newsletter, 1997; Stirling *et al*, 1996; Yassine; Al-Rjoub; Musamat, *pers. comm.*). Though not sold commercially, olive pressing waste used as fuel by potters in Tunisia is sometimes preburned to make charcoal (Sethom, 1964). Several companies in Jordan sell bags of briquettes made from *jift*. The *jift* is often purchased from companies doing chemical oil extraction. I purchased bags of this charcoal from two different companies, the Bila'l Company (Figure 3.56) and the Arab Coal company (Figure 3.57), and a box of Royal Charcoal. All companies made a point of claiming the charcoal was made from olive *jift* (the Arab Coal bag says from the "olive tree") or in the case of Royal Charcoal "made from Pure Olive Seeds." The Arab Coal bag stated that the charcoal "gives you high heat without a lot of smoke, does not [contain] have any

FIGURE 3.56: BILA'L OLIVE COAL (GREEN BAG). LABEL READS "JORDANIAN OLIVE *JIFT* COAL [NARGILAH – CLASSICAL ARABIC/ MODERN ARABIC argilah] COAL. ½ KILO. PRODUCT OF THE BILA'L FACTORY FOR *JIFT* COAL. PH# 689059 OWNER'S PORTABLE PH# 07-934113"

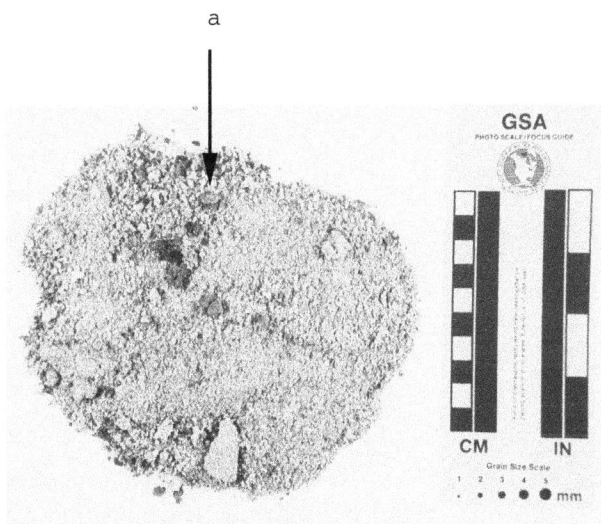

FIGURE 3.55: ASH FROM TABUN, NOTE CHARRED OLIVE STONE (a)

FIGURE 3.57: ARAB COAL (YELLOW BAG). LABEL READS
"ARAB COAL, REGISTERED TRADEMARK. NARGILAH AND
BARBEQUE. IT GIVES YOU A HIGH HEAT WITHOUT A LOT OF
SMOKE. DOES NOT [CONTAIN] HAVE ANY CHEMICAL MATERIALS.
HEALTHY AND CLEAN. MADE FROM THE OLIVE TREE.
PRODUCED BY THE ARAB FACTORY FOR COAL, MUTEA KHALIL
BAKER AND PARTNER CO. PO BOX 420271, AMMAN, 11042,
FACTORY ADDRESS."

chemical materials," and is "healthy and clean." The Royal Charcoal box had labels that said: "Easy Ignition," "Long Burning" and "Smokeless." I found the Bila'l and Royal Charcoal charcoal brands sold in a Middle East food store in Columbia, Missouri, proof enough that it is a preferred type of charcoal.

I attempted to contact both the Bila'l and Arab Coal companies, without success. In my attempts to contact the companies to see and discuss the process, I was told that the companies did not want anyone to see their process for fear of having their methods and secrets stolen.

The *jift* charcoal is used in braziers and the like for cooking; the Arab Coal bag specifically mentions barbeque and shows a picture of a brazier. The charcoal is also especially preferred for use with the traditional Arab water pipe (*argîlah, narghila*, or *narjilah*) (Avitsur, 1994; R. Frankel, *pers. comm.*; K. Yassine, *pers. comm.*; K. Nuimat, *pers. comm.*). Both bags mention water pipes and have pictures

of water pipes on their labels, and the Royal Charcoal is primarily for waterpipe use. Again, the reason for the preference is that *jift* charcoal produces a good steady heat and burns to ash. It also produces no smell or taste, an important feature since flavored tobacco is commonly smoked in water pipes and people do not want the taste of the tobacco altered by the charcoal.

Crushed olive stones are also transformed into activated charcoal (Australian Olive Grower, 1999; Lafi, 2001; Roldán, 2000). This activated charcoal is in demand by an expanding industry dealing with the purification of liquids and gases (Australian Olive Grower, 1999) including the possible purification of water supplies in Jordan (http://calvin.standrews.ac.uk/external_relations/news_article.cfm?reference=58, 2000).

3.3.5.2 Jewelry and Cosmetics
The use of olive pressing waste material for jewelry and cosmetics is little known or documented, which could account for the lack of literary references. One of the practices, using olive stones for jewelry, leaves very identifiable marks on the remains; while the other, cosmetics, leaves practically no evidence or remains at all.

My contact in Madaba, Jordan, who used a rotary hand quern to grind the olives, said that the olives were pitted before grinding them. When asked what she did with the olive stones, the contact said they (she and others using this method) pit the olive stones (removing the seed kernel inside the stone) and use the pitted stones for jewelry and prayer beads. The contact's husband, an elderly Bedouin Haj and Sheik, gave me his set of olive stone prayer beads (Figure 3.58). The set of prayer beads consists of three sections of thirty-three olive stones strung length-wise (the string goes through the stone along the long axis of the stone), with each section of thirty-three separated by a stone strung sideways (the string goes through the middle of the stone along the short axis). Strings of prayer beads come in sets of ninety-nine or thirty-three; when praying with the beads you either do one set of ninety-nine or three times a set of thirty-three. J. Zias (*pers. comm.*) observed Palestinian "detainees" making sets of prayer beads. The detainees took cleaned olive stones and filed off the ends. The kernel was removed using a thin piece of wire and the stones strung into sets of prayer beads. Another contact mentioned that his grandmother, living in the Irbid area, also made prayer beads with olive stones. Tulumba.com, a Turkish on-line store, mentions rosaries (*tesbih*) made from olive stones in their rosary sales pitch ("all you want to know about rosary"), as does the Ataman Hotel site (atamanhotel.com). Modifications to the olive stone such as these should be readily apparent in archaeological remains. However, the survivability of the olive stones in the archaeological record must also be considered. For instance, if the stones (as jewelry) are grave goods in a burial, and are not charred, they may not survive.

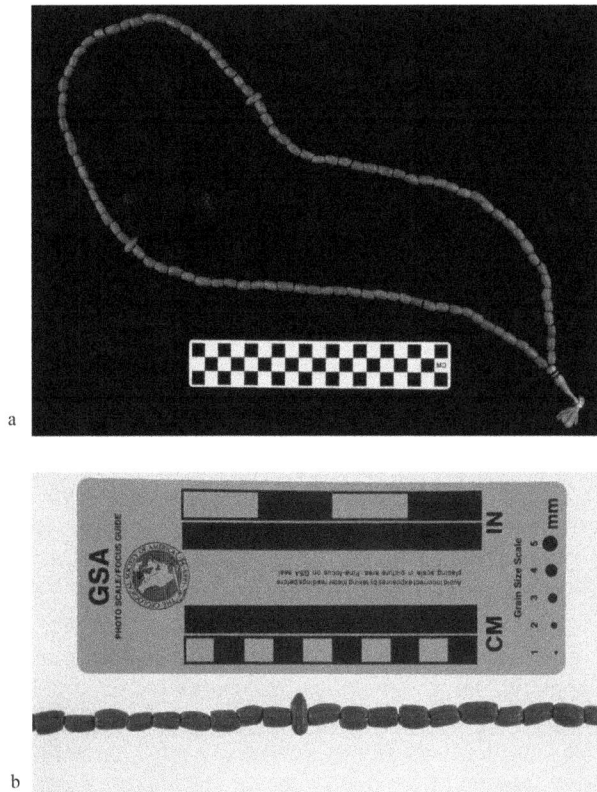

FIGURE 3.58: OLIVE STONE PRAYER BEADS
a: THREE SECTIONS OF 33 OLIVE STONES STRUNG LENGTHWISE,
SEPARATED BY ONE STONE STRUNG SIDEWAYS
b: CLOSE-UP OF LENGHTWISE STONES AND A SEPARATOR STONE

E. Ayalon (*pers. comm.*), at the Eretz Israel Museum in Tel Aviv, was informed by some Yemeni Jews that they used burnt olive stones as a cosmetic. The burnt stones are crushed and ground into a fine black powder and used primarily as an eye-liner, called *kohl*. *Kohl* is the heavy black eye-liner favored by women around the Middle East. According to Ayalon the Yemeni Jews realized that the galina ore previously used in *kohl* was lead based and poisonous and switched to using burnt olive stones. This practice destroys the olive stones, and would leave next to nothing in the archaeological record. The amount of olive stones needed for making kohl is unknown; unless it is made for commercial purposes, the number of olive stones involved is likely fairly limited. Korres Natural Products produces an Olive Stones Natural Face Scrub, made from finely ground olive stones (sold by several cosmetics companies, including Sephora, a leading retail beauty chain in Europe) (Sephora.com). The Carneros Inn in Napa, California, offers an Orchard Olive Stone and Honeydew Exfoliation made from crushed olive stones and olive oil (thecarnerosinn.com), while the Four Seasons Hotel in Chicago has a Four Seasons Elixir Paraffin Wrap which also includes an exfoliation with finely ground olive stones (fourseasons.com).

3.3.5.3 Animal Feed
The use of *jift* as animal feed is mentioned by a number

of sources (Amouretti and Comet, 1992; Australian Olive Grower, 1999; Burgess, 1999; Fuller, 1986; Hadjipanayiotou, 1999; I.O.O.C., n.d.; Lazreg, 2001; Mattingly, 1996; Olives Australia Newsletter, 1997; Roldán *et al*, 2000; Sansoucy, 1985) and a few contacts in my study. Cato (*De Re Rustica* 103) had the lees mixed with cattle feed to improve their health. The United Nation's Food and Agriculture Organization (FAO) has investigated the potential use of *jift* as animal feed around the Mediterranean basin (Sansoucy, 1985). Amouretti and Comet (1992) mention the use of *jift* as swine feed in southern France and as a component of cattle feed. Some contacts mention mixing *jift* with minerals and feeding it to sheep, while others reported giving it to lambs. Al-Rjoub, Musamat and Jibril (*pers. comm.*), at the Ramtha Agricultural Experiment Station near Irbid, reported that since lambs will occasionally eat the ash from burnt *jift*, some of the ash is spread out for them. One contact said that animals might eat it off the ground (where it was spread as fertilizer), but they were not fed it. Some reports (Hadjipanayiotou, 1999; I.O.O.C., n.d.) mention removing the stones from the *jift* before using it as livestock feed. Conversely, Fuller (1986) reports that ground olive stones are fed as fodder to animals. Some contacts mention that if animals eat pure *jift* the animal's teeth fall out, but that the animals are protected from external parasites. Along the same lines, putting *jift* on the bodies of animals protects the animals from external parasites.

In Jordan, experiments with *jift* as a feed additive are being carried out at the Ramtha Agricultural Experiment Station, outside Irbid. The people I interviewed there, both station staff and local farmers involved in the feeding experiments, provided information and opinions on the use of *jift* as animal feed. The use of *jift* is one of several experiments using various agricultural industries' by-products as components of animal feed; for instance, other experiments include by-products from the tomato paste or chicken processing industries. Hadjipanayiotou (1994; 1999) also mentions similar ingredients added to *jift*: including ground corn, molasses, poultry litter and tomato pulp. In Morocco, olive pressing wastes were mixed with sugarcane wastes and fermented, then used as animal fodder (Hibler, 2003).

The contacts at the Agriculture Experimental Station believe that using *jift* as animal fodder is new and was not practiced much in the past, a view shared by other contacts. One farmer said that his father has had sheep since 1948 and it was very rare to feed *jift* to the animals, mainly because there has always been plenty of pasturage and there is no pressure to use *jift* as feed. Plus, *jift* is useful for so many other things.

When *jift* is used as feed, it is mixed with calcium, other minerals and grain in varying amounts, rather than comprising the total animal feed component (Sansoucy, 1985; Al-Rjoub and Musamat, *pers. comm.*). Other sources mention a 10:90 ratio of *jift* to forage in experimental cattle feed mixes (Omari and Azraie, 1994; Al-Omari and Al-Azraie, 1995; Okla and Azraie, 1994; Loubani and Azraie, 1994). In sheep-feeding experiments, *jift* replaces barley in a multi-component feed mix at different replacement ratios (10%, 20% and 30% replacement) with the 20% working best (Al-Rjoub and Musamat, *pers. comm.*). A Tunisian study reported that higher levels of pressing waste in feed or the waste itself caused weight loss in livestock (Olives Australia Newsletter, 1997). According to Hadjipanayiotou (1999) a major problem in using pressing waste as a feed component is that it deteriorates rapidly and becomes rancid or moldy.

The dung of sheep that are fed *jift* is passed in chunks rather than the usual small pellets (Al-Rjoub and Musamat, *pers. comm.*). Sheep can eat olive stones and the stones do pass through the digestive system (Jibril, *pers. comm.*). The dung of a number of domesticated animals (sheep/goat, cattle, camel and donkey) in the Middle East, if utilized, is used as a fuel first and for fertilizer only as a second option. If sheep are kept in an enclosure or pen, the dung must be collected every two or three days, otherwise it gets too deep. The dung is then dried in the sun and is used in heating houses, and in *tabuns* and cooking fires.

The use of *jift* as animal feed provides a potential route for the inclusion of charred olive stones into the archaeological record. While I have found no evidence for the solid pressing wastes to be used as animal food, the possibility does exist that the practice might have occurred. As olive stones are not digested but are passed out in the dung, and since dung is frequently used as fuel (Madella, *pers. comm.*; Miller and Smart, 1984: Smith, 2001; Warnock, personal observation), charred olive stones could result from dung use as fuel. Dung fuel is frequently used in similar circumstances as *jift* fuel, especially in domestic settings, which may further complicate analyses and interpretation. Discovering charred olive stones might suggest using *jift* as fuel, when the olive remains are actually from dung fuel. Using dung from *jift*-fed animals as fuel could result in charred olive stones from the *jift* in the burnt dung. However, dung fuel, like *jift*, frequently burns completely to ash, resulting in no surviving remains.

3.3.5.4 Fertilizer

Another common use of *jift* is as fertilizer. The *jift* is often returned to the same orchards where the olives producing the *jift* originated, completing a circuit from orchard to mill to orchard again. A number of contacts in my study refer to this practice, and some mention specific methods or restrictions on using *jift* fertilizer, along with the reasons behind the practices. One contact said that olive trees remove a good deal of potassium from the soil and that putting *jift* around the base of the tree helps put the potassium back into the ground. However, another said that when you put the *jift* in the olive orchard you spread it around. If you pile the *jift* around a tree the *jift* gives off heat that is bad for the roots. Another contact agreed that when you put the *jift* in the orchard you spread all over because it prevents the

grass from growing. The journal for a documentary film, *Salt of the Earth*, mentions "As we walked by the now-lush fields, we noticed black and burned-looking patches. This is land polluted by the by-products of olive pressing. At the olive press, when a farmer takes his olive oil, he must also take the solid (olive cake) and liquid waste from the process. Because there are no facilities for accommodating these wastes, farmers often just dump them where they can – on roadsides and on corners of their land. It takes years for the land to recover" (Journal in the Holy Land, Feb. 2001: 2/18/01). In retrospect, I did not notice much ground cover under many olive trees or in olive orchards. The *jift* may also control nematodes as well (Roldán *et al*, 2000).

The practice of using the *jift* as fertilizer is referred to numerous times in the literature (Amirante and Pipitone, 2002; Amouretti and Comet, 1992; Australian Olive Grower, 1999; Burgess, 1999; Davis, 1996; Dolamore, 1994; Mattingly, 1996; Olives Australia Newsletter, 1997). Cato (*De Re Rustica* 37.1,2) suggests that olive pressing waste be used as fertilizer for trees, but not arable crops, supporting the idea that *jift* kills the grass.

While *jift* fertilizer might initially appear to be a means of incorporating olive stones into the archaeological record, this is misleading. Inspection of soils in olive orchards and under olive trees did show olive stones in the soil, however, the stones were only in or on the surface soil and were in a highly friable, decomposing state. Uncharred stones rapidly decay and do not leave any long-lasting macroremains. The stones could also represent fruit that had fallen from the trees and was not collected.

A recent suggested use, similar to using *jift* for fertilizer, is as a substrate for growing edible mushrooms (Roldán *et al*, 2000).

3.3.5.5 Ash

As has been mentioned previously, *jift* is preferred as a fuel because it burns to ash. Even this ash has its uses. Many contacts mention that after burning *jift* the resulting ash is also used as fertilizer, especially in the olive orchards. According to Kiritsakis (1990), the *jift* ash makes good fertilizer due to the high potassium, phosphorus and calcium content. As discussed above, the ash, like the *jift* used as fertilizer, is usually spread around. Like the *jift*, the ash is supposed to put potassium back into the soil. Cato (*De Re Rustica* 37.2) suggests using burned olive stones or pressing waste as fertilizer, but whether or not this refers to ash from burnt *jift* is unclear. One contact informed me that *jift* ash is either used as fertilizer by itself or is mixed with manure and then the mixture used as fertilizer. The same contact identified large bags containing a white substance, which he said was *jift* ash being used as fertilizer at a new orchard. Sterling and Lazreg (2001) suggest that since wood was a valuable commodity at the site of Leptiminus in Tunisia, it is not surprising that the by-products of burning wood were also of value. They suggest that ash from the site could have been used as fertilizer. Several amphora found at Leptiminus were filled with ash and carbonized olive stones. This suggests that ash from olive *jift* was also being used in antiquity for fertilizer or other purposes.

If the unconsumed inclusions in ash were not sifted out, the use of ash as fertilizer could be a means by which charred olive stones were deposited into the archaeological record. However, since the ash is spread on the surface of the ground, taphonomic factors could alter or destroy the stones. Further, since the activity of fertilizing occurs in areas not commonly sampled in archaeology, i.e. orchards, gardens and fields, recovery of olive remains representing this activity would likely be minimal.

In Tekkök-Biçken's (2000) ethnoarchaeological study on traditional pottery production in Turkey, fine ash from the firing chamber is used in the clay preparation process. The ash prevents the clay from sticking to a surface while the clay is worked to remove air bubbles. It is reasonable to suggest that this use occurred elsewhere in time and space.

Another use of ash produced by burning olive pressing wastes is in the glass industry. The ash produced from olive pressing wastes as fuel in the glass industry at Sepphoris, Israel might have been reused as a fluxing agent in making glass, as plant ash was used in the Arab I (A.D. 640–950) and Arab II (A.D. 950–1516) periods (Fischer and McCray, 1999).

3.3.5.6 Soap

Olive oil soap is a special case in the use of olive pressing wastes, for the process utilizes both the raw *jift* as well as ash resulting from burning *jift*. A number of contacts informed me that they sold *jift* from the mills to the soap industry. The raw *jift* is pressed a second time for its residual oil, which is used in making olive oil soap. *Jift* from the second pressing is stored and used as fuel in the soap making process (E. Ayalon, *pers. comm.*) and to power equipment. The ash from the *jift*-fueled fires is used as a component of the soap itself, not unlike medieval European bakers selling the ash from their ovens for making lye (Toussaint-Samat, 1992). The olive oil soap is made from low grade oil, ash, and lime, which are boiled together for a week to ten days. This process consumes around three and a half tons of *jift* fuel (Avitsur, 1994). After the liquid soap mixture has cooled it is poured, at the desired thickness of the soap bar, over a stone floor. When dried, it is cut into cubes, with the manufacturer's name often stamped on them (Figure 3.59).

Palestine has been famous since medieval times for its olive oil soap (Avitsur, 1994), which is favored by Muslims and Jews since it is free of pork fat. The center of Palestinian soap making was Nablus, and the soap was often called "Nablus soap" (Avistur, 1994). The name is still synonymous with quality soap, and one can purchase, as I did, olive oil soap in the many small stores and markets

in Jordan by asking for Nablus soap (Figure 3.59). I also found this traditional olive oil soap in the Near Eastern food market in Columbia, Missouri. Several contacts mention selling *jift* to factories in Nablus, though the contacts in Jordan now sell to a soap company in Irbid.

FIGURE 3.59A-B: NABLUS SOAP
a: SOAP BLOCK AND WRAPPER
b: NABLUS SOAP LABEL "EXCELLENT NABLUS SOAP. OSTRICH BRAND TRADEMARK. TEL 370027. FAMILY OF THE TAHER MASSRI IN NABLUS. USE IT, ITS PURE."

FIGURE 3.59c: NABLUS SOAP WITH IMPRINT

FIGURE 3.60: HOMEMADE SOAP FROM JUDEIDA, ISRAEL

Olive oil soap is still made at home. This soap also utilizes olive oil and the ash from burnt *jift*. Several people mention making homemade soap by boiling down ("boiling for a long time") olive oil and ash, then pouring the mix into molds (Frankel, J., 1996; Zias, *pers. comm.*). Other contacts describe the process as mixing caustic soda and olive oil together and letting the mix sit for 24 hours. The mix is then heated and some water added. This mixture is stirred as it heats. Care is taken during this step as the soda and fumes from the mixture will burn the eyes. The mix is heated until it bubbles. The mixture is tested by rubbing some on the hand. When the mix is ready, it is poured into a wooden form on a flat hard surface (floor, driveway). Some of the water runs off as it dries. In two days the soap is solid and is cut into pieces (Figure 3.60). The contacts said the soap dries well. Rosenblum (1996) mentions soap making in Nablus using a similar recipe and methods, as does Howard (2001) on Crete.

No one mentioned if the burnt *jift* is sifted to remove inclusions such as unashed stones, but the contacts may assume that this is understood. Such inclusions are not a desirable ingredient in the soap. Unashed material might then be thrown away, thus ending up in the archaeological record, or returned to the fire to be rendered to ash. Since the soap-making process uses both the *jift* as fuel, and then the ash as a component of the soap, it is conceivable that no evidence of olive oil processing or *jift* use might remain.

I did find several instances where the *jift* was used as a component in the soap, providing an abraiding agent to remove dead skin. Noveya sells an Olive Soap made from "Pure Israel Virgin Olive Oil, Gefet (Pomace pulp leftover from pressings)" (www.noveya.com/olive.html). Oasis Day Spa's website (www.oasisdayspanyc.com) sells L'Occitane brand olive exfoliating shower cream where "crushed olive pits gently exfoliate the body as A.O.C. olive oil nourishes the skin." Shipshewana Shops also offer a Olive Leaf Exfoliating Body Polish which has "fine olive pit granules" that "exfoliate gently to reveal skin's natural radiance" (www.Shipshewana.com). I found a number of

other companies on-line selling similar creams and body polishes.

3.3.5.7 Construction
Several other uses of olive pressing remains are suggested in both the literature and by my contacts. Olive remains in various forms are used in construction and repair. Stones are used as a component of heat resistant bricks, bakelite, and in materials for cleaning facades (Australian Olive Grower, 1999). Olive stones are used as a strengthening agent for mortar (E. Ayalon, *pers. comm.*). Carbonized olive stones were used as a binding agent or temper in mortar at Carthage (Hoffman, 1981) and Leptiminus (Lazreg, 2001; Smith, 2001). At sites in Tunisia (Leptiminus and Thapsus), some of the mortar found in standing structures, especially cisterns, contained ash and carbonized olive stones (Smith, 1998; Stirling and Lazreg, 2001). Several amphora were found filled with ash, carbonized olive stones and twigs, possibly for use as fertilizer and in making mortar (Stirling and Lazreg, 2001). In Jordan, ash is used in plastering and repairs. The ash is mixed with a small ratio of clay and applied as a plaster/sealant repair material to close holes, cracks, etc., in mud brick houses (Al-Rjoub; Musamat, *pers. comm.*).

The use of olive wastes as construction materials provides yet another example concerning the difficulty in identifying olive oil processing remains. Use as construction materials removes the olive remains to locations away from the processing area. Directly linking the olive remains to olive oil processing could be difficult. Further, the effects from being incorporated into mortar and plaster might alter the remains, making identification of individual processing practices impossible. However, olive remains used as construction components at sites lacking evidence of olive oil processing would support the idea of intersite exchange of raw materials.

3.3.5.8 Waste Water Usage
There were uses in antiquity for the waste water (lees or amurca) from pressing as well. Cato (*De Re Rustica* 91-103; 128-130) recites a number of uses for amurca, including making plaster and in the construction of threshing floors (White, 1984). The use of amurca to prepare freshly laid floors is also mentioned by Vitruvius (*De Architectura* 7.1.7) and Columella (*De Re Rustica* 1.6.12-15). The application of amurca on floors was tested on samples from the Great Temple of Amman, using pollen analysis (Warnock and Pendleton, 1994). Other uses of the amurca include coating new oil vats, pest control (for caterpillars, and to keep moths from clothes), and for oiling leather goods, presumably for waterproofing and suppleness.

Cato also mentions the use of the lees or amurca as fertilizer (*De Re Rustica* 37.1, 2) and suggests diluting by half with water. This practice continues in Spain (Rosenblum, 1996). The modern use of olive oil processing wastewater for irrigation and as fertilizer has been proposed (Di Giovacchino *et al*, 2002; Di Giovacchino, 2005). The *jift* may also control nematodes as well (Roldán *et al*, 2000; Tamburino *et al*, 1999). The processing wastewater is mixed with conventional water sources and contains organic wastes useful as fertilizer. A number of contacts (on the internet) also mention the use of processing wastewater as fertilizer. Most think that the wastewater returns nutrients to the soil (primarily potassium and phosphorus).

Also, the wastewater has a phytotoxic effect on other plants (Chandler, 2000; Kaddour *et al*, 2005; Tamburino *et al*, 1999), and one contact mentioned the microflora as well. Varro (*Rerum Rusticarum* 1.40.7) mentions using the lees to kill noxious weeds. This collaborates the statement made by a contact using *jift* as fertilizer where the *jift* prevented grass from growing in the orchard.

Unlike solid olive remains, it is difficult to test for the uses of the liquid wastes of olive oil processing. Modern analyses, such as pollen analysis, can be used to test and verify ancient textual references into the use of liquid olive oil processing wastes.

3.3.6   Other Aspects of the Olive Tradition

These last few sections cover information that, while not necessarily pertinent to the main focus of the research, provides important ethnographic information on the olive tradition in the Near East. This information includes: eating olives, taste preferences, economic and social implications, and folk stories about the olive and olive oil.

3.3.6.1   Eating Olives

A major question is 'which came first, the olive or the oil?' In other words, in what form was the olive first utilized, for eating the fruit or for the oil? As discussed in Chapter 2, when humanity first discovered the olive as a food source is unknown. Adding to the confusion is the fact that the fruit is considered inedible raw (Artzy, 1996; Borowski, 1987; Dolamore, 1994; Forbes & Foxhall, 1978; Klein, 1994; Rogers, 1995). Not all people may consider fresh, unprocessed olives distasteful, however, from personal experience I know that eating a green to slightly black olive fresh off the tree is a very unpleasant and distasteful experience, not to be repeated. Raw, unprocessed olives are exceedingly bitter. "Unlike grapes, you cannot put fresh-picked olives on the table unless you are troubled with sadism; they are excruciatingly bitter" (Rosenblum, 1996:13). According to Johns (1994:46), "Wild food plants often contain chemical constituents that make them pungent, astringent, sour, or bitter; for someone unaccustomed to a particular plant food its ingestion can be a unpleasant experience."

Fresh olives are inedible straight from the tree because they contain oleuropein, an extremely bitter alkaloid compound which must first be broken down or altered before olives are palatable. As Johns (1994:46) points out, "many human populations consume by choice foods that are by most accounts distasteful." People in antiquity

may not have always considered a "bitter" taste bad, but rather preferable. Oils made from green olives may have a sharp, bitter flavor, which is preferred by some people. Due to the way it is produced, some Moroccan olive oil has a high acidity, but because people are used to it they have developed a taste for it (Hibler, 2003). The contact accompanying me when I ate the raw olive also ate one off the tree and stated that it was very tasty. It is impossible to determine what ancient humans might have considered tasty; they might have been more ambivalent to the palatability of wild food plants and may have enjoyed raw bitter olives. Singer (1996:29) states that "Man ate from the fruit of the olive tree even before he knew how to preserve it or to remove the bitter taste from the fruit." He goes on to state that during the ripening process the bitterness diminishes and that after the ripening process is finished and the olives are over-ripe they are edible without special preparation. However, he does not provide any documentation or references for his statements.

Nesbitt (*pers. comm.*) reports that semi-rotten and fermenting fruit are eaten off the ground in Turkey. My fieldwork confirms this practice. One contact said that one could eat olives off the tree, but only when they were ripe. They are pressed with the fingers and the oil squeezes out immediately, they would be edible. This was for black olives only; the ones which look dried out but are still on the tree. Other contacts said some people will eat the olives off the tree, but only at the end of the picking season. Only the very ripe olives still on the tree can be eaten. At the end of the season all the water is gone from the olives and only the oil is left, it is "like the olives are pickled on the tree." Ripe olives are considered better for pressing due to the higher oil content. The practice of eating olives off the tree is not a "commercial" practice, but is done only when out picking in the groves (Takruri, *pers. comm.*). The dropped olives ("*jarjir*") which have fermented on the ground can also be eaten. However, Frankel (*pers. comm.*) mentioned a monastery on Cyprus where there is an olive variety that can be eaten off the tree. The olives of this variety do not have to be ripe, they can be eaten off the tree at any time.

During my field research, a number of contacts mentioned methods of processing (pickling) olives for consumption. The Moroccans interviewed by Rosenblum (1996) treat eating olives in ways similar to the Palestinians. When Rosenblum asked a Moroccan how many ways there were to prepare olives for eating, he was told, "How many households are there?" Every culture, region, and family have their own way of processing eating olives.

There are some standard procedures adhered to; in almost every case the olives are slightly crushed (bruised) or cut during the process. The idea is to break the skin to better allow the pickling solution into the fruit and to neutralize the bitter alkaloids. In locations selling olives in Jordan, such as roadside stalls or near oil mills in the Ajlun and Irbid areas, special machines for crushing the fruit are available for those who wish to save the time of crushing them at home. A hopper or bin feeds the olives down to two slightly knobby rollers with the space between them slightly smaller than an olive. Turning a crank handle moves the olives between the rollers, slightly crushing the fruit.

One contact told of her mother-in-law's method of making home-pickled olives: Using a large wooden pestle about a foot tall, with a handle about an 1 to 1½ inches in diameter and a base of approximately 6-7 inches around by 4-5 high (quite heavy according to the contact) they crush the olives for pickling in a large stone mortar. I was told that one is not supposed to crush the stone, since breaking the stone gives a bad taste and makes the olives bitter. This statement supports the idea that breaking the stone during crushing prior to pressing gives the oil a bad flavor.

Green and black olives are pickled differently. The more bitter green olives are processed longer, usually with salt water or lye (Sandy, 1989). The green olives are crushed and pickled in brine with pieces of lemon. Sometimes hot or bell peppers are also added (Amiry & Tamari, 1989; Rosenblum, 1996) (note that peppers are a New World plant and would not be found in antiquity). One contact reported that after crushing the green olives just enough to break the skin, they are soaked in salt water for a week or two. The water is changed two to three times. During the last water change, the lemon and peppers are added. Two months after the last water change, the olives are ready to eat. Sandy (1989) also says changing the water frequently gives better quality.

Black (ripe) olives are not treated with lye (Sandy, 1989) or salt water, instead, black olives are pickled only in olive oil. Rosenblum (1996) mentions similar methods. According to the contacts in my study, these olives cost twice as much as green ones. Amiry and Tamari (1989) mention a different method: the black olives are heavily salted, stored for a couple of weeks, then soaked in hot boiling water to remove bitterness and finally stored in jars filled with water and olive oil. Some contacts say black olives are sometimes specially prepared by removing the stone and stuffing the hole with nuts (walnuts) or bits of green pepper.

In ancient times olives were made palatable by pickling, drying or salting, which removed some but not all the bitterness (Simpson and Ogorzaly, 1986). Columella gives detailed instructions on how to pickle olives (*De Re Rustica: De Arboribus* 12.49-51). Runnels and Hansen (1986) state that table olives are prepared by soaking them in brine. However, they are unsure if this procedure was actually practiced, and if so, when the practice was introduced in antiquity. Ridgeway (1996:7) states that the olive's "history is so ancient no one knows who first ... thought of softening and preserving the fruit in salt or soda," a sentiment echoed by Dolamore (1994). Galili *et al* (1997) assume that salty Mediterranean water available off the Carmel Coast sites may have been used to prepare

olive for consumption (also seconded by Dolamore, 1994). Some scholars (Renfrew, 1973; Zohary and Hopf, 2000) claim (although undocumented) that raw olives were eaten before the Hellenistic or Roman periods. However, Borowski (1987) disagrees. He maintains a Hellenistic or Roman introduction for this practice. Borowski (1987) states that the Old Testament has absolutely no references to raw olives being eaten. According to him, prior to Hellenistic or Roman times, olives in the diet would probably have been used for oil only. All of the Biblical passages mentioning the olive refer to the olive as a source for oil, but never as a fruit for consumption. Evidence from early (pre-Iron Age) Greece suggests that olives were processed for uses other than dietary (Vickery, 1936). The majority of Vickery's evidence suggest the use of olive oil as a fuel, however, he suggests they were eaten, but presents no evidence supporting the position. The lack of early Greek references to olive oil as a food-stuff supports Borowski's position. The general scarcity of olive stones at many early period archaeological sites around the Eastern Mediterranean may suggest that people did not eat them on a regular basis (Haldane, 1990).

3.3.6.2 Preferences

The vast majority of people I talked with, especially at traditional mills and in the small villages, said that the traditionally-made oil, the "old oil," tastes better. This includes oil made with boiled, dried or smoked olives. Some contacts argued that oil collected by hand was best. And, of course, everyone thought that their village or mill made the "best" oil. According to contacts, traditional oil even smells better; one can "taste" the oil with the nose. Another argument against modern processing by the traditional pressing supporters is that modern methods add too much water to the olive mash, which alters the quality of the oil.

Several people mention that modern oil gives heartburn, while traditional oil does not. One can eat as much of the traditional oil as one wishes; if one eats too much modern oil, it will give one a stomach ache or heartburn. Some suggest that the heartburn is caused by centrifuging the oil. The modern centrifugal pressing method "burns" the oil; if the centrifugal mill is not monitored, the centrifuge can overheat and break down the oil. This causes a bad taste (I.O.O.C., n.d.; Rosenblum, 1996; Takruri, *pers. comm.*). The overheated oil I tasted was very unpleasant and bitter. Oil made from green olives is often darker green and has a sharper, more bitter taste. This is due to bitter alkaloids remaining in the green, not fully ripe, fruit. Oil from riper fruit will be more of a golden color, with a mellower flavor. Due to all the varieties of oil available, the range of color and taste is enormous, and personal preference is a determining factor in oil choice.

As Rosenblum (1996) points out, taste preferences for oil, pressing methods, and so on are all subjective; different people like different things. Older people point out that younger generations want things quicker, and in doing so miss the quality. The introduction of mass-produced and mass-marketed oils such as corn or soybean oil into the local markets changes consumers perception of "good" oil. People buy and become accustomed to these other oils. People then think that the modern clear oil is better, rather than the dark, cloudy traditional oils. The older traditions and styles are vanishing, in part due to the time it takes and the low volume traditional methods produce. There is a growing market for such traditional oils, however, as more people acquire the knowledge and a real taste for quality olive oils (Dolamore, 1994; Knickerbocker, 1997; Ridgeway, 1996; Rosenblum, 1996). There is even an "Extra Virgin Olive Oil of the Month Club" selling oils from smaller specialty mills from around the Mediterranean basin.

3.3.6.3 Distribution of Oil

The distribution of the olive oil after pressing varies from press to press and farmer to farmer. Olive oil production is based on weight, rather than liquid volume. At the end of pressing, the oil is put into containers, which are then weighed. I saw both metal tins and plastic barrels being used. The weight is in metric kilograms (kilos), with the press owners taking a percentage of the oil rather than a cash payment for processing the olives into oil. The percentage taken varies.

The oil is divided up differently each year. At the press at Al Mazar the split was 10 to 1 (for 1996), ten kilograms to the farmer and one kilogram to the press owner. In 1995 the split was 11 to 1. A split of 10 to 1 or 11 to 1 appeared standard (Rafi Bataaneh, *pers. comm.*), though at the majority of presses I visited in 1996 the split was 10 to 1. At only one press was the split 11 to 1.

One of my main contact's father buys olives from other small farmers. Since the contact's father deals in volume and brings in more olives than a single farmer would (delivering what four to five farmers might bring in), he gets a discount price for dealing in volume. Instead of the usual 10 to 1 split, he gets an approximately 12 to 1 split.

3.3.6.4 Beliefs Surrounding Olive Oil

During my research, a number of contacts, especially some of the older ones, told me that olive oil endows strength upon its users. Traditionally processed olive oil, more than modern oil, gives one strength. "You would become strong [as in powerful, give you muscles] like stones [like the millstones that crush the olives]." Also, you become strong like the "stone that presses the oil!" Modern processed oil is "not as strong." Rosenblum (1996) writes of an 110 year old Arab man who eats olives and rubs himself with the oil. If Rosenblum were to fight the old man, Rosenblum was told the old man would beat him. In another story (told me by an Israeli contact), a small group of Israelis had gotten a jeep stuck in a hole and could not lift it out. An Arab on a donkey came by and offered to get the jeep out. As the Israelis went to assist him, he told them "no, he could do it by himself." The Arab bent down and picked up the back

of the jeep and lifted it out of the hole. He then thumped his chest and said "olive oil!"

Spaniards say that olive oil not only makes one strong, but it will give one children; suggesting that olive oil has aphrodisiacal properties as well (Rosenblum, 1996).

3.4 Discussion

The ethnographic work I conducted provides important information on processing practices and the disposal of olive oil pressing wastes, some of which is previously undocumented. Olive oil production includes several steps: picking, pre-crushing preparations, crushing, pressing, and the disposal of pressing wastes. Production practices vary depending on where production occurs and who is doing it. Not all steps may be included, such as pre-crushing preparations. There is also variation in the disposal of pressing wastes, i.e., for fuel, domestic and industrial, for fertilizer, and so on.

Based on the ethnographic evidence, the two stages where alteration of the olive stones will most likely occur is during the crushing stage of processing, and in various uses of the pressing wastes. Information on processing practices was important in my decisions concerning which processing methods to replicate experimentally. Knowledge about the various processing techniques offers insight on how those methods may affect the olive remains. More detail will be given on the effects of processing in the next Chapter. Processing techniques also may determine how the stones and pressing wastes are used. Disposal of the pressing wastes will ultimately determine where and in what form the olive remains will be incorporated into the archaeological record, if at all.

Olive pressing wastes may be disposed of in a number of ways. Tables 3.1, 3.2 and 3.3 summarize the possible ways olive remains are incorporated into the archaeological record for domestic processing and deposition (Table 3.1), commercial processing and domestic deposition (Table 3.2), and commercial processing and deposition (Table 3.3) and illustrate pathways that may lead non-depositing remains. As seen in all three figures the predominant use of olive pressing wastes is as a fuel (Table 3.1 B; 3.2 B; 3.3 A1.3, B). Non-fuel uses of olive pressing wastes include uses as varied as fertilizer (Table 3.2 A; 3.3 C) to jewelry (Table 3.1 C). Olive stones from olives eaten as food and not processed for oil can show up in waste deposits (Table 3.1 A). Potential preservation for these remains is low as uncharred olive remains appear to decompose fairly quickly. Recovery of olive remains used as fertilizer is also limited due to the place of deposition, orchards, which are seldom excavated.

The primary use of olive pressing wastes, *jift*, is as a fuel source (Table 3.1 B; 3.2 B; 3.3 A1.3, B). Few uses of the pressing wastes leave charred olive stones or parts of stones available for incorporation into the archaeological

```
                              ┌──────────────┐   A    ┌──────────────────┐
                              │    Olives    │────────│ Pickled for eating │
                              └──────┬───────┘        └──────────────────┘
                                     │
              C           ┌──────────┴──────────┐
      ┌───────────────────│   Oil Processing    │
      │                   │ (usually small amounts) │
┌─────┴────────┐          └──────────┬──────────┘
│   Stones     │             B       │
│ removed prior│  ───────────────────┼────────────────────────────────┐
│  to eating   │          ┌──────────┴──────────┐                      │
└─────┬────────┘          │ Residue (stones, pulp = jift) │             │
      │                   │ used as fuel in tabuns and │                │
┌─────┴────────┐          │      braziers       │                      │
│ Stones used for│        └──────────┬──────────┘                       │
│   jewelry    │                     │                         ┌────────┴────────┐
└─────┬────────┘          ┌──────────┴──────────┐              │ Stones thrown out. │
      │                   │  Jift burns to ash  │              │ Deposition in waste │
┌─────┴────────┐          │ (some stones may be │              │    deposits.     │
│  Eventually   │         │      charred,       │              │   Uncharred-     │
│ discarded or buried │   │     not ashed)      │              │ survivability low │
│ (grave goods), but │    └──────────┬──────────┘              │   Charred-       │
│  usually only │                    │                         │ survivability good │
│ preserved if charred │  ┌──────────┴──────────┐              └─────────────────┘
│ (trash burning, etc., │ │   Disposal of ash   │
│   i.e. in midden) │     └──────────┬──────────┘
└──────────────┘           B1      B2    B3
```

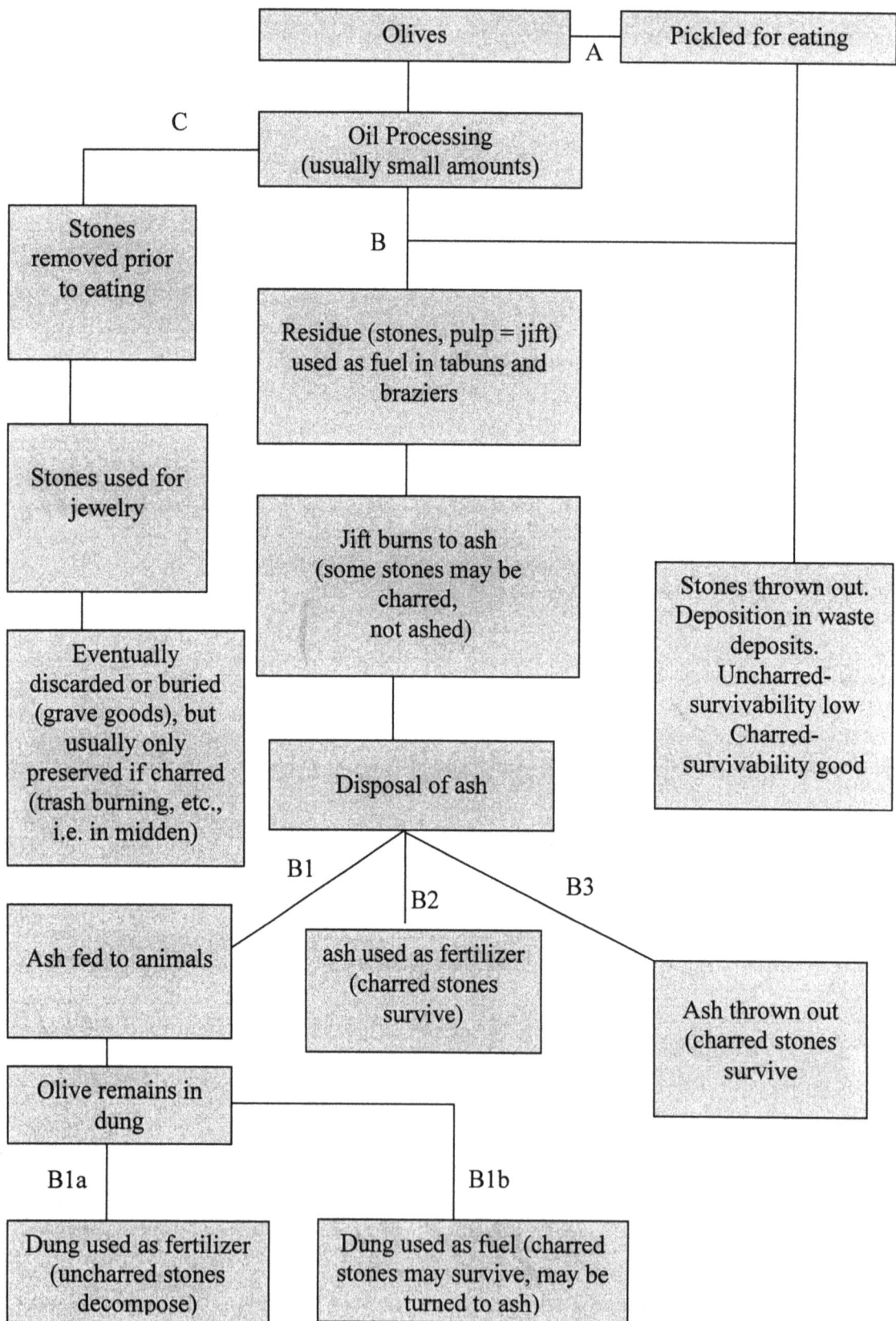

Table 3.1: Domestic Processing Residues and Deposition of Olive Remains

Olives

Mill

C

Household use of wastes

A

Animal feed

B

Fuel (tabuns, stoves, etc.) jift burns to ash (some stones may be charred, not ashed)

Fertilizer uncharred, decomposes quickly

Olive stones in dung

1. Dung used as fertilizer (uncharred stones decompose)

2. Dung used as fuel (charred stones may survive, may be turned to ash)

Uses of ash

B1

Fed to animals

B2

Soapmaking

B3

Construction

B4

Thrown out

B5

Fertilizer

Olive stones in dung

Ash used in making plaster and mortar

Deposition in agricultural fields

1. Dung used as fertilizer (charred stones survive)

Remains incorporated into archaelogical record (i.e. into bricks, walls, floors)

2. Dung used as fuel (charred stones may survive, may be turned to ash)

Ash used in making soap (large inclusions, charred stones. sifted out of ash

Deposition in middens

B2a

Soap (no remains)

B2b

Sifted-out inclusions (thrown out, deposited in middens, or returned to fire to be turned to ash)

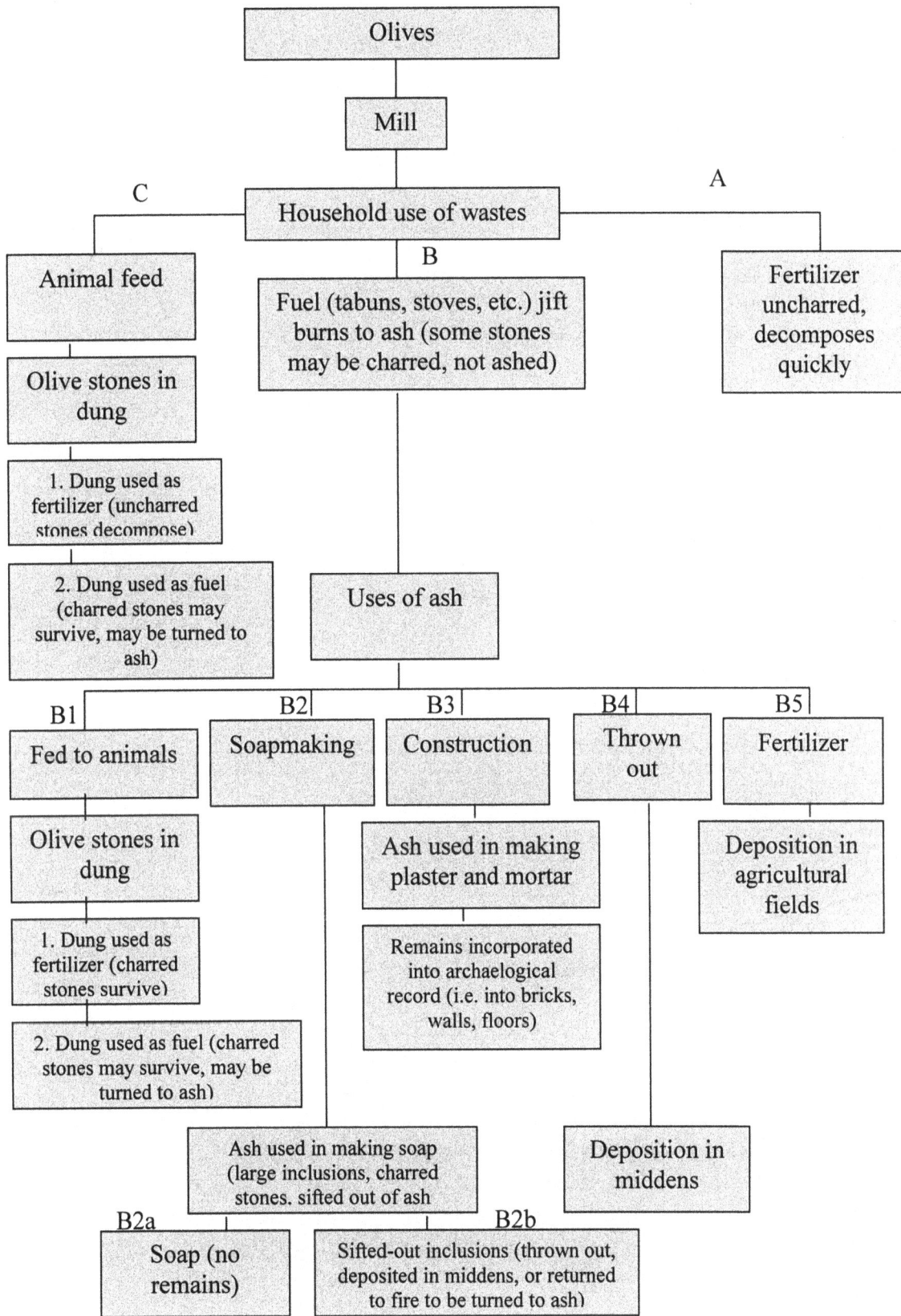

Table 3.2: Domestic Use of Commercial Processing Wastes

```
                          ┌──────────────────┐
                          │     Olives       │
                          └──────────────────┘
                                   │
                          ┌────────────┐  A1  ┌──────────────────────┐
                          │    Mill    │──────│ Companies doing chemical │
                          └────────────┘      │      processing       │
                                              └──────────────────────┘
```

| D | C | B | | A2 | | | | |

- **D** — Animal feed
- **C** — Fertilizer → Uncharred decomposes quickly
- **B** — Used as fuel at mill

A2:
- **A3** — Soapmaking (commercial) → Jift as fuel burns to ash → Ash used to make soap → No remains
- **A4** — Kiln fuel (pottery, glass)
- **A5** — Charcoal (commercial) → Bags of briquettes sold in stores → Burns to ash → No remains

D:
- Olive remains in dung → Dung used as fertilizer (uncharred stones decompose) → Dung used as fuel (charred stones may survive, may be turned to ash)

E — Jift burns to ash (some stones may be charred, not ashed)

- **E1** — Fed to animals → Olive stones in dung →
  1. Dung used as fertilizer (charred stones survive)
  2. Dung used as fuel (charred stones may survive, may be turned to ash)
- **E2** — Thrown out → Deposition in middens
- **E3** — Construction → Ash used in making plaster and mortar → Remains incorporated into archaelogical record (i.e. into bricks, walls, floors)
- **E4** — Fertilizer → Deposition in agricultural fields

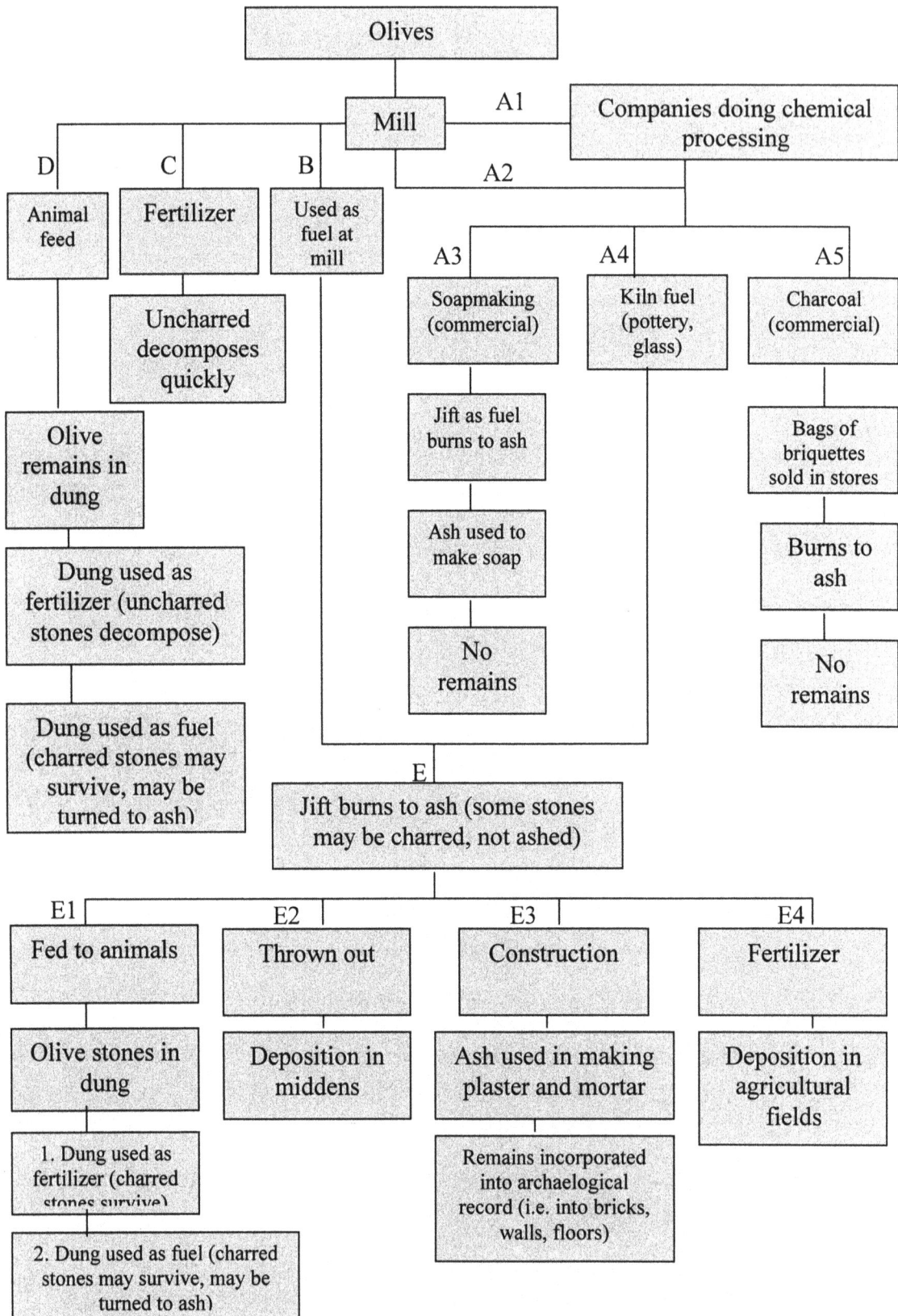

Table 3.3: Commercial Use of Commercial Processing Wastes

record. Especially since *jift* burns almost completely to ash. This resulting ash may be used as well. The use of *jift* or *jift* ash may also occur in settings not usually investigated archaeologically (as in the previous mention of *jift* used in orchards) (Table 3.1 B1.2; 3.2 B3, B5; 3.3 E1, E4).

While *jift* burns almost completely to ash, *jift* used as fuel may leave some charred stones or stone fragments (Table 3.1 B; 3.2 B; 3.3 E). These charred remains can appear in middens (Table 3.1 B3; 3.2 B2b, B4; 3.3 E2), as a component in ash used as fertilizer (Table 3.1 B2; 3.2 B5; 3.3 E4), or as a component in construction materials (mortar, bricks) (Table 3.2 B3; 3.3 E3). These forms of deposition include both domestic and commercially produced remains, though midden deposits appear more likely for domestic remains. The volume of waste material may have an impact on the material's deposition, i.e., a small amount of domestic waste may end up in a midden (Table 3.1 B3), while a large amount of commercial waste gets used as fertilizer (Table 3.3 E4).

The ash resulting from *jift* fuel may be thrown away and end up in midden soils (Table 3.3 E2). However, rather than wasting the *jift* ash, it is usually used in a variety of ways. The ash is a component of olive oil soap (both domestic and commercial) (Table 3.2 B2; 3.3 A3), it is used in construction materials (mortar, plaster), and is used as fertilizer. The use of *jift* ash in soap means that any inclusions (charred stones or stone fragments) are sifted out, either to be reburned or thrown out (Table 3.2 B2b). No remains will result from the soap (Table 3.2 B2a). Inclusions in construction material will show up, as the archaeological record illustrates (Table 3.2 B3). Discovery of remains in ash fertilizer are dependant on sampling those places *jift* ash is used, such as orchards.

Domestic processing (Table 3.1) usually involves only small amounts of olives (a handful to a few kilos) and may involve processing methods which leave whole stones or larger fragments (see Chapter 4). Two of the steps illustrated in Table 3-1, A and C, have the stones either remaining in the fruit (A, olives for eating) or removed whole (C, stones removed prior to processing). If the olives are pickled for eating (Table 3.1 A), the stones are disposed in normal household wastes or tossed out onto the ground (eating outdoors, picnics, and so on). In either case, the stones are not usually charred, unless deposited in a midden that is burned, and simply decay normally. Nothing is incorporated into the archaeological record. In step C, the stones are removed prior to processing. They may be used for jewelry or discarded. If the stones are discarded into a waste situation that is burned, they may be preserved. If the stones are used for jewelry, they may end up in a burial, but since they are not charred, natural decay will eventually destroy them.

Only in step B, processing with the stones still in the fruit, are the processing residues more likely to be burned as a fuel. While most of the wastes may be burned to ash, some stones may only be charred. However, since domestic processing utilizes only small amounts of olives there are few resulting remains for disposal. The most likely sequence for domestic processing in traditional households (if the stones are not removed prior to pressing) is the sequence ending in Table 3.1 B3. Limited olive remains would be expected, though some stones might be charred and not ashed.

Domestic uses of commercial processing wastes (Table 3.2) utilize much greater quantities of pressing remains. These uses include spreading large quantities of *jift* into the orchards as fertilizer (Table 3.2 A) and feeding the waste to animals, sometimes mixed into animal feed (Table 3.2 C). Animal dung may be used as either fertilizer or fuel (or left where deposited by the animals). The only way olive remains might be preserved from either A or C is if the animal dung was burned as fuel (Table 3.2 C2).

However, the primary domestic use of processing wastes is as a fuel (Table 3.2 B). Although burning *jift* consumes most of the *jift* to ash, some stones might be only charred. The multiple uses of the ash (Table 3.2 B1.5) include some uses where the unashed stones might yet be turned to ash (Table 3.2 B1 step 2; B2b). Some uses will leave no remains (Table 3.2 B2a), or use the remains in locations seldom sampled (Table 3.2 B5). Few uses of the ash lead directly to incorporation into the archaeological record (Table 3.2 B3.4).

While the domestic uses of commercial wastes utilize a larger volume of remains, the supplementary uses of the processing wastes (Table 3.2 A & C) are not likely to be charred and preserved into the archaeological record and the primary use as a fuel consumes most of the remains to ash. The few stones that are not totally consumed and remain charred may not end up in the archaeological record due to uses of the ash which may result in those stones being consumed in a fire, or deposited in locations seldom sampled archaeologically.

Commercial uses of commercial wastes (Table 3.3) utilize the greatest amount of olive pressing wastes produced by mills. Uses as fertilizer (Table 3.3 C) and as animal feed (Table 3.3 D) result in deposition as described previously (For Table 3.2 A & C). Similarly, use as fuel (Table 3.3 A3.4; B) results in pressing wastes being consumed to ash. The incorporation of remains into the archaeological record from uses of *jift* ash for commercial uses of commercial wastes parallel those described in the domestic use of commercial wastes (Table 3.2) previous. Only the use of wastes that is different from those mentioned previously is the manufacture of charcoal (Table 3.3 A5). In this use, the remains also burn completely to ash, more so in fact than in other fuel uses.

Even though the commercial uses of commercial wastes utilize the greatest amount of pressing wastes, there are no end uses which significantly increase the amount of charred remains which can be incorporated into the archaeological record. Both domestic and commercial usage of commercial processing remains utilize the wastes in somewhat similar patterns (fertilizer, animal feed and fuel), as are uses of the residual ash. There are no uses in which large numbers of whole charred olive stones are incorporated into the archaeological record.

The multiple uses of *jift* and *jift* ash help explain the lack of olive remains in the archaeological record. As discussed in Chapter 1 (Figure 1.2) olive stones and stone fragments occur at a variety of sites over a long time period. The remains from the cited sites in Figure 1.2 do not make up a major portion of recovered plant remains. Of course, sampling strategies and recovery techniques must be taken into consideration. Understanding that as fuel *jift* burns almost completely to ash is vitally important in viewing the presence and absence of olive remains. That *jift* burns to ash also helps interpret finds of ash in some instances. This characteristic of *jift* fuel does raise the question of what do the olive remains recovered at archaeological sites actually represent? In the reverse, does the lack of olive processing installations necessarily mean oil was not produced at that location, at least for domestic purposes?

Comprehending *jift*'s multiple uses also raises questions concerning cultural practices, such as the movement of raw materials such as fuels or construction components around and between sites.

The ethnographic research also shows that even after new processing techniques are introduced, older methods continue in use. A variety of methods may be in use simultaneously. This is clearly demonstrated by the fact that almost all of the known ancient processing techniques have survived and are either still in use or have just recently fallen out of use. Many of the older methods of processing are used for small yield domestic processing, usually in more rural areas. Necessity for faster techniques able to handle larger volumes is the trend for the industrial or commercial processing methods.

Overall, the ethnographic research provides the basis for performing the experimental processing methods, and documents information on traditional practices which soon may disappear. The information also provides a better understanding of both ancient and traditional olive oil processing, domestic and commercial, and suggests that important issues yet remain to be resolved concerning the interpretation of remains.

CHAPTER 4

EXPERIMENTAL RESEARCH

4.1 Introduction

The second phase of my research involves experimental studies to determine how different processing methods affect the olive remains and their incorporation into the archaeological record. The experiments follow examples set by Hillman (1973; 1984), Miller and Smart (1984), Moore, Hillman and Legge (2000, see figs. 12.14 and 12.15); Samuel (1993), and selections in Anderson (1999) (especially chapters by Harlan, Sievert, Anderson, Unger-Hamilton, Skakum, Ataman, Grégoire, and Meurers-Balke and Lüning). Deciding which processing methods to include in the experiments was based on information gathered from literature searches (Avitsur, 1994; Ayalon, 1994a; Eitam, 1993; Frankel, 1987; 1994; Mattingly, 1988), discussions with other scholars (including several mentioned in the preceding literature reviews), and through ethnographic research as discussed in Chapter 3.

As discussed earlier, a number of pre-pressing and pressing techniques exist. For my experiments I focus only on the processing stage that affects the olive stone, i.e. crushing the fruit. I conducted experiments on eight different crushing methods. Method 1 is crushing the olives by treading or stomping on them by foot. Three different grinding or pounding methods were tested, all using a stone pestle: Method 2-1, mortar and pestle, used a metal bucket as the mortar; Method 2-2 used a plastic basin; Method 2-3 used a stone mortar. Method 3 was grinding or pounding the olives on a flat surface with a pestle. Method 4 was crushing the olives on a flat surface with a roller. Two basin and roller methods were tested, Method 5 used a small basin and hand roller, and Method 6 used a larger basin and push roller. Olive remains were collected for comparative purposes during the ethnographic research. Pressing wastes were taken from a Roman rotary mill (Method 7) at the Israel Olive Oil Museum, several of the traditional stone rotary presses, and from a modern commercial press outside Irbid, Jordan.

The Israel Olive Oil Museum in Haifa (Zisling, 2000) allowed me to use several Bronze and Iron Age artifacts in my olive crushing experiments. Similar artifacts to those that I used are on display at the Eretz Israel Museum in Tel Aviv. The remaining experiments were performed at the American Center of Oriental Research (ACOR) in Amman, Jordan, with help from its staff. Olives were purchased from the Israel Olive Oil Museum for experiments conducted

there, while the olives used in the ACOR experiments were purchased from farmers selling olives outside a modern commercial mill near Ajlun, Jordan.

I should point out that there are limitations to the experiments I performed. There is no way to know if I replicated exactly the ancient or traditional methods. For instance, in the treading (Method 1) experiments, I used a large metal container instead of an open treading area simply because I did not have access to a larger, open treading area. The roller used in the roller on a flat surface (Method 4) was smaller to those shown in the Matson photographs because I could not find a stone of the size shown. Limitations such as these may have affected the results of some of the experiments. I worked with what I was able to obtain under the circumstances.

Some of the experimental processing remains were used in secondary experiments. Subsamples were taken from several sets of remains and tested to see how secondary use, such as a kiln fuel, affected the remains. Experimental processed remains were burned and charred in an open hearth and a small kiln. Samples of similar secondary usage were obtained from secondary use activity sites during the ethnographic research.

The goal of the experiments was to determine how different processing methods affect the olive stone. The hypothesis was that the varied processing methods affect the olive stone in different ways, and that ultimately, these differences allow each method of processing to be identified in the archaeological record. Method 1, treading by foot, was expected to do little or no damage to the remains. I did not believe that the amount of pressure applied would break the stones and the crushing force would be dissipated. Using a mortar and pestle should have produced highly fragmented and crushed remains. The direct crushing force of a pestle was expected to completely fracture the olive stone. Rollers were expected to break the stones, though into larger fragments than those in mortar and pestle crushing. Mill crushing using horizontal stone wheels on a stone platform was expected to fall into a mid-range of alteration. I expected that the two extreme forms of alteration (either little or none, and large amounts of change) to be associated with smaller-scale domestic processing (treading or mortar and pestle). Large scale industrial processing (milling) would then be evidenced by the mid-range level of alteration.

4.2 The Experiments

The first six methods were performed at the American Center of Oriental Research (ACOR) in Amman, Jordan, while the last two were done at the Israel Olive Oil Museum in Haifa, Israel. The first six methods involve using equipment made or purchased for the experiments, while the methods done at the Olive Oil Museum utilize several Bronze and Iron Ages artifacts on display at the museum.

4.2.1 Treading

As noted in the previous chapter, special sandals are used for treading or crushing olives. With assistance from Abdul Adawi of the ACOR staff, I constructed wood sandals which fit under my tennis shoes. The sandals were approximately 33 cm long, 10 cm wide, and 2.5 cm thick, with a 3 cm wide rubber strip attached 6.5 cm from the sandal's front. This rubber strip formed a loop into which the shoe's toe fit. Notches were cut into the bottom of the sandal 6 cm from the back. Cord run through the notches was tied up around the ankle to hold the sandal on at the back (Figure 4.1). The olive treading experiment was performed using a large metal tub (43 cm diameter by 27.5 cm deep) to contain the olives.

I performed the treading experiments (Method 1) three times. In the first trial, eight liters of olives were placed into the basin. The basin was not large enough to tread with two feet effectively, so I used one foot to tread the olives (Figure 4.2). A straight up and down "marching" motion was used. After 15-20 minutes of treading, I inspected the results. A number of whole olives remained and no broken stones were observed. In the second trial, eight liters of olives were also used. This time I used a twisting motion: stomping down, then twisting the foot. This method crushed the olives more effectively. Fewer whole olives were observed after treading. Again, no broken stones were seen. For the third trial, another 8 liters of olives were used, along with the same motion as in the second (stomp and twist). The mash from this trial had very few whole olives, almost all were crushed or had the skin broken. The mash from all three trials was dried in a dryer in the ACOR conservation laboratory.

The "mash" from the second and third treading experiments was saved for further analysis. A quarter of the first trial's "mash" was charred in the muffle furnace at the ACOR lab. The remaining two thirds of the first treading experiment's mash was burned along with commercial olive *jift* charcoal (Figure 4.3).

4.2.2 Mortar and Pestle

The next three experiments involved grinding or pounding the olives in a mortar with a pestle. In all cases the pestle was made of stone, while the mortars or basins were either made of metal (Method 2-1), plastic (Method 2-2) or

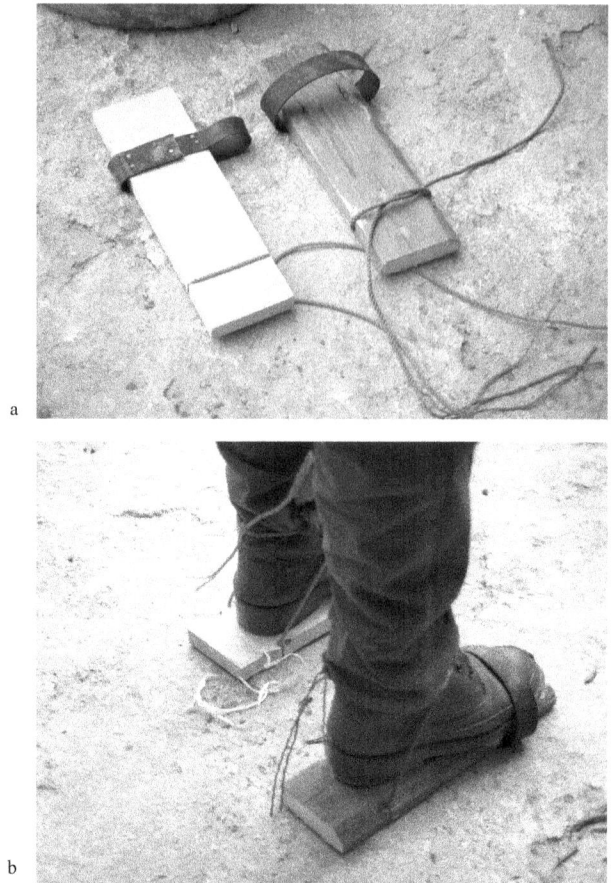

FIGURE 4.1a-b: OLIVE TREADING SANDALS
a: BOTTOM VIEW, LEFT, TOP VIEW, RIGHT
b: SANDALS ON FEET

stone (Method 2-3). Two liters of olives were processed each time; this was the most effective size sample for the containers.

The first form of crushing using a mortar and pestle (Method 2) involved a stone pestle and a metal bucket for a mortar (Figure 4.4). The pestle was made of limestone, a scrap purchased from a business selling decorative stonework. The pestle was oblong, similar to an elongated teardrop, measuring 25 cm high x 6 cm diameter at the top and 10 cm at the widest bottom point. The bottom was rounded with the bottom-most surface flattened. The mortar was a metal bucket (tin/aluminum) 23 cm deep x 17 cm diameter wide at bottom and 23.5 cm diameter at the top. The use of a metal bucket was for convenience only, as was the larger plastic basin. Finding stone depressions of appropriate size and shape was not an option due to time and financial constraints.

Method 2 was run three times, using a fairly straight "up and down" motion. This method crushed/pulped the olives quite well, producing a somewhat uniform "mash." During the crushing, I heard occasional crunching sounds, and on inspection some of the stones in the mash were broken. However, when the mash was spread on newspaper to dry,

FIGURE 4.2a: TREADING EXPERIMENT (METHOD 1)

FIGURE 4.2b: TREADING EXPERIMENT (METHOD 1)

FIGURE 4.3: BRAZIER (KANON) WITH COMMERCIAL *JIFT* CHARCOAL (LEFT) AND FOOT TREADING *JIFT* (RIGHT)

FIGURE 4.4: METAL BUCKET AND STONE PESTLE (METHOD 2-1)

FIGURE 4.5: STONE MORTAR AND STONE PESTLE (METHOD 2-3)

I did see a number of whole pits as well. The mash from one of the mortar and pestle experiments (experiment #2, trial #2) was burned.

Method 2-2 was run once, with the same pestle as in Method 2-1, but using a slightly larger plastic basin. The basin measured 35 cm top diameter/29 cm bottom diameter x 16 cm deep. Initially, a rotary grinding method was used (similar to stirring around the inside edge of the basin). Frankel (1999) believes that crushing using a mortar and pestle involves a partial rotary action. This was not attempted with the metal pail, as the pail was too small. The rotary grinding method had very little effect on the olives: it did not crush, pulp or break the fruit. The olives were pushed along rather than being crushed. After several minutes of attempting this method it was abandoned, and the up and down crushing motion was used. The resulting mash was identical in appearance to that produced by Method 2-1.

Method 2-3 used a stone mortar and stone pestle (Figure 4.5). The stone mortar was slightly oval and measured approximately 25 cm by 20 cm, and was 12 cm deep. I performed this experiment twice. The stone mortar had a slight inward overhang to the inside lip of the rim. Where this lip was intact, it helped keep the mash inside the mortar. Due to the small size of the mortar, the whole two liters was not crushed at once. One liter was crushed first, then the second liter added and crushed. More than two liters would have been very difficult to do. In a more open container it would have been difficult to keep the mash in the bowl.

During the second trial of Method 2-3 I tried using the grinding motion as attempted with the plastic basin. Again, the grinding motion was ineffective. The round, oval shape of the olive allows it to move away from the pestle. Instead of crushing the olives, I ended up chasing them around the basin. I believe that this would also occur in a smooth-sided stone basin. A rough-sided container might prevent some of the slippage. The rotary motion does not put enough pressure on the olives to break the skin. In order to crush the olives one has to pound on them.

While performing the two Method 2-3 trials, using the pounding motion, I heard many "popping" and "cracking" noises. However, I am not sure if the sound was the stones being broken or was the fruit's skin rupturing (sometimes letting the stone pop out), or both. Observing the results, a number of the stones were crushed into smaller fragments, though a number of stone were not broken (at least not visibly) .

4.2.3 Pestle on a Flat Surface

Method 3 involved the same pestle as in the previous experiments, but used a flat crushing surface rather than a mortar or basin as in Methods 2-1, 2-2, and 2-3 (Figure 4.6). Numerous ethnographic contacts mentioned using a

FIGURE 4.6: STONE PESTLE ON FLAT STONE SURFACE (METHOD 3)

FIGURE 4.7: STONE ROLLER (METHOD 4)

During the crushing process I heard many cracking sounds, and noticed that a high number of the stones were fractured. Many stones were smashed into a number of smaller fragments. This method definitely alters the stones' structure, and it looks like it broke up olives more than the mortar and pestle method did.

4.2.4 Roller and Flat Surface

Method 4 used a small stone roller to crush olives on a flat surface (similar to, but smaller, than those in Figures 3.27, 3.28). The flat surface was the cement floor/driveway outside the ACOR sub-basement garage. The roller was made of limestone and purchased at the same place as the flat slab and pestle. The roller measured 40 cm long x 15 cm in diameter. It had a slightly rough surface (some pock-marks), one end was flat and the other broken and rough (Figure 4.7).

Three trials were run using this method (Figure 4.8). The first trial used four liters of olives, while the last two used two liters each. While processing, I heard some cracking noises as the roller crushed the olives. Some breakage was observed, though it seemed the majority of pits were not damaged or broken. I did have a problem with the roller pushing the mash ahead of the roller rather than rolling over the olives. I am not sure if a larger stone would have the same problem, but I believe it would.

4.2.5 Rollers and Basins

The final two crushing methods (Method 5 and Method 6) involved crushing the olives in stone basins with rollers. Method 5 used a hand pushed roller in a smaller stone basin, while Method 6 used a handle pushed larger roller within a larger stone basin. The Israel Olive Oil Museum, located at Shemen Industries in Haifa, allowed me to use several Bronze and Iron Age artifacts for these crushing experiments, and similar artifacts were viewed at the Eretz Israel Museum in Tel Aviv. Dr. David Eitam, the museum director, provided input on using the artifacts. The olives used in the experiments were purchased from the museum's supplies. These same supplies provided the

stone to crush olives, usually on a flat surface or simply on the hard ground. This is the method of preference by people making only a small amount of oil, such as that for a single serving or meal.

A large, flat limestone slab (46 cm x 29 cm x 5 cm), purchased at the same location as the pestle, was used as the flat crushing surface. Two liters of olives were crushed using the same stone pestle used in the mortar and pestle experiments. Three trials were run using this method. The mash of two trials was dried and the third was charred.

Using this method proved more difficult than using a mortar. The major problem was that the olives kept sliding or squirting off the flat surface. Crushing the olives was not an easy task; I had to continually chase down the olives. It proved to be more difficult to mash the olives using this method than in the mortar, instead, the olives appeared to be crushed or have the skin split. I could not crush many olives at one time since they would start to slide off the edges of the flat slab when the olive mash spread out on crushing. The best means was to do one, two or three handfuls at a time, scoop up and transfer the crushed olives to a container, then do another couple of handfuls.

FIGURE 4.8a: STONE ROLLER (METHOD 4)

FIGURE 4.8b: STONE ROLLER (METHOD 4)

olives for hands-on displays for tour groups and school trips given by the museum.

In Method 5 a stone, hand-pushed roller was used to crush olives in a small stone basin (Figures 3.31, 4.9). The stone

basin was somewhat egg shaped with an overall length of 88 cm and width of approximately 83 cm. The dimensions of the inner crushing basin were 65 cm (top of basin) and 53 cm (bottom of the basin) in length, with a width at the narrowest point of 23 cm (top and bottom) and 60 cm (top of basin) and 42 cm (bottom of basin) at the widest point. Depth of the basin was approximately 25 cm. The basin is similar in size and shape to one found at Kfar Samir, Israel (Galili *et al*, 1997) (see Figure 3.32). The roller was not completely rounded, instead it was almost trapezoidal box with slightly rounded edges. The roller measured approximately 42 cm long by approximately 16 cm wide in cross-section.

I performed the Method 5 experiment three times, using three and a half liters of olives per trial. Dr. Eitam observed the crushing for a short time, and suggested more crushing was necessary to really pulp the olives. After several minutes, I could see an oily film on the surface of the liquid expressed from the olives. Most of the olive stones I observed during the processing were broken, however, some remained whole. After the crushing, some of the mash was pressed on one of the small portable presses at the museum (see Figure 3.39). The result was an oily liquid that given time looked like it would separate into water and oil.

The bottom of the basin was rough, making me question whether or not a roller was used in it. However, Dr. Eitam assured me it was a crushing basin using a roller. The roller I used may not have been contemporary with the basin. If a roller had been used in the basin, I would have expected the inner surface to be more worn and smoother than it was. I scraped my hands a number of times on the rough surface. Some of the stone basin surface crushed and broke during use, mixing in with the olive mash.

The other roller and basin method, Method 6, utilized a handle pushed larger roller within a larger stone basin (Figure 4.10). This form of processing was used at the Iron Age oil production center at Tel Miqne-Ekron, Israel (Gitin, 1989) and continued through to Roman times (the *canalis et solea*) (www.pacificsunoliveoil.com/ancient_mills.html). The basin was basically a rectangle with outer dimensions of 145 cm in length x 102 cm in width, inner dimensions of 116 cm in length x 75 cm in width, and about 36 cm deep. Similar basins found at Tel Miqne-Ekron measure approximately 101-180 cm long x 51-100 cm wide, with the majority in the 141-160 cm length x 81-90 cm width range (Eitam, 1996). Similar olive processing basins were excavated at Tel Batash (Timnah), Israel (Kelm and Mazar 1996). The roller was about 30 cm in diameter, with depressions in the center of either end of the cylinder. A push handle was attached to the roller at these depressions (Figure 4.10). Using the handle, the roller could be pushed and pulled over the olives in the basin. Both the basin and roller were excavated at Tel Miqne.

a

b

FIGURE 4.9a-b: SMALL BASIN WITH HAND ROLLER (METHOD 5), OLIVE OIL MUSEUM, HAIFA, ISRAEL

Two trials were done using this processing method (Figure 4.11). Dr. Eitam suggested using a minimum of nine liters of olives for the most efficient operation of the roller. Rosenblum (1996:72) recounts talking with Natan Eidlin, museum curator at Kibbutz Revadim near Tel Miqne/ Ekron; "Olives were crushed under granite cylinders, like huge rolling pins, which millers pushed back and forth for about 20 minutes." I crushed the olives for 30 to 45 minutes. While this method did mash the olives quite well,

I had a problem with the roller pushing the pile of mashed olives rather than rolling over it. I thought that crushing even larger amounts of olives would have made moving the roller even more difficult. This method seemed to crack a number of the stones, but the process left whole stones as well. Some of the mash was pressed in an antique hand powered screw press (see Figure 3.43). This was done in order to squeeze out some of the liquid to speed up drying the mash.

FIGURE 4.10: LARGE BASIN WITH PUSH ROLLER (METHOD 6, ROLLER AND BASIN FROM TEL MIQNE/EKRON. OLIVE OIL MUSEUM, HAIFA, ISRAEL

FIGURE 4.11: LARGE BASIN WITH PUSH ROLLER (METHOD 6)

While at the Israel Olive Oil Museum I also crushed a comparative sample using a restored Roman rotary mill (Method 7) (Figure 4.12a, also see 3.36). Crushed remains from this Roman mill and from the traditional rotary mills visited during the ethnographic research were compared to the experimental samples. The Roman period mill was a single stone rotary mill. The mill stone was 30 cm wide x 86 cm high. The mill base was 146 cm in diameter (outer dimensions) and about 113 cm in diameter for the inner (crushing) surface. Both the base and the roller were made of limestone. The crushing surface of the base had some cross-hatch patterns on it, possibly to help prevent the olives from sliding when crushed (photo 4.12b).

Three liters of olives were crushed with the Roman mill. The Roman mill crushes olives quite well. It took little effort to push the stone around. With the exception of a few stones, the majority of olive stones were crushed and broken using this process. Some of the mash was pressed in the hand powered screw press to facilitate drying.

4.3 After-crushing Experiments

Samples of several of the experimental crushing methods and some of the commercial olive *jift* charcoal obtained in local stores were burned in an open brazier to observe burning and the resulting residue. Samples from early experimental crushing's were also charred in a sealed muffle furnace (charred without oxygen). However, since all evidence encountered thus far points to the use of pressing wastes in open fires rather than in banked fires, muffle furnace charring was discontinued.

a

b

FIGURE 4.12a: ROMAN SINGLE STONE MILL (METHOD 7). OLIVE
OIL MUSEUM, HAIFA, ISRAEL
b: CROSS-HATCH SURFACE PATTERN ON MILL BASE

FIGURE 4.13: COMMERCIAL *JIFT* CHARCOAL ASH

The coals and ash of the experimental material were sifted after cooling down. There were a few unburned stones and a number of stone fragments. From the commercial charcoal end there were several unburned charcoal pieces, though most of it had been turned to ash (Figure 4.13). I also burned 0.5 kilos of commercial charcoal by itself in the brazier. The *jift* charcoal produces a very hot, smokeless and odorless fire. The ash was sieved to observe what remained after burning.

Observation of the experimental burnings provides another important piece of information concerning the effects of post-processing activities on the olive remains. Whole olive stones show a tendency to burst when subjected to high heat and burning. It is possible that heat causes the air, moisture or kernel inside the olive stone to expand and "pop," much like the water in a popcorn kernel turns to steam, causing popcorn to pop. Since the olive stone is hard and thick, the "popping" causes the olive stone to break. The breakage appears to follow the fracture lines observed in the cleaned and sorted samples (discussed in section 4.5). The fact that olive stones break when burned suggests that any olive remains used as a fuel source will be altered. Processing methods leaving large numbers of whole stones, which are then burned and fracture, could be misinterpreted as another processing method, i.e., one that fractures the stones more frequently. Such a problem clouds interpretation of olive remains.

The mash from one of the mortar and pestle experiments (Method 2-1, trial #2) was burned in an open grill or brazier (called a *kanon*). The mash was dried on newspaper first. When the mash was burned, it had some of the newspaper stuck to it, but the newspaper was oil soaked from the pressing and burned quickly away. There were a large number of whole stones in this experimental residue. The mash burned with a lot of flame and several loud "pops" were heard. One pop was immediately followed by a partial olive stone thrown out of the brazier and away from the fire. I also observed that in areas not immediately aflame or burning, several of the olive stones were glowing pink/red and a number of others were observed to be white (possibly turning to ash).

In a second burning experiment, 1.5 kilos of commercial olive *jift* charcoal was burned in the brazier. While burning the *jift* charcoal, approximately three quarters of the dried mash from one foot treading experiment (Method1, #1, trial #1) was also burned (see Figure 4.3). The *jift* charcoal occupied one end of the brazier and the experimental material the other. The experimental mash had a large proportion of unbroken stones. As the experimental mash burned, I again heard a number of "pops," probably olive stones bursting from the heat and breaking.

4.4 Natural Decay

Since one of the uses of *jift* is as fertilizer, I inspected the soil in orchards to determine the survivability of olive remains in the orchard soils. One of my primary contacts and I inspected the soil at the grove where I helped pick olives, and I also inspected the soil in a grove in which *jift* was used around the trees. I took soil samples from under trees, digging about 10 to 20 cm down. My contact observed that olive stones that have fallen to the ground rot and decay fairly quickly. As I watched, he dug up a couple of stones and said "they appeared soft" and crumbled easily in his hand. The wet, cool winters make the soil damp, aiding in decomposition. Even charred remains become friable and crumble easily after a short period of time in the soil. Olive remains used as fertilizer either sit on the surface, or are incorporated into the surface soil layers. The remains are thus subjected to taphonomic processes which work to rapidly break them down, which in retrospect, is the whole idea behind using them as fertilizer. The use of other paleoethnobotanical data, such as pollen or phytoliths (non-silica type) might help identify the use of *jift* as fertilizer. However, since olives are wind pollinated plants, olive pollen would be expected in an olive orchard. And since there are olives which naturally end up in the orchard soils (dropped before picking began, missed during picking, etc.), one would also expect olive phytoliths in the orchard soils. A comparison study between *jift* fertilized and unfertilized soils would be recommended.

4.5 Analysis Of Experimental Samples

4.5.1 Methods

The dried olive pressing waste (*jift*) from my experiments was analyzed in the paleoethnobotany laboratory at the University of Missouri-Columbia. A 1 liter subsample of each experimental sample was sorted. A random sample splitter was used to subsample the waste. The stones and stone fragments were then separated from the olive fruit pulp. The stones and stone fragments were passed through a series of standard testing sieves: #4 sieve – 4.75 mm openings, #5 sieve – 4.00 mm openings, and #10 sieve – 2.00 mm openings. Initially a 1.00 mm sieve was also used, but was eliminated due to the lack of material smaller than 2.00 mm. The volume and weight of the stone material were recorded for each sieve size (Table 4.1). It should be noted that the amount of material for each sieve size represents the material which was small enough to pass through the previous sieve (greater than 4.75 mm, greater than 4.00 mm and greater than 2.00 mm), but was too large to fit through the sieve it ended up within (for example, the material in the 4.00 mm sieve represents material which fell through the 4.75 mm mesh sieve, but was too large to pass through the 4.00 mm sieve). The number of whole stones and fractured stones was also recorded. Fractured stones were those stones which appeared whole but had visible fracture lines, suggesting that the stones would probably break apart at a later date. The whole and fractured stones are included in the volume and weight totals.

An interesting fracture pattern was observed in the olive stones. Many of the fractured, but still whole, stones exhibited fracture lines on a quarter section of the stone (Figure 4.14). Further, included in the larger sieve fragments, especially from the 4.75 mm and 4.00 mm sieves, are stones which are three-quarters whole, as well as quarter fragments. This fracture pattern suggests a genetic adaptation that allows the germinating olive seedling to break out of the protective stony endocarp through a fracture or fault line inherent in all olive stones.

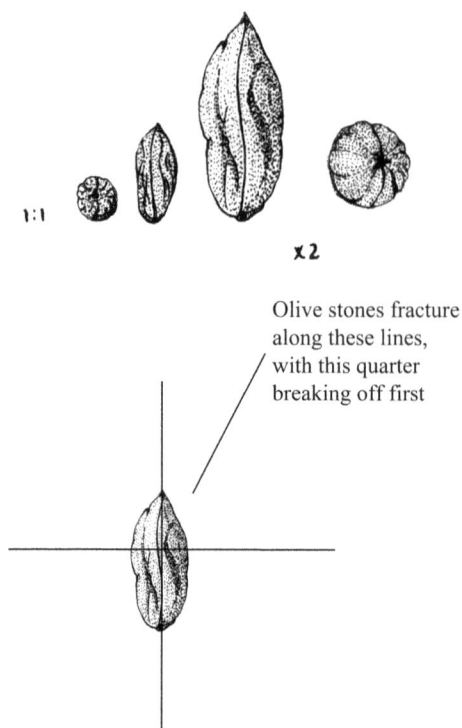

FIGURE 4.14: OLIVE STONE FRACTURE PATTERN
(KAREN JACOBSEN)

Most other olive stone fragments appeared to be pieces of these two initial stone fragments.

4.5.2 Discussion of Results

The data for the experimental tests are summarized on Table 4.1, which shows the results of individual experiments grouped by Method, while Table 4.2 shows the averages for each type Method. Before looking at statistical comparisons, several trends are apparent based on the raw numbers.

The foot treading experiments (Method 1) contained only whole stones and have no fragments. The mortar and pestle (Method 2-1, 2-2 and 2-3), flat pound (Method 3), and flat roller (Method 4) experiments all show similar trends: high numbers for the 4.75 mm sieve and lower, and approximately equal numbers for the 4.00 and 2.00 mm sieves. The small basin (Method 5) show high numbers for the 4.75 mm sieve, low for the 4.00 mm sieve, and higher again for the 2.00 mm sieve, though not as high as the 4.75 mm sieve. The large basin (Method 6) results are similar to the small basin, however, the 2.00 mm sieve numbers are slightly lower compared to the small basin amounts. The Roman mill (Method 7) had no whole stones, and while the volume for the 4.75 mm sieve is high, the weight is very low. The Roman mill shows an opposite trend relative to the other processing methods: the high numbers for the Roman mill are at the 2.00 mm sieve end rather than at the 4.75 mm sieve end. Reflecting on the experimental

All samples based on 1 liter of experimental remains

Method	Experiment	Olive Stones		Volume and Weight of Olive Stone Fragments						Pulp
		Whole stones	Fractured stones	> 4.75 mm		4.00 mm		2.00 mm		weight
				ml	g	ml	g	ml	g	g
#1	Foot Tread #2	59	1	388	228	0	0	0	0	313
#1	Foot Tread #3	56	0	400	236	0	0	0	0	NA
#2-1	Mortar & Pestle #1	17	5	175	103	30	16	50	22	280
#2-1	Mortar & Pestle #3	27	2	210	127	25	15	25	15	294
#2-2	Mortar & Pestle #4	28	14	160	131	20	9	20	9	239
#2-3	Mortar & Pestle #5	31	4	250	147	15	7	10	5	287
#2-3	Mortar & Pestle #6	29	5	300	145	15	6	10	6.5	267
#3	Flat Pound #1	32	9	300	161	10	5	15	6	237
#3	Flat Pound #2	29	21	275	147	10	5	10	4	320
#3	Flat Pound #3	30	15	225	154	15	4	10	5	303
#4	Flat Roller #1	43	2	270	182	15	6.5	15	10	366
#4	Flat Roller #2	40	0	300	193	5	2	5	2	358
#4	Flat Roller #3	42	0	281	180	0.5	1	1	1	304
#5	Small Basin	24	5	250	148	60	33	175	94.5	385
#6	Large Basin #1	34	7	225	129	25	13	50	25	228
#6	Large Basin #2	16	3	150	89	50	29	100	56	221
#7	Roman Mill	0	0	320	32	92	112	880	480	168

Table 4.1: Results of individual experiements grouped by Method

All samples based on 1 liter of experimental remains

Method	Experiment	Olive Stones		Volume and Weight of Olive Stone Fragments						Pulp
		Whole stones	Fractured stones	> 4.75 mm		4.00 mm		2.00 mm		weight
				ml	g	ml	g	ml	g	g
#1	Foot Tread	57.5	0.5	394	232	0	0	0	0	NA
#2-1,2,3	Mortar & Pestle	26.4	6	219	130.5	21	10.6	23	11.5	273.4
#3	Flat Pound	30.3	15	266.7	154	11.7	4.7	11.7	5	286.7
#4	Flat Roller	41.7	0.7	283.7	185	6.8	3.2	7	4.3	342.7
#5	Small Basin	24	5	250	148	60	33	175	94.5	385
#6	Large Basin	25	5	187.5	109	37.5	21	75	40.5	224.5
#7	Roman Mill	0	0	320	32	92	112	880	480	168

Table 4.2: Averages of experiments grouped by Method

processing experiments, the above trends make sense. The foot treading and Roman mill experiments have little in common with any other method. Similarities would be expected between the mortar and pestle and flat pound experiments as they used the same crushing implement, the pestle, with the major difference being the surface on which the olives were prepared (a mortar or flat surface). It is interesting to note that the flat roller experiment gave results more similar to those of the pounding experiments rather than the basin and rollers experiments, as I expected.

The basin and roller experiments (small and large basin) gave results more similar to each other than to the other experiments. Both basin experiments show a pattern of high large and small fragments and lower amounts of mid-size fragments. None of the other experiments show this pattern. The Roman mill sample had no whole stones but a large amount of small fragments, suggesting that all the olive fruit had been crushed. Crushing all the fruit is a preferred outcome in any olive oil processing, as oil is not obtained from uncrushed fruit. The effectiveness of the Roman-style mill was probably one reason why

Treatments	Slope	Significance	Curve	Significance
1,2	28002.9	**	8960.95	**
1,3	11592.6	**	3864.2	NS
1,4	8354.4	**	2691.2	NS
1,5	33920.3	**	880.111	NS
1,6	39762	**	7072.67	*
1,7	303372	**	42987.1	**
1,8	51745.3	**	9604	**
1,9	51745.3	**	4715.11	*
2,3	3263.44	NS	945.312	NS
2,4	6000	*	1901.25	NS
2,5	6100.42	*	1531.25	NS
2,6	5040	*	34.2857	NS
2,7	238140	**	92480	**
2,8	16006.7	**	1388.89	NS
2,9	16006.7	**	22222.2	**
3,4	330.75	NS	132.25	NS
3,5	12150	**	312.5	NS
3,6	12269.4	**	897.8	NS
3,7	249084	**	72390.1	**
3,8	24384.4	**	3003.12	NS
3,9	24384.4	**	14878.1	**
4,5	15150.4	**	91.125	NS
4,6	16137.6	**	1620	NS
4,7	262086	**	68080.5	**
4,8	28566	**	3960.5	NS
4,9	28566	**	12960.5	**
5,6	456.333	NS	1521	NS
5,7	100806	**	42126.8	**
5,8	1406.25	NS	3502.08	NS
5,9	1406.25	NS	7252.08	*
6,7	150528	**	76176	**
6,8	4181.33	*	860.444	NS
6,9	4181.33	*	18860.4	**
7,8	78400	**	69921.3	**
7,9	78400	**	14421.3	**
8,9	0	NS	20833.3	**

Table 4.3: Orthogonal Contrasts, Volume

this method superseded other methods as the primary processing method.

The data from Table 2 were used in the statistical analyses. Statistical analysis of the samples was done with the help of Dr. Mark Ellersieck of the University of Missouri Statistics Department. Standard statistical methods (Snedecor and Cochran, 1989) were utilized. The goal of the statistical analyses was to see if the trends observed in the data, i.e. differences and similarities in the shape and direction of the curves, held up to statistical analysis. In other words, while certain methods (mortar and pestle and flat pound) may be similar, is it possible to differentiate between major technology groups (foot treading, pounding, basins, and Roman mill)? We would be looking for similarities between some methods (such as the various mortar and pestle methods) and differences between others (such as foot treading vs. the Roman mill).

First, an analysis of variance was performed. The analysis of variance was a nine by three factorial arrangement of treatments. The nine represents the fragment averages of the different experimental processing methods, and the three represents the different sieve sizes (4.7 mm, 4.00 mm and 2.00 mm). The linear statistical model contained the effects of methods, sieve size and the interaction of methods times sieve size. Since the interaction term was significant ($p<01$), linear and quadratic polynomial contrasts were performed to test linear and curvature effect and if linear and curvature response were different between methods. The polynomial comparisons are discussed by Snedecor and Cochran (1989). All analyses were performed using the SAS System. This analysis was used to determine if there was a slope or curve for each processing method. For each treatment, the null hypothesis was that there was either no slope or no curvature (each was tested). Two separate analyses were performed, one for volume (ml) and one for weight (g).

A second test was then performed with the null hypothesis being that the slope and curvature of the treatments were similar. All hypotheses were tested using one degree of freedom F-tests. Levels of significance were tested at two levels of alpha (.05 and .01). The calculated levels of significance were (.05) 4037 and (.01) 7518. Tables 4.3 (volume) and 4.4 (weight) show the results of the comparisons between the various experimental processing methods and the two archaeological samples. The "treatments" represent the comparison between experiment types: 1 represents foot tread (Method 1), 2 represents mortar and pestle (Method 2), 3 represents flat pound (Method 3), 4 represents flat roller (Method 4), 5 represents small basin (Method 5), 6 represents large basin (Method 6), and 7 represents Roman mill (Method 7). If the calculated number for the treatment (the comparison between Methods) is lower than both the .05 and .01 calculated level of significance numbers, then the test is Not Significant, meaning that the slope or curvature are identical. If the calculated treatment number is lower than the .01 level number but is higher than the .05 level number, referred to by an asterix (*), then the test is significant at the .05 level but not the .01 level, which means the slope or curvature is only slightly similar. If the calculated number is higher than both the .05 and .01 level numbers, then the test is significant at both the .05 and .01 levels, referred to by a double asterix (**), meaning that the slope or curvature of the two Methods being compared are not similar to each other. A post hoc analysis determined whether the rates of either the volume or weight changed in the same fashion over different sieve sizes. The data were analyzed as a charted line with the Y-axis (vertical) representing volume or weight and the X-axis (horizontal) representing the three sieve sizes (see

Treatments	Slope	Significance	Curve	Significance
1,2	8960	**	2986.67	**
1,3	4133.4	**	1377.8	**
1,4	1560.6	**	480.2	NS
1,5	10680.3	**	336.111	NS
1,6	13448	**	2562.67	**
1,7	1541333	**	348.444	NS
1,8	13068	**	20544.4	**
1,9	38081.3	**	7627.11	**
2,3	788.438	*	262.812	NS
2,4	3488.44	**	1240.31	**
2,5	1870.42	**	451.25	NS
2,6	1931.43	**	34.2857	NS
2,7	134427	**	3920	**
2,8	3081.67	**	14045	**
2,9	21281.7	**	19427.2	**
3,4	768	*	289	NS
3,5	3456	**	98	NS
3,6	3936.6	**	336.2	NS
3,7	133653	**	2415.13	**
3,8	4959.38	**	15051.1	**
3,9	24384.4	**	14878.1	**
4,5	6144	**	4.5	NS
4,6	7661.4	**	1125	*
4,7	148365	**	1378.13	**
4,8	8103.38	**	18145.1	**
4,9	30888.4	**	12090.1	**
5,6	75	NS	529	NS
5,7	62750.3	**	1026.75	*
5,8	90.25	NS	11718.8	**
5,9	6320.25	**	8374.08	**
6,7	88752	**	3600	**
6,8	385.333	NS	10404	**
6,9	10092	**	16555.1	**
7,8	58081	**	19683	**
7,9	29241	**	3536.33	**
8,9	4900	**	39905.3	**

Table 4.4: Orthogonal Contrasts, Weight

Figure 4.15 as an example). It is possible for a sample to have a slope but no curve. Methods with both slope and curvature statistically similar would therefore be alike.

For the foot treading experiment (1), there are no similarities to the slopes of any other experiment for either volume (mls) or weight (g). The curve of the slope is similar to three other experiments at the 5% level and two at the 1% level for volume, and three at the 5% level for weight. Since slope and curve are not both similar, the foot treading experiments are not statistically similar to any other experiment method, which agrees with qualitative observations of the data.

For the mortar and pestle experiments (2), there are some similarities to other methods. Using the weight data, the mortar and pestle (2) and flat pound (3) experiments are similar at the 1% level for slope and 5% level for

curvature. The volume data are even closer, as both volume and weight are statistically not significant at the 5% level; non-significance meaning we should accept the test hypothesis that the experiments have very similar results. Comparison with other experiments shows that there are no similarities of slope for weight, though curvature matches at the 5% level with both basin types (5, 6). Volume shows closer contrasts with all but the Roman mill (7), with the slope being not significant at the 1% level and the curvature not significant at the 5% level for all three remaining types (flat roller, 4; small basin, 5; large basin, 6). Based on the statistical analysis, the mortar and pestle and flat pound methods are very similar to each other (i.e. no statistical differences between the methods). There are minor similarities between the mortar and pestle methods and the remaining processing methods, except for the Roman mill. Again, this matches with the qualitative observations.

The flat pound experiments (3) show a very close similarity to the flat roller experiments (4) and the mortar and pestle (2, above). Both weight and volume curvatures are similar at the 5% level, while the slopes are similar at 1% for weight and 5% for volume. There is no similarity to the slopes of any other methods, though the curves are similar to both basin experiments. The qualitative observations also predicted this outcome.

Somewhat unexpectedly, the flat roller experiments (4) show few similarities with any other experiments except for the match with the flat pound experiments (3, above), though the volume (but not weight) data for mortar and pestle (2) suggest some similarity. There are no matches in slope with another experiment. The curvature is similar to both basin experiments in weight (5% for small basin, 1% for large) and volume (5% for both), however, since there is no correlation in slope, this does not provide a match. The statistical data agree with the qualitative observations that the flat pound and flat roller are somewhat similar.

The two basin experiments, small (5) and large (6), match up with each other statistically (at the 5% for both slope and curvature), but have no other statistical matches with another experimental method. The weight curvature is slightly similar to the Roman mill, but that alone is not a match. Based on the general qualitative observations, the two basin experiments were somewhat similar, which agrees with the statistical data.

The Roman mill (7) shows no close similarities to any other processing method. The Roman mill and foot treading experiments form separate, definite distinct data sets unlike any other methods. Once again, this observation was noted in the qualitative data review.

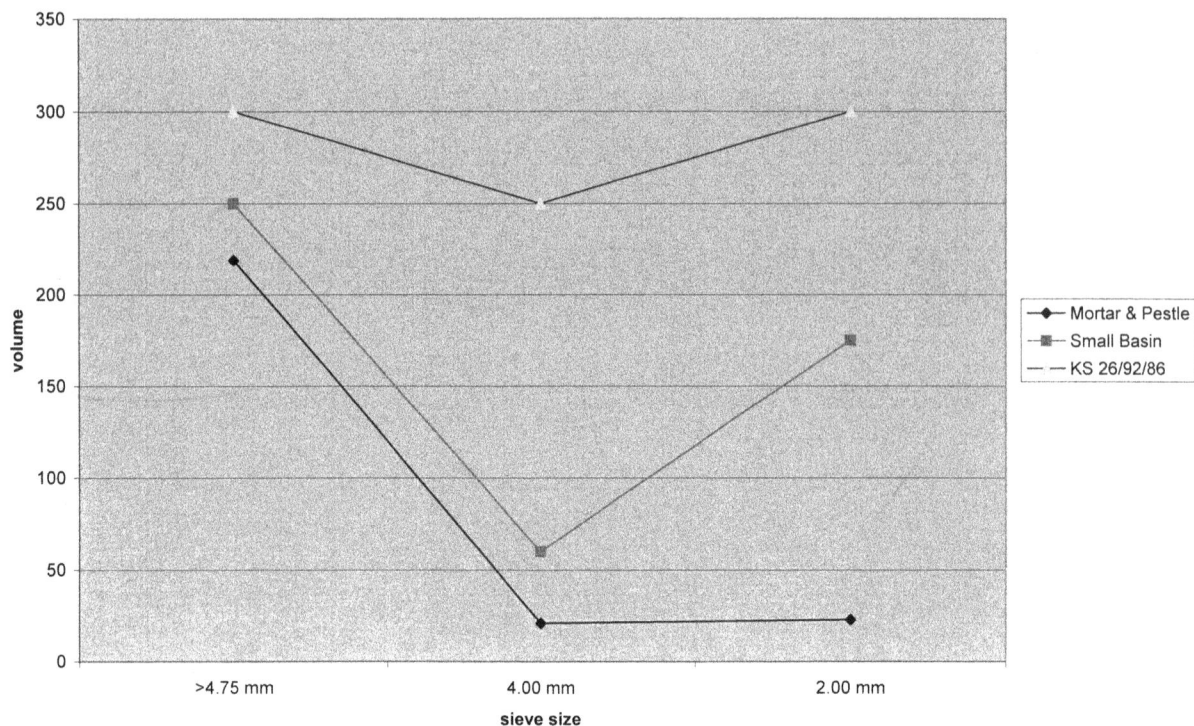

FIGURE 4.15: GRAPHED RESULTS

4.6 Conclusions

Based on the results of the experimental olive oil processing methods, it is possible to differentiate between various methods of traditional olive oil processing. Some of the methods clearly stand alone, such as foot treading and the Roman style mill. Other methods show some similarities to each other, i.e., the basin methods to each other, and those methods using the pestle. Based on the experimental data, the processing methods break down into four broad groups: 1) foot treading; 2) using a pounding device, either in a mortar or on a flat surface, and including a roller on a flat surface; 3) using a roller in a basin; and 4) milling, such as the Roman style mill. Within these broad groups, there is some slight differentiation, such as the roller on a flat surface versus the pounding methods or between the two types of basins. Overall, however, it is possible

to differentiate traditional olive oil processing methods from one another.

The foot treading and Roman mill methods stand apart from other methods both qualitatively and quantitatively. The predominant feature of foot treading is a preponderance of whole stones, while the exact opposite is true for the Roman mill method, which produces a greater amount of small fragments compared to other methods. The other two groups, using a pounding device and using a roller in a basin, are qualitatively closer together and thus harder to differentiate. However, the roller and basin methods do have a greater proportion of smaller fragments. Statistically, when plotted against each other, it is possible to differentiate the different methods. Using the experimental methodology, it is possible to compare an archaeological sample to the experimental results in order to determine the processing method used on the archaeological sample.

CHAPTER 5

TESTING AN ARCHAEOLOGICAL SAMPLE

5.1   Introduction

The third phase of my research involves applying the results of the experimental processing studies to aid in interpreting an archaeological sample of olive pressing remains. The goal is to see whether an analysis of the fracture pattern of the archaeological sample provides insight into the type of crushing method that may have been used. Based on the processing equipment found at the site, a small basin, a crushing pattern match with the basin experiments would be expected. A match between the experimental and archaeological remains would support the research goal of identifying processing techniques through the botanical remains (olive stones).

The archaeological samples were provided by Ehud Galili, director of the Marine Branch of the Israel Antiquities Authority. The olive remains had been recovered from two pit features at a submerged Late Neolithic, early Chalcolithic site at Kfar Samir, off the Mediterranean coast of Israel near Haifa (see Figure 2.2). Examination of the features suggests they represent the remains of olive oil processing (Galili and Sharvit, 1994-5; Galili *et al*, 1997; Galili *et al*, 1989) (Figure 5.1). The olive remains consisted of whole and broken olive stones and olive pulp. Mat fragments and woven baskets found in the features imply a similar function to mats and baskets used in the traditional upright presses. Olive oil processing equipment had been found at the site during earlier underwater surveys (Galili, *pers. comm.*) (Figure 5.2). Both pit features were excavated and the olive remains preserved in sea water. Upon initial inspection of the remains, the stones and fragments were in an excellent state of preservation. The broken edges of fragments had distinct lines and sharp points. Due to their long submergence in seawater, the remains were somewhat friable.

The Kfar Samir olive remains were selected for study for several reasons. First, the remains from this site presented a unique opportunity to study remains from ancient olive oil processing in situ. As shown in Chapter 3, olive pressing wastes have multiple uses. These uses require movement of the olive remains away from the processing areas. Further, olive remains are organic, and unless charred, do not survive long in the archaeological record. For land sites, finding archaeological olive remains which can be definitely tied to processing would mean that the processing area, materials, and probably the site

itself, had to be destroyed (and thus preserved) by fire. Not only destroyed by fire, but destroyed during the olive oil pressing season. The Kfar Samir remains represent ancient olive oil processing which has been uniquely frozen in time, and preserved without destructive force (fire).

Secondly, the Kfar Samir site is significant in that the time period it represents, the Late Neolithic/early Chalcolithic, is the period many scholars believe olive cultivation begins (Eitam, 1987; Galili *et al*, 1989; Galili *et al*, 1997; Galili and Sharvit, 1994-5; Liphschitz, 1996; Stager, 1985; Zohary and Hopf, 2000; Zohary and Spiegel-Roy, 1975). The samples represent olive remains potentially processed at the beginning of the olive oil industry in the ancient Near East. I was surprised at the early date with consideration to the olive oil processing features and artifacts found at

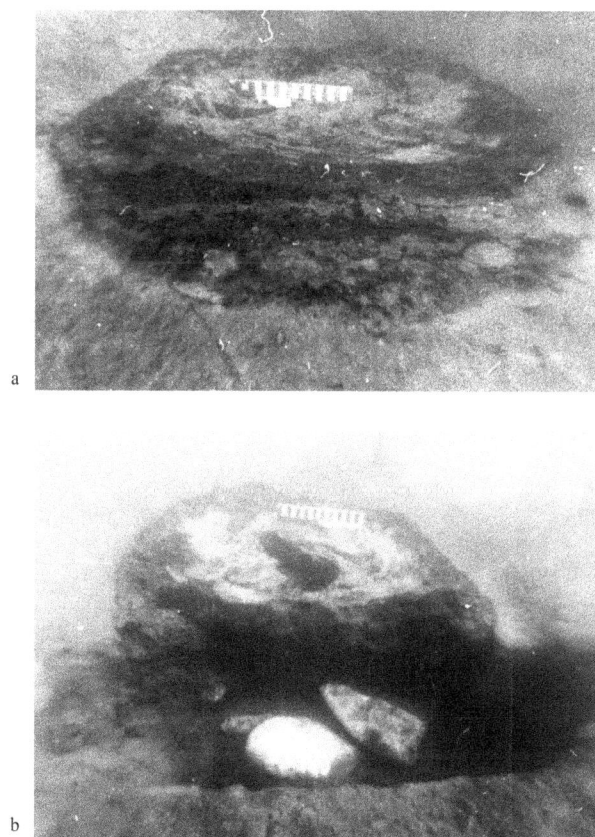

FIGURE 5.1: UNDERWATER PIT CONTAINING CRUSHED OLIVE REMAINS, KAFR SAMIR, ISRAEL
a: PIT BEFORE EXCAVATION (GALILI)
b: PIT DURING EXCAVATION (GALILI)

FIGURE 5.2: BASIN FROM KAFR SAMIR, ISRAEL (GALILI)

Kfar Samir. The use of processing equipment that handle larger quantities of olives might suggest that there was a change from the use of wild olives to the use of cultivated olives earlier than previously thought. The dating of the Kfar Samir materials might also suggest an earlier start to large scale processing intended for trade or exchange. At the same time, older methods and techniques were probably still employed for domestic use, processing smaller amounts of olives.

5.2 Analysis of Samples

5.2.1 Methods

Approximately 27 liters of olive remains were removed from one pit, structure 6, and a third of another pit, structure 7, was excavated. Half of the ca. 27,000 cubic centimeters of material removed from structure 7 was olive stones and pulp. A ruffle separator was used to get a random sample of remains from each feature (Figure 5.3). Approximately 1 liter of material from each feature was taken for analysis. The samples were kept wet to prevent alteration of the remains, primarily those effects caused by drying. The samples were transported in sealed containers to the lab facilities at the University of Missouri. The samples were then passed through the same set of sieves as were the experimental remains, 4.75 mm, 4.00 mm, and 2.00 mm. While processing the archaeological samples, care was taken to keep the remains wet.

Due to the wet condition of the samples, the remains did not filter through the sieves as easily as did the dry experimental remains. Also, due to the somewhat fragile nature of the remains, greater care was taken in shaking the sieves. It should be noted that the wet condition of the remains caused the fragments to clump and stick together, preventing them from falling through the sieve openings. The water from the samples was used to wash them through

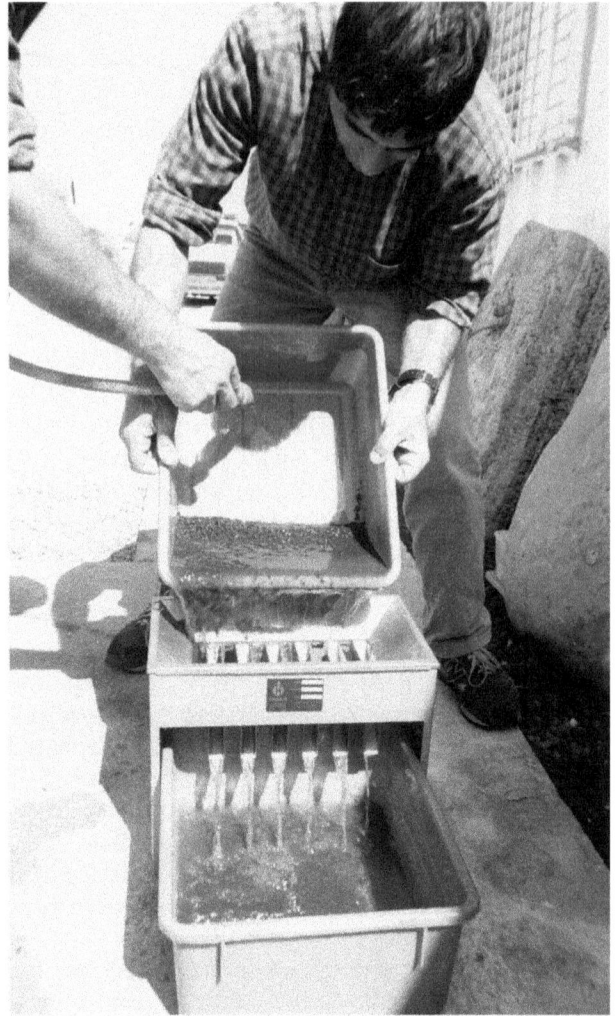

FIGURE 5.3: USING RUFFLE SEPARATOR TO RANDOMIZE SAMPLE, MARINE BRANCH, ISRAEL ANTIQUITIES AUTHORITY

the sieves, this was done several times over. Washing the samples was done to compensate for the lessened amount of shaking and to keep the samples wet. Washing the samples appeared to move the fragments through the sieves, and I believe that the amount of material that did not settle into the appropriate sieve pan did not significantly alter the overall numbers. Weight, volume and a count of whole olive stones was done, as for the experimental samples.

5.3 Discussion of Fracture Patterning

The data from the archaeological samples are at the bottom of Table 5, with the experimental data displayed for comparison. Table 5.1 shows the results of individual experiments grouped by Method, along with the two archaeological samples. The data from Table 5.2, averages of experiments grouped by Method, were used for the statistical comparisons. Observation of the raw data, especially for sample KS 30/93/30 (9), suggested similarities between the archaeological samples and the basin experiments, especially the small basin type. Note, for example, that both KS 30/93/30 and the small basin

All samples based on 1 liter of experimental remains

Method	Experiment	Olive Stones		Volume and Weight of Olive Stone Fragments						Pulp
		Whole stones	Fractured stones	> 4.75 mm		4.00 mm		2.00 mm		weight
				ml	g	ml	g	ml	g	g
#1	Foot Tread #2	59	1	388	228	0	0	0	0	313
#1	Foot Tread #3	56	0	400	236	0	0	0	0	NA
#2-1	Mortar & Pestle #1	17	5	175	103	30	16	50	22	280
#2-1	Mortar & Pestle #3	27	2	210	127	25	15	25	15	294
#2-2	Mortar & Pestle #4	28	14	160	131	20	9	20	9	239
#2-3	Mortar & Pestle #5	31	4	250	147	15	7	10	5	287
#2-3	Mortar & Pestle #6	29	5	300	145	15	6	10	6.5	267
#3	Flat Pound #1	32	9	300	161	10	5	15	6	237
#3	Flat Pound #2	29	21	275	147	10	5	10	4	320
#3	Flat Pound #3	30	15	225	154	15	4	10	5	303
#4	Flat Roller #1	43	2	270	182	15	6.5	15	10	366
#4	Flat Roller #2	40	0	300	193	5	2	5	2	358
#4	Flat Roller #3	42	0	281	180	0.5	1	1	1	304
#5	Small Basin	24	5	250	148	60	33	175	94.5	385
#6	Large Basin #1	34	7	225	129	25	13	50	25	228
#6	Large Basin #2	16	3	150	89	50	29	100	56	221
#7	Roman Mill	0	0	320	32	92	112	880	480	168
#8	KS 26/92/86	268	0	300	278	250	360	300	244	NA
#9	KS 30/93/30	218	0	400	347	100	153	400	453	NA

Table 5.1: Results of individual experiments grouped by Method, plus archaeological samples

All samples based on 1 liter of experimental remains

Method	Experiment	Olive Stones		Volume and Weight of Olive Stone Fragments						Pulp
		Whole stones	Fractured stones	> 4.75 mm		4.00 mm		2.00 mm		weight
				ml	g	ml	g	ml	g	g
#1	Foot Tread	57.5	0.5	394	232	0	0	0	0	NA
#2-1,2,3	Mortar & Pestle	26.4	6	219	130.5	21	10.6	23	11.5	273.4
#3	Flat Pound	30.3	15	266.7	154	11.7	4.7	11.7	5	286.7
#4	Flat Roller	41.7	0.7	283.7	185	6.8	3.2	7	4.3	342.7
#5	Small Basin	24	5	250	148	60	33	175	94.5	385
#6	Large Basin	25	5	187.5	109	37.5	21	75	40.5	224.5
#7	Roman Mill	0	0	320	32	92	112	880	480	168
#8	KS 26/92/86	268	0	300	278	250	360	300	244	NA
#9	KS 30/93/30	218	0	400	347	100	153	400	453	NA

Table 5.2: Averages of experiments grouped by Method, plus archaeological samples

experiments show a pattern of large numbers of remains for the 4.75 mm sieve, a smaller amount for the 4.00 mm sieve, and large amounts again at the 2.00 sieve.

The statistical analysis of similarity between the archaeological and experimental samples was performed as described in Chapter 4. Tables 4.3 and 4.4 show the statistical correlation between the experimental and archaeological samples. Sample KS 26/92/86 (8) shows a similarity in slope for weight to the small basin experiment (5). Both archaeological samples show a similarity in slope for volume to the small basin results. Sample KS 26/92/86

(8) is similar in curvature to the small basin results (5) in volume only, and sample KS 30/93/30 (9) is only slightly similar (at the 1% level) in volume. However, this is the best match between the archaeological samples and any of the experimental results. There is less of a match between the archaeological samples and the large basin experiments (6), which are the next closest similarity. The slope for weight and the curvature for volume match up for KS 26/92/86 (8) and the large basin experiments (6), but there is no similarity in curvature for weight, and only a slight (at the 1% level) match for slope with volume. KS 30/93/30 (9) has only a slight match (1% level) for volume slope and no other similarities with the large basin method. Overall, the comparison between the Kfar Samir archaeological samples and the small basin experimental samples suggests that the small basin processing method was the method employed in the processing of the Kfar Samir remains.

5.4 Conclusions

After taking a random sample of olive remains recovered from the underwater site of Kfar Samir, Israel, the olive remains were processed and analyzed in the same manner as the experimental samples: sorted through 4.75 mm, 4.00 mm, and 2.00 mm sieves, with the different fractions measured for both weight and volume, and the results statistically analyzed. The statistical tests looked for similarities in slope and curvature between the Kfar Samir archaeological samples and the experimental samples.

A comparison between the archaeological samples from Kfar Samir and experimental methods reveals a similarity between the Kfar Samir sample and the small basin processing method, especially for sample KS 26/92/86 (8). I had initially expected KS 30/93/30 (9) to be more similar than KS 26/92/86 (8) to the small basin method, based on raw observation. However, the statistical comparisons show that the archaeological samples fall into the small basin method of processing.

This interpretation is supported by the archaeological processing artifacts found at the site (see Figure 5.2). The stone basin found at the Kfar Samir site is very similar in size to the small basin used (see Figures 3.29, 3.31, 4.9) in Method 7, the small basin with hand roller experiments. Since the Kfar Samir remains were potentially processed in the small basin found at the site, the fracture patterns of those remains should be similar to the fracture patterns of olives processed in a similar feature, i.e., the small basin from the Olive Oil Museum used to process olives in Method seven. Comparison of the remains showed this to be true.

The results of this study show that it is possible to model the type of processing method used from the fracture patterns of the botanical remains (olive pressing wastes). It should be noted that it is possible that an unknown, or untested, method could have produced these results. Corroborating evidence is necessary.

It should be noted that the archaeological remains used in the comparison were unique. The manner of preservation, waterlogged and buried under sediment on the sea floor rather than charred, and the temporal context, frozen during the oil production process, are unlikely to be found at land-based archaeological sites. However, it is possible that concentrations of olive pressing wastes may be found. Concentrations of olive pressing wastes, preferably with pulp residue intact, could be analyzed just as the Kfar Samir materials were studied. Sifting ash sediments, which appear to be from burnt olive wastes, might produce enough unashed olive stone remains to analyze for processing method. Concentrations of olive stones, however, do not necessarily indicate olive oil processing, some indication of said concentration of stones being utilized for oil is necessary. Concentrations of whole olive stones, especially within containers such as amphorae, would likely suggest olives as foodstuffs. Understanding the olive oil processing method and the uses of pressing wastes does help in determining where olive pressing remains might be found, in association with presses, kilns, construction materials, etc. Any concentration of charred crushed olive remains might be worth analyzing.

Also, the fact that olive oil pressing wastes are a multi-use commodity likely to be used as fuel, further limits the possibility of discovering intact assemblages of olive oil pressing wastes. Should such assemblages of pressing wastes be found, this study shows that it may be possible to determine the processing method.

The experimental/archaeological comparison shows that it is possible to identify different processing methods based on the olive stone fracture pattern ratios caused by the processing methods. The information from this research can be applied to olive remains from the crucial period time of the Chalcolithic through the Iron Age in Syro-Palestine, when processing technologies changed drastically. Large scale processing evolves from mortar and pestle and small basins in the earlier periods and ends with large basins and rollers at olive oil processing complexes. These processing changes coincide with an expansion of trade and state building in the region. My research offers a means of understanding the role of olive oil production in this expansion.

CHAPTER 6

OLIVE OIL, TRADE AND THE CITY-STATE

6.1 Introduction

Understanding the developmental changes occurring in ancient olive oil processing technology and in the ancient olive oil industry has important implications in understanding trade, trade networks, and the ancient economies of the region. Better understanding of the ancient olive oil industry and trade broadens our knowledge of the ancient economy, social structure, geopolitical relationships and many other aspects of the rise of city states (Heltzer and Eitam, 1996). A number of researchers hypothesize that the change from household production to expanded industrial olive oil production was important in the establishment of localized "states" in Palestine, based in part on the trade of olive oil (Gitin, 1989; Kelm and Mazar, 1995; Mazar, 1990). By studying the variables (botanical remains, features, artifacts) involved in olive oil production one could predict the level of production at a site, using the results of my current research as a guide, adding important information to our knowledge of archaeological sites and cultures.

6.2 Olive Oil and Trade

The olive and olive oil played a crucial role in the economic history of the Mediterranean region (Frankel, 1999). The trade in olives and olive oil was prevalent throughout the ancient eastern Mediterranean, especially to Egypt and the Aegean (Artzy, 1996; Bothwell and Bothwell, 1998; Bunimovitz, 1996; Eitam, 1996; Herr, 1997; Lines, 1995; Stager, 1985). Egypt was a major recipient of olive oil (Ahituv, 1996), probably due to Egypt's close proximity to Syro-Palestine. "Given the probable late date of introduction of olive into Egypt, it has been assumed that olive oil was one of Egypt's earliest imports" (Serpico and White, 2000:399), a statement that Frankel (1996) agrees with. An Egyptian-Canaanite trade connection can be documented as early as the beginnings of the Old Kingdom in Egypt (during the Early Bronze II–III period, ≈ 2,680 B.C.) (Emery 1987; Leonard, 1996; Mazar, 1990; Stager, 1985,) and may have formed part of a trade complex reaching as far west as Crete. Beginning in the Middle Bronze Age (≈ 2,200 B.C.) the wide distribution of Canaanite jars gives evidence to extensive trade between Palestine and the lands of the Mediterranean basin (Zemer, 1978). Textual evidence from clay tablets found at Ugarit support trade in oil to Egypt from Ugarit in the Middle and Late Bronze period (≈ 2,200 B.C–1,200 B.C.) (Heltzer, 1996). The

Canaanite jar was introduced to Egypt as a consequence of exporting agricultural products, likely including olive oil, from Palestine to Egypt (Zemer, 1978). Canaanite jugs and jars exported to Egypt in the Late Bronze period (≈ 1,550–1,200 B.C.), and "Canaanite Jars" found in Greece and Egypt (Frankel, 1999) are further evidence of an early olive oil trade. These ancient trade connections are supported by the proposed shipping route of the Late Bronze period Kas wreck (Bass, 1987). Botanical evidence supports the trade in olives and probably olive oil in the Late Bronze period (Haldane, 1993). Part of the Kas wreck's cargo included a Canaanite jar full of olive pits (Haldane, 1990; Bass, 1991). The Canaanite jar was the first container used in wide scale sea transport, and finding the jars in Egypt and Mycenaean Greece supports the hypothesis that the jar was made for transport and storage by sea routes (Zemer, 1978). The trade in olive oil resembles the "neotechnic ecotype" suggested by Wolf (1966), in which a regional specialized cultivated component is linked with maritime trade. The maritime trade in olives and olive oil undoubtedly influenced the spread of oleoculture west from the eastern Mediterranean to the Aegean, North Africa, Italy and Spain (Hadjisavvas, 1992; Liphschitz, 1996; Mattingly, 1996).

Some scholars suggest a strong link between Bronze Age orchard cultivation and urbanization, arguing that orchards and urbanization go hand in hand (Lines, 1995). Production of olive oil is an important part of the city-state economy, as the tax from olive oil helped establish the city-state (Heltzer, 1996). Stager (1985) believes that urbanization and horticulture were intertwined with commerce as well, through interregional and maritime trade. Specialized horticulture and an increasing dependence on "cash crops" such as olive oil was due to involvement in international trade, and is indicative of societies which have advanced past basic subsistence economies (Esse, 1991; Stager, 1985). Olive cultivation is considered to be one of the main reasons for the prosperity of Yarmouth in the Early Bronze period (Miroschedji, 1999). Economies developed past simple subsistence strategies with little surplus to efficiently organized production systems that allowed for the export of large surpluses (Herr, 1997). Hadjisavvas (1992) sees a parallel situation on Cyprus during the Late Bronze period, in which small scale household processing is replaced by large scale centralized production aimed at export. The same is true for Palestine (Finkelstein, 1999). The complex operations needed for production and trade could only occur through division and specialization of labor. Further, the hierarchy necessary to control such operations suggests increasingly socially complex cultures.

6.3 Trade and City-states

Throughout the Bronze and Iron Ages the evolution of strong economic city-states coincides with trade networks in the eastern Mediterranean. Leonard (1996) believes the Late Bronze period ($\approx$ 1,550–1,200 B.C.) was the first true period of internationalism that the cultures of the eastern Mediterranean had yet experienced. Foreign trade reinforced the development and maintenance of economic hierarchies, and presumably political and social ones as well (Esse, 1991). At Middle and Late Bronze Age ($\approx$ 2,000–1,200 B.C.) Ugarit, taxes were paid in olive oil, and the main production centers were part of the royal agricultural economy (Heltzer, 1993). Foreign trade of commodities, including olive oil, was also a state monopoly at Ugarit (Heltzer, 1993). The change from small scale processing to centralized and large scale processing was "observable throughout the eastern Mediterranean, as foreign trade became increasingly a royal monopoly," (Blitzer, 1993:167). As Scarre and Fagan (1997) point out, trade was an important component in the rise of states.

While the city-states in Syro-Palestine were somewhat autonomous, control of the region alternated between Egypt and Assyria. A unified Egypt with a strong trade system is suggested to have provided the primary impetus toward city-state formation in late Early Bronze period (Levy *et al*, 1997). The reurbanization of Palestine in the Middle Bronze period is paralleled by the emergence of the Egyptian Middle Kingdom ($\approx$ 2,134–1,991 BC) and a reestablished centralized authority (Dever, 1987). While trade in olives and olive oil occurred earlier, it was not until the Iron Age ($\approx$ 1,200–586 B.C.) that Syro-Palestine became a major exporter of olive oil. Frankel (*pers. comm.*) does not believe there was an olive oil "industry" prior to the Iron Age, basing his argument on press features and linguistics. Prior to the Iron Age II ($\approx$ 1,000–586 B.C.) the same term is used for both olive oil and wine presses. After the Iron Age II, there are separate terms. It is during the Iron Age that large scale oil production centers appear in Syro-Palestine, at sites such as Batash, Beit Mirsim, Timnah and Tel Miqne/Ekron. Tel Miqne/Ekron is the largest identified center for olive oil production in the ancient Near East (Gitin, 1989; Herr, 1997).

Tel Miqne-Ekron switched back and forth between Egyptian and Assyrian dominance due to its location on the border between the two empires. Tel Miqne-Ekron was a major olive oil production center, shipping oil to Egypt, Cyprus and Phoenicia (Gitin, 1989). The large scale production suggests a strong long-term economic relationship between ports (for maritime trade) along the coastal plain of Palestine and inland production sites such as Tel Miqne-Ekron. Olive oil production artifacts and features suggest a wealthy economic trade (Gitin, 1996). The chief stimulus

for the phenomenal physical and economic growth of the city was the production of olive oil (Gitin, 1996). While some have argued for the local use of Tel Miqne-Ekron produced oil, Gitin (1996) believes that the purpose of Tel Miqne-Ekron's mass production was to produce a surplus of olive oil for trade. The site flourished, probably due to the stability offered under Assyrian rule. The commercial policies of the Assyrian Empire were the dynamics behind the economic growth in the Eastern Mediterranean basin during the 7th century B.C. (Gitin, 1996). These policies helped precipitate new market conditions, developing household industries into industrial ones.

The olive oil trade was an integral piece of the complex economic and socio-cultural situation in the ancient Near East. Trade networks around the eastern Mediterranean linked the Aegean, Egypt and the Syro-Palestinian coast. Olive oil was a major commodity fueling the rise of economic city-states in Syro-Palestine. The rise of these states hinged greatly upon the exchange of surplus goods. Increased organization and production for trade helped city-states to evolve. Production of olive oil helped production sites, as well as ports, gain wealth and power. Olive oil played a major factor as a trade commodity, and helped promote socio-cultural evolution in the region.

6.4 Questions

Most of the olive remains found in the archaeological record come from contexts outside of oil processing, as evidenced by the suggested uses of olive pressing remains (discussed in the ethnographic chapter). Few olive remains have been found in association with press features, based on the many archaeological references previously cited. I would suggest that this is further proof of the pressing wastes' value and varied uses.

An important example of the aforementioned statement is the elaborate olive oil production site in the Iron Age of Tel Miqne/Ekron, located in the southern coastal plain of Israel (Eitam, 1996; Gitin, 1989; 1996). Unlike the olive remains from Kfar Samir, the remains from Tel Miqne/Ekron are charred. While the remains are mostly whole, they are highly friable and broke easily when collected (Gitin, *pers. comm.*). The majority of olive remains were not found in close association with the olive oil press areas, though they were usually found in nearby rooms. These rooms may have been store rooms and also contained loom weights. Gitin (*pers. comm.*) does not believe the massive destruction found at the site occurred during the fall olive harvest and oil pressing season.

Because the Tel Miqne/Ekron olive remains were not found in direct association with olive oil production, as were the Kfar Samir remains, and were represented by whole rather than broken stones, we again ask a fundamental question concerning finds of olive remains: what do the olive remains represent? Did the Tel Miqne/Ekron olive remains represent olives stored for eating or olives waiting to be crushed? The olive crushing equipment at Tel Miqne/ Ekron was the large basin with push roller type (Method 8). Since the Tel Miqne/Ekron remains are whole, they do not, in all probability, represent pressing wastes as the large basin method breaks over half of the stones.

Since only about four percent of Tel Miqne/Ekron has been excavated, one cannot say for sure if there were any industries at the site which may have used pressing wastes as a fuel source. Little ash has been found in what little has been excavated, in contrast to Gezer III, where olive wastes and an ash level were associated with a possible oil press (Gitin, *pers. comm.*). However, Gitin would agree that due to the size of the city, pressing wastes could probably have been used as a domestic fuel source (home heating and tabuns).

Several questions do arise concerning the production of olive oil at Tel Miqne-Ekron. The presses at Tel Miqne-Ekron are consolidated in one area within the city, forming a small "industrial complex." Even though the production level was an "industrial" one with large numbers of pressing facilities centered in one area, what type of organization actually operated the production centers? Were the production facilities family operations assigned to a number of individual family groups, or were they "factory" production centers located in a number of small associated buildings (Herr, 1997)? Olive oil production at Tel Miqne-Ekron does not seem to be the "cottage industry" format associated with small independent family operated businesses, but rather larger production facilities supported and organized by the Assyrians through local intermediaries (Herr, 1997). However, Herr does feel that the family was at the heart of the operation. Production was supported, organized and administered from a central source, but individual families ran the production for a contracted share. The family was the important social grouping and Herr (*pers. comm.*) thinks it likely that the business was run out of the home, much like today, with the shop below and living quarters above.

The huge oil complex at Tel Miqne/Ekron brings to my mind a question based on the uses of pressing wastes suggested from the ethnographic research. Would the pressing wastes produced by such a large industrial complex have been utilized at Tel Miqne/Ekron alone? As only a small percentage of the site has been excavated, we do not know what other industries, including those which might utilize pressing wastes, occur at the site. Certainly some of the wastes fueled Tel Miqne/Ekron's domestic fires. However, the site of Ashdod is about 15 miles away from Tel Miqne/Ekron and has a series of potter's kilns, suggesting a potters' quarter. Would it have been economically and physically feasible to transport pressing wastes from Tel Miqne/Ekron to Ashdod in antiquity? I have shown that pressing wastes are utilized as kiln fuel. Unfortunately, we know little about the movement and use in antiquity of agricultural by-products such as olive oil pressing wastes.

Excavations at Delos in Greece have produced both an olive oil press and perfumeries (Brun, 2000). The oil mill excavations produced charred olive stones among the remains. The presses found at the perfumeries (and the mortars also found at the site) could have been used for pressing olives for oil, but Brun (2000) suggests that they were for perfume production, including the production of the olive oil used as a base. Similar techniques are suggested for the perfumery in Paestum, southern Italy, and in Campania region during the Roman period. Both the extraction of some essences and the preparation of perfume required heating (Brun, 2000). Olive pressing wastes from the manufacture of the perfume's olive oil base could very easily have been used as fuel for heating and mixing the perfumes, unguents and oils.

6.5 Proposed Testing

I propose a series of ideas to be considered for further research concerning the investigation of ancient olive oil production. What range of distances would the transportation of resources, such as pressing wastes or ash, be economically viable? Are there other ancient sites within this distance range that have ancillary industries (such as glass or pottery) which might make use of olive pressing wastes? If so, what types of olive remains do such sites exhibit?

Since one major problem in the analysis of olive pressing remains is the multiple use and dispersal of those remains, finding the distance from the pressing site that remains would travel for a particular post-pressing use would help in searching for remains. Some research has been done concerning the monetary supply and demand of biofuels (Kumar *et al*, 2001). An ethnographic study similar to the one done to investigate post-processing waste uses would be a way to investigate this.

Predicting what types of remains from a site prior to discovering olive remains is possible. From the experiments I have fracture patterns which can be applied to both olive remains and archaeological features. For instance, the Tel Miqne-Ekron oil complex used the large basin with push roller style crushing method (Method 8). I would, therefore, expect olive remains with a crushing pattern exhibited by the Large Basin experiments (Method 8): a large amount of large fragments (> 4.7n mm sieve), few medium fragments (4.00 mm sieve) and a moderate amount of small fragments (2.00 mm sieve) (especially since the materials used to perform the experiment [the basin and push roller] at the Israel Olive Oil Museum were from the Tel Miqne-Ekron site). Thus, a site with many mortar and pestle style artifacts (such as 'Amqa, in the western Galilee [Frankel, 1994]) would expect to have a majority of large fragments (> 4.7n mm sieve), and very few medium (4.00 mm sieve) and small fragments (2.00 mm sieve).

Since the ethnographic study showed that a variety of methods, especially those used to make small amounts of oil for immediate household use, remained in use over time, it might be worthwhile to date olive remains from different sites and from different processing methods. C-14 dating would be the likely method of dating the specimens. Dating olive remains would help put a temporal fix on different processing methods and would show the use overlap of various methods compared to each other.

Even if deposits of olive stone fragments cannot be found, evidence of associated debris from post-processing usages could be helpful. At a site with large deposits of fine ash, the ash should be analyzed for olive stone fragments. A few fragments might be able to suggest the type of processing initially performed, though I would suggest at least a half-liter to a liter. A site with large numbers of olive stone inclusions in construction mortar would suggest an olive oil industry somewhere close by. Again, analyzing a small sample of such fragments might help discern the

processing method. Also, since the burning process may cause the stones to fracture, studying the affects of fire on fracturing should be investigated.

To reliably analyze olive remains from a site to determine processing method, I would suggest the following: at least a half-liter of olive remains from a localized area, such as a square meter. Ash deposits should be screened or analyzed for olive stone fragments. If olive fragments are a common aggregate of construction material (i.e. mortar or plaster), say greater than 10 fragments per 25 cm of mortar (give or take a few), picking the fragments out and measuring them can be done. Any features or processing artifacts would also offer predictions as to the type of processing done at a site. The type and number of processing installations, features and artifacts will help determine whether primarily domestic or commercial processing was occurring as well.

CHAPTER 7

CONCLUSIONS

7.1 Introduction

This research focused on identifying olive oil processing methods based on archaeological remains. The ultimate goal was to see if the olive oil processing method used at a site can be determined by its olive remains. Comparison of archaeological remains to experimental data shows that this can be done. This study was important because the olive and its oil was one of the most versatile plant resources available to Mediterranean cultures in antiquity. Olive oil was important not only for its dietary uses, but also for its uses as the main lighting fuel source, a major perfume and unguent base, body oil, and use in holy ceremonies. However, despite the olive's importance in antiquity it is much less studied than other major Near Eastern food crops, such as grains. The methods used in this study are applicable to other archaeological and paleoethnobotanical problems.

The research presented here combined three different methods of anthropological investigation: ethnographic, experimental and archaeological. Few other studies have combined these three methods in the analysis of one problem. The ethnographic study documented various methods of traditional and possible ancient methods of olive oil processing, and the effects these methods had on the olive remains. The ethnographic portion of the project established which experimental processing methods would be done. The ethnographic research also revealed the large number of problems involved in dealing with olive processing remains such as the secondary and tertiary uses of pressing wastes, the movement of wastes away from processing sites, and the primary usage of pressing residues as a fuel source, which burns almost completely to ash. This research helps understand how olive remains are incorporated into the archaeological record.

The experimental portion of the project attempted to replicate various olive oil processing methods, mainly those used prior to the Roman-style rotary mill. The olive remains from these experiments were then analyzed to test the hypothesis that different processing methods would fracture the olive stones in different discernible patterns. Statistically identifiable breakage patterns were observed for the different processing methods.

The final portion of the research, the archaeological analysis, compared samples from an archaeological site with well preserved olive pressing remains in-situ to the experimental results. The remains were recovered from an underwater site consisting of olive oil processing pits, with associated materials and artifacts (basketry, crushing basin). The goal of this portion was to see if there was a match between the fracture pattern of the archaeological remains and any of the experimental studies. The archaeological remains did match with one of the experimental studies, a correlation which was further solidified by the associated features from the archaeological site. The match verified that it is possible to determine ancient olive oil processing methods based on their remains.

The analysis of olive oil processing methods allows us to approach the larger picture, that of the complex issue of olive oil and its role in the evolution of city-states in ancient Syro-Palestine. Olive oil was an integral part of early Eastern Mediterranean trade and the establishment of city-states. Technological change in olive oil processing methods allowed for olive oil to become a major trade commodity. Understanding the evolution of processing technology will help identify where and when the changes occurred.

7.2 Issues Raised in the Research

My research generated a number of research issues and exposed problems in identifying olive remains, some of which have no clear answer. The ethnographic research showed that the primary use of olive oil pressing wastes is as a fuel. Further, an appreciated quality of the waste as fuel is that it burns almost completely to ash, which may also have its uses. The pressing wastes may be moved from the location where it is produced (the oil mill) to a site of secondary usage (fuel source), and to a tertiary use site (fertilizer, etc.). If these practices were carried out in antiquity, what do the olive remains from archaeological sites, especially oil production sites, represent? If pressing residues are used as fuel, potentially moved away from the oil processing area, and burned to ash, do the olive stones found indicate olive oil processing, olives for consumption, or another unidentified use? Serious consideration concerning the context of olive remains, especially understanding deposition of remains, both primary and secondary (or even tertiary) needs to be made. Site formation issues and taphonomic processes which may also affect remains (for instance, the friability of the Tel Miqne-Ekron remains) also need to be addressed.

The research suggests we need to know more about the inter- and intra-site movement of organic raw materials, such as agricultural by-products. Most information about the movement of raw materials deals with inorganic remains, such as lithics. Such materials played a major role in ancient everyday life. Could there have been an exchange of materials such as olive pressing wastes, which has the potential to be a fuel source for various industries (pottery, glass, etc.)? The ethnographic research shows that it is a prized fuel for such industries. More research needs to be done on the uses of bio-wastes, and their role in the ancient economy.

Because of the nature of olive remains recovered from archaeological sites, unless the correct circumstances occur, it is quite difficult to identify the relationship of the olive remains to olive oil processing. As I mentioned above, olive pressing remains are likely to be moved or destroyed. Only in unique cases are they preserved (charred or waterlogged), and especially at a processing site as in the case of the Kfar Samir remains.

Finally, there are the questions of domestic versus industrial processing methods, and the evolution of olive processing methods. I hypothesized that high volume processing for commercial purposes undoubtedly caused the evolution of processing methodology, however, older techniques were probably not completely replaced by newer technologies. There would be an overlapping of methods as new techniques evolved and were introduced (Frankel, *pers. comm.*; Kislev, *pers. comm.*). This was directly observed, as both traditional and modern mills are in operation in the Near East in the present.

The techniques used by families today to produce a small amount of oil are similar to traditional methods used in antiquity. Here too we have older methods in use at the same time. There is an overlap of methods, from the most ancient and basic, to the modern. This overlapping of processing methods can further cloud the issue when looking at archaeological remains. Do the remains represent olives pressing using the most "modern" means for commercial purposes, or do they represent remains from a single household pressing for daily food? As numerous techniques may be found at any one time at any one place, determining which method the remains actually represent may be difficult. It may be possible to determine which techniques were used at a site based on the olive remains and processing features. If separate sets of olive remains recovered from the same level of a site display fracture patterns of two different processing methods, one could predict that both of those processing methods were in use during the period represented by that level. Discovery of different styles of processing features might suggest the same thing.

On the topic of domestic versus commercial production, what we might associate as "industrial" production; where the olives are grown, brought to the press, pressed, and the oil sold by a large corporation, may be difficult to discern. In many places there is no true "industrial" or "commercial" enterprise. In modern Jordan, families will pick their own olives and have them pressed. The press owner gets a share of the oil, which he then sells. Is this really commercial? Some families will keep all their oil, some will sell all of it. This also may change from year to year, depending on olive yields and other factors. In many areas, olive oil production is dependent on small scale family farming and production, making it difficult to determine true commercial production.

Phytolith remains are a potential aid in determining the presence of olive pressing remains. Tyree (1999) found olive and grape phytoliths from modern and ancient wine and olive oil sediments. Phytolith analysis could be used to determine the function of features: determining if a press was used for olive or grape pressing, or both. However, since the solid pressing wastes are commonly used as a fuel, tests should be performed to see what happens to olive phytoliths when burned or charred. For instance, does the resulting ash contain olive phytoliths? The ability to identify ash deposits and layers as burnt pressing wastes would help identify pressing activities or use of pressing wastes at a site. Phytolith analyses are becoming more common in the Near East (Rosen, 1999), and has great potential in research similar to that presented here.

7.3 Conclusions

It is possible to determine an olive oil processing method based on the olive remains recovered from a site. Different processing methods fracture olive stones in distinct patterns. These patterns can be linked to specific methods and processing features. I have also explored the post-processing uses of olive pressing wastes and presented valuable information on the uses of olive pressing wastes. I believe the potential exists for using the same methodologies applied in this research on other botanical remains. I have also exposed potential problems which should be considered when doing such research, and have raised questions concerning interpretation of remains from archaeological sites. This research contributes greatly to the field of paleoethnobotany in the Near East and elsewhere.

BIBLIOGRAPHY

AJA   =   *American Journal of Archaeology*
BA/NEA =   *Biblical Archaeologist (name changed to Near Eastern Archaeologist in 1998)*
BASOR   =   *Bulletin of the American Schools of Oriental Research*
JAS   =   *Journal of Archaeological Science*
OXJ   =   *Oxford Journal of Archaeology*

Adan-Bayewitz, David
1993   *Common Pottery In Roman Galilee*, Bar-Ilan University Press, Jerusalem.

Ahituv, Shmuel
1996   Observations on Olive Oil in Ancient Egypt, In: Eitam and Heltzer (eds.) *Olive Oil in Antiquity: Israel and Neighbouring Countries from the Neolithic to the Early Arab Period*, History of the Ancient Near East/Studies – Vol. VII, Sargon, Padova, pp. 41-43.

Alexiades, Miguel N.
1996   Collecting Ethnobotanical Data: An Introduction to Basic Concepts and Techniques, In: Alexiades (ed.) *Selected Guidelines for Ethnobotanical Research: A Field Manual*, New York Botanical Garden, New York, pp. 53-94.

Al-Omari, Faisel and Jaber Al-Azraie
1995   *Project - TCP/JOR/4452 (T), Training in Management of Forest and Range Lands, Part II: Management Of Forests And Range Lands Of Jerash Agricultural District 1996-2005*, Jordanian Ministry of Agriculture and Forestry, Amman.

Al-Rub, Ala'a Izzat Farid Abu
1992   A Comparative Study of the Chemical & Physical Properties of Samples of Nabali - Virgin Olive and Olive Kernel Oils, MA thesis, Jordan University.

Amirante, P. and F. Pipitone
2002   Re-use of the by-products of olive growing and olive oil production, *OLIVÆ* 93:27-32.

Amiry, Suad and Vera Tamari
1989   *The Palestinian Village Home*, British Museum, London.

Amouretti, Marie-Claire
1986   *Le pain et l'huile dans la Gréce antique*, Les Belles Lettres, Paris.

Amouretti, Marie-Claire and Georges Comet
1992   *Le livre de l'Olivier*, Édisud, Aix-en-Provence.

Anderson, Patricia (ed.)
1999   *Prehistory of Agriculture: New Experimental and Ethnographic Approaches*, Institute of Archaeology Monograph 40, UCLA Institute of Archaeology Press, Los Angeles.

Anderson, S. and F. Ertug-Yaras
1998   Fuel, fodder and faeces: an ethnographic and botanical study of dung fuel use in central Anatolia, *Environmental Archaeology: The Journal of Human Paleoecology* 1:99-109.

Anderson-Stojanovic´, Virginia R.
1997   *Dye Works or Olive Press: A Reconsideration of Installations in the Rachi Settlement at Isthmia*, Paper presented at the Archaeological Institute of American's Annual Meeting, Chicago.

Artzy, Michal
1996   On the Storage of Olive Oil in Antiquity, In: Eitam and Heltzer (eds.) *Olive Oil in Antiquity: Israel and Neighbouring Countries from the Neolithic to the Early Arab Period*, History of the Ancient Near East/Studies – Vol. VII, Sargon, Padova, pp. 45-48.

Australian Olive Grower
1998   Olive Power!, *Australian Olive Grower* 8:22.

Australian Olive Grower
1999   El Tejar Attacks Waste Problems, *Australian Olive Grower* 11: 4-5.

Australian Olive Grower
2000   Olive waste to fuel Turkish power station, *Australian Olive Grower* 19:14.

Avitsur, Shmuel
1994   Olive Oil Production in the Land of Israel: Traditional to Industrial, In: Ayalon (ed.), *History and Technology of Olive Oil in the Holy Land*, Oléarius, Arlington, pp. 91-157.

Ayalon, Etan
1994a   Reconstucting a Traditional Olive Oil Plant at the Eretz Israel Museum, Tel Aviv, In: Ayalon (ed.), *History and Technology of Olive Oil in the Holy Land*, Oléarius, Arlington, pp. 159-188.

Ayalon, Etan (ed.)
1994b   *History and Technology of Olive Oil in the Holy Land*, Oléarius, Arlington.

Ayoub, Salam
2001   The Green Gold of Jordan, *Ajloun Food Processing Company Llc website* (www.tableoil.com)

Bar-Yosef, Ofer and Richard H. Meadow
1995   The Origins of Agriculture in the Near East, In: Price and Gebaur (eds.) *Last Hunters-First Farmers: New Perspectives on the Prehistoric Transition to Agriculture,* School of American Research Press, Santa Fe, pp. 39-94.

Bass, George
1987   Oldest Known Shipwreck Reveals Splendors of the Bronze Age, *National Geographic* 172(6):693-733.

Bass, George
1991   Evidence of Trade from Bronze Age Shipwrecks,

In: N.H. Gale (ed.) *Bronze Age Trade in the Mediterranean*, Jonesered, P. Åström, pp. 69-82.

Batsell-Fuller, Neathery
1986 Analysis of the Ethnoarchaeological Studies, In: Fuller, Michael (ed.), *Abila Reports: 1980-1984*, St. Louis Community College, St. Louis, pp. 305-323.

Baussan, Olivier and Jacques Chibois
2000 *Olive Oil: A Gourmet Guide*, Flammarion, Paris.

Bernard, H. Russell
1994 *Research Methods in Anthropology: Qualitative and Quantitative Approaches* (2nd Ed.), Sage Publications, Thousand Oaks.

Besnard, Guillaume and André Berville
2000 Multiple origins for Mediterranean olive (*Olea europaea* L. ssp. *europaea*) based upon mitochondrial DNA polymophisms, *Life Sciences* 323:173-181.

Besnard, Guillaume, Ph. Baradat, D. Chevalier, A. Tagmount and André Berville
2001 Genetic differentiation in the olive complex (Olea europaea) revealed by RAPDs and RFLPs in the rRNA genes, *Genetic Resources and Crop Evolution* 48:1-18.

Besnard, Guillaume, B. Khadari, P. Villemur and André Berville
2000 Cytoplasmic male sterility in the olive (*Olea europaea* L.), *Theoretical and Applied Genetics* 100:1018-1024.

Besnard, Guillaume, A. Moukhli, H. Sommerlatte, H. Hosseinpour, M. Tersac, P. Villemur, F. Dosba and André Berville
1998 Origins and Domestication of Mediterranean Olive Determined through RAPD Marker Analysis, In Damania, Valkoun, Willcox and Qualset (eds.) *The Origins of Agriculture and Crop Domestication: The Harlan Symposium*, ICARDA, Aleppo, pp.224-232.

Blitzer, Harriot
1993 Olive Cultivation and Oil Production in Minoan Crete, In: Amouretti and Brun (eds.) *Oil and Wine Production in the Mediterranean Area,* Bulletin De Correspondance Hellénique Supplément XXVI, De Boccard, Paris, pp. 163-175.

Boardman, J.
1977 The olive in the Mediterranean: its culture and use, In: Hutchinson *et al* (eds.) *The Early History of Agriculture*, Oxford University Press, Oxford, pp. 187-196.

Borowski, Oded
1987 *Agriculture in Iron Age Israel*, Eisenbrauns, Winona Lake.

Bothwell, Don and Patricia Bothwell
1998 *Food in Antiquity: a survey of the diet of early peoples, expanded edition*, Johns Hopkins Press, Baltimore.

Bottema, Sytze
1984 The composition of modern charred seed assemblages, In: Van Zeist and Casparie (eds.), *Plants and Ancient Man: Studies in Palaeoethnobotany*, Balkema, Rotterdam, pp. 207-212.

Bottema, Sytze and Henk Woldring
1995 The Environment of Classical Sagalassos: A Palynological Investigation, In: Waelkens and Poblome (eds.), *Sagalassos III: Report on the Fourth Excavation Campaign of 1993*, Acta Archaeologica Lovaniensia Monographiae 7, Leuven University Press, Leuven, pp. 327-340.

Brun, Jean-Pierre
2000 The Production of Perfumes in Antiquity: The Cases of Delos and Paestum, *AJA* 104:277-308.

Bunimovitz, Shlomo
1996 Minoan-Mycenaean Olive Oil Production and Trade – A Review of Current Research, In: Eitam and Heltzer (eds.) *Olive Oil in Antiquity: Israel and Neighbouring Countries from the Neolithic to the Early Arab Period*, History of the Ancient Near East/Studies – Vol. VII, Sargon, Padova, pp. 49-53.

Burgess, Andrew
1999 Waste In Our Olive Industry, *Australian Olive Grower* 11: 6-7.

Buxo, R.
1996 Evidence for vines and ancient cultivation from an urban area, Lattes (Hérault), southern France, *Antiquity* 70:393-407.

Cato, Marcus Porcius and Marcus Terentus Varro
De Re Rustica, Translation by H. B. Ash and W. D. Hooper, Loeb Classical Library, Harvard University Press, Cambridge (revised 1935, reprinted 1967).

Chabour, Mustapha
2004 Olive oil extraction methods in Algeria: changes and surviving traditions, *OLIVÆ* 99:50-55.

Chandler, Cap
2000 Cleaning up olive cast-offs, *New Times, The Charles Stuart University Magazine* Spring 2000, Vol. 10(2).

Columella, Lucius Junius Moderatus
De Re Rustica: De Arboribus, Translated by H. B. Ash, E. S. Forester and E. Heffner, Loeb Classical Library, Harvard University Press, Cambridge .

Cotton, C.M.
1996 *Ethnobotany: Principles and Applications*, Wiley and Sons, New York.

Cotton, M.A.
1979 The Late Republican Villa at Posto, Francolise. *Papers of the British School at Rome, Supplemental Volume.* The British School at Rome, London.

Davis, Lindsey
1996 *A Dying Light in Corduba*, Century Books, London.

Di Giovacchino, L.
2005 Characteristics of olive oil mill wastewater and prospects for its rational re-use, *OLIVÆ* 104:55-63.

Di Giovacchino, L., C. Basti, N Costantini, G Surricchio, M Ferrante and D. Lombardi
2002 Effects of spreading olive vegetable water on soil cultivated with maize and grapevine, *OLIVÆ* 91:37-43.

Dolamore, Anne
1994 *The Essential Olive Oil Companion*, Interlink Books, Brooklyn.

Donnan, Christopher B. and C. William Clewlow, Jr. (eds.)
1974 *Ethnoarchaeology*, Monograph IV, Archaeological Survey, Institute of Archaeology, University of California, Los Angeles.

Doumani, Beshara
1995 *Rediscovering Palestine: Merchants and Peasants in Jabal Nablus, 1700-1900*, University of California Press, Berkeley.

Eitam, David
1993 «Between The [Olive] Rows, Oil Will Be Produced, Presses Will Be Trod ...» (Job 24, 11), In: Amouretti and Brun (eds.) *Oil and Wine Production in the Mediterranean Area*, Bulletin De Correspondance Hellénique Supplément XXVI, De Boccard, Paris, pp. 65-90.

Eitam, David
1996 The Olive Oil Industry at Tel Miqne-Ekron in the Late Iron Age, In: Eitam and Heltzer (eds.) *Olive Oil in Antiquity: Israel and Neighbouring Countries from the Neolithic to the Early Arab Period*, History of the Ancient Near East/Studies – Vol. VII, Sargon, Padova, pp. 167-196.

Eitam, David
2000 Olive Culture in Ancient Israel, *Gems in Israel* (www.GemsinIsrael.com), Oct.-Nov. 2000.

Eitam, David and Michael Heltzer
1996 *Olive Oil in Antiquity: Israel and Neighbouring Countries from the Neolithic to the Early Arab Period*, History of the Ancient Near East/Studies – Vol. VII, Sargon, Padova.

Epstein, Claire
1993 Oil Production in the Golan Heights During the Chalcolithic Period, *Tel Aviv* 20:133-146.

Esse, Douglas
1991 *Subsistence, Trade, and Social Change in Early Bronze Age Palestine*, Studies in Ancient Oriental Civilization No. 50, Oriental Institute of the University of Chicago, Chicago.

Feinbrum-Dothan, Naomi
1978 *Flora Palaestina, Part Three: Text*, Israel Academy of Sciences and Humanities, Jerusalem.

Finkelstein, Israel
1999 State Formation in Israel and Judah: A Contrast in Context, A Contrast in Trajectory, *NEA* 62(1):35-52.

Fischer, Alysia and W. Patrick McCray
1999 Glass Production Activities as Practised at Sepphoris, Israel (37 BC – AD 1516), *JAS* 26(8): 893-905.

Forbes, Hamish A. and Lin Foxhall
1978 "The Queen of All Trees": Preliminary Notes on the Archaeology of the Olive, *Expedition* 21(1):37-47.

Forbes, R. J.
1965 *Studies in Ancient Technology*, 2nd Edition, E. J. Brill, Leiden.

Ford, Richard and Naomi Miller
1978 Palaeoethnobotany I, In: J.H. Humphrey (ed.) *Excavations at Carthage 1976 conducted by the University of Michigan, vol. IV*, Kelsey Museum, University of Michigan, Ann Arbor, pp. 181-189.

Foxhall, Lin
1995 Bronze to Iron: Agricultural Systems and Political Structures in Late Bronze Age and Early Iron Age Greece, *The Annual of the British School at Athens* 90: 239-250.

Foxhall, Lin
1998 Snapping up the Unconsidered Trifles: the Use of Agricultural Residues in Ancient Greek and Roman Farming, *Environmental Archaeology* 1:35-40.

Frankel, Jehoshua
1996 Oil and Olives in the Land of Israel (Palestine) in the Early Muslim Period (634-1099), In: Eitam and Heltzer (eds.) *Olive Oil in Antiquity: Israel and Neighbouring Countries from the Neolithic to the Early Arab Period*, History of the Ancient Near East/ Studies – Vol. VII, Sargon, Padova, pp. 55-62.

Frankel, Rafael
1987 Oil Presses in Western Galilee and the Judaea – a Comparison, In: Heltzer and Eitam (eds.), *Olive Oil in Antiquity: Israel and Neighbouring Countries from the Neolith to the Early Arab period*, Conference 1987, Haifa, pp. 63-80.

Frankel, Rafael
1994 Ancient Oil Mills and Presses in the Land of Israel, in: Ayalon (ed.), *History and Technology of Olive Oil in the Holy Land*, Oléarius, Arlington, pp. 19-89.

Frankel, Rafael
1996 Oil Presses in Western Galilee and Judaea: A Comparison, In: Eitam and Heltzer (eds.) *Olive Oil in Antiquity: Israel and Neighbouring Countries from the Neolithic to the Early Arab Period*, History of the Ancient Near East/Studies – Vol. VII, Sargon, Padova, pp. 197-218.

Frankel, Rafael
1997 Olives, In: Meyers (ed. in chief) *The Oxford Encyclopedia of Archaeology in the Near East*, Oxford University Press, New York, pp. 179-184.

Frankel, Rafael
1999 *Wine and Oil Production in Antiquity in Israel and Other Mediterranean Countries*, JSOT/ASOR Monograph Series 10, Sheffield Academic Press, Sheffield.

Fuller, Michael
1986 An Ethnoarchaeological Study of Harvesting Techniques, Harta, Jordan, In: Fuller, Michael (ed.), *Abila Reports: 1980-1984*, St. Louis Community College, St. Louis, pp. 305-323.

Gal, Zvi and Rafael Frankel
1993 An Olive Oil Press Complex at *Hurbat Ros Zayit (Ras ez-Zetun)* in Lower Galilee, *Zeitschrift des Deutschen Palästina-Vereins* 109(2):128-140.

Galili, Ehud and Jacob Sharvit
1994-5 Evidence of Olive Oil Production from the Submerged Site at Kfar Samir, Israel, *Mitekufat Haeven, Journal of the Israel Prehistoric Society* 26:122-133.

Galili, Ehud, Daniel J. Stanley, Jacob Sharvit and Mina Weinstein-Evron
1997 Evidence for Earliest Olive-Oil Production in Submerged Settlements off the Carmel Coast, Israel, *JAS* 24:1141-1150

Galili, Ehud, Mina Weinstein-Evron and Daniel Zohary
1989 Appearance of Olives in Submerged Neolithic Sites Along the Carmel Coast, *Mitekufat Haeven, Journal of the Israel Prehistoric Society* 22:95-97.

Geraty, Larry T. and Oystein S. LaBianca
1985 The Local Environment and Human Food-Procuring Strategies in Jordan: The Case of Tell Hesban and its Surrounding Region, In: Hadidi (ed.) *Studies in the History and Archaeology of Jordan II*, Department of Antiquities of Jordan, London, pp. 323-330.

Gitin, Seymour
1989 Tel Miqne-Ekron: A Type-Site for the Inner Coastal Plain in the Iron Age II Period, In: Seymour Gitin and William Dever (eds.) *Recent Excavations in Israel: Studies in Iron Age Archaeology*, Annual of the American Schools of Oriental Research Vol. 49 (Eric Meyers and William Dever, eds.), Eisenbrauns, Winona Lake, pp. 23-58.

Gitin, Seymour
1996 Tel Miqne-Ekron in the 7th Century B.C. City Plan Development and the Oil Industry, In: Eitam and Heltzer (eds.) *Olive Oil in Antiquity: Israel and Neighbouring Countries from the Neolithic to the Early Arab Period*, History of the Ancient Near East/ Studies – Vol. VII, Sargon, Padova, pp. 219-242.

Goor, A.
1966 The Place of the Olive in the Holy Land and its History Through the Ages, *Economic Botany* 20:223-243.

Gould, Richard A. (ed.)
1978 *Explorations in Ethnoarchaeology*, University of New Mexico Press, Albuquerque.

Greene, Joseph A.
1996 The Beginnings of Grape Cultivation and Wine Production in Phoenician/Punic North Africa, In: McGovern *et al* (eds.) *The Origins and Ancient History of Wine*, Gordon and Breach, Canada, pp. 311-322.

Gubrium, Jaber F. and James A. Holstein
1997 *The New Language of Qualitative Method*, Oxford University Press, New York.

Hadjipanayiotou, M.
1994 Laboratory evaluation of ensiled olive cake, tomato pulp and poultry litter, *Livestock Research for Rural Development* Vol. 6(2), on-line edition.

Hadjipanayiotou, M.
1999 The Ensiling Technique: A Simple, Safe, and Low-cost On-farm Tool for Storing and Feeding Crude Olive Cake, *OLIVÆ* 76:31-34.

Hadjisavvas, Sophocles
1992 *Olive Oil Processing in Cyprus: From the Bronze Age to the Byzantine Period*, Studies in Mediterranean Archaeology Vol. XCIX, Paul Åströms Förlag, Göteborg.

Haldane, Cheryl
1990 Shipwrecked Plant Remains, *BA* 53(1):55-60.

Haldane, Cheryl
1993 Direct evidence for organic cargoes in the Late Bronze Age, *World Archaeology* 24 (3):348-60.

Hammersley, Martyn and Paul Atkinson
1983 *Ethnography: Principles in Practice*, Tavistock Publications, New York.

Heltzer, Michael
1993 Olive Oil and Wine Production in Phoenicia and in the Mediterranean Trade, In: Amouretti and Brun (eds.) *Oil and Wine Production in the Mediterranean Area*, Bulletin De Correspondance Hellénique Supplément XXVI, De Boccard, Paris, pp. 49-54.

Heltzer, Michael
1996 Olive Growing and Olive Oil in Ugarit, In: Eitam and Heltzer (eds.) *Olive Oil in Antiquity: Israel and Neighbouring Countries from the Neolithic to the Early Arab Period*, History of the Ancient Near East/Studies – Vol. VII, Sargon, Padova, pp. 77-89.

Heltzer, Michael and David Eitam
1996 Introduction, In: Eitam and Heltzer (eds.) *Olive Oil in Antiquity: Israel and Neighbouring Countries from the Neolithic to the Early Arab Period*, History of the Ancient Near East/Studies – Vol. VII, Sargon, Padova, pp. 1-2.

Herr, Larry
1997 The Iron Age II Period: Emerging Nations, *BA* 60(3):114-183.

Hibler, Michelle
2003 Improving Morocco's olive industry, from harvest to waste disposal, *Science in Africa – Africa's First On-Line Science Magazine*, July-August.

Hillman, Gordon
1973 Crop husbandry and food production: modern models for the interpretation of plant remains, *Anatolian Studies* 23:241-244.

Hillman, Gordon
1984 Interpretation of archaeological plant remains: The application of ethnographic models from Turkey, in: W. Van Zeist and W.A. Casparie (eds.), *Plants and Ancient Man: Studies in Palaeoethnobotany*, Balkema, Rotterdam, pp. 1-42.

Hillman, Gordon and M.S. Davies
1992 Domestication rate in wild wheats and barley under primitive cultivation: Preliminary results and archaeological implications of field measurements of selection coefficient. In *Préhistoire de l'Agriculture: Nouvelles Approaches Experimentales at Ethnographiques*, P.C. Anderson (ed.) Monographie du Centre de Recherches Archeologiques, no. 6. Paris: Éditions du CNRS, pp. 113-58.

Hoffman, E.S,
1981 Paleoethnobotany II: Plant remains from Vandel and Byzantine deposits in three cisterns, In: J.H.

Humphrey (ed.) *Excavations at Carthage 1977 Conducted by the University of Michigan, Volume VI*, Kelsey Museum, University of Michigan, Ann Arbor, pp. 259-268.

Hole, Frank
1979 Rediscovering the Past in the Present: Ethnoarchaeology in Luristan, Iran, In: Kramer, Carol (ed.), *Ethnoarchaeology: Implications of Ethnography for Archaeology*, Columbia University Press, New York, pp. 192-218.

Hora, Bayard (ed.)
1980 *The Oxford Encyclopedia of Trees of the World*, Cresent Books, New York.

Howard, Rachel
2001 Doing as Cretans Do, *National Geographic Traveler* 18(3):116-120.

International Olive Oil Council (I.O.O.C.)
n.d. *The Olive Tree, The Oil, The Olive*, I.O.O.C., Madrid.

James, T.G.H.
1996 The Earliest History of Wine and Its Importance in Ancient Egypt, In: McGovern *et al* (eds.) *The Origins and Ancient History of Wine*, Gordon and Breach, Canada, pp. 197-213.

Johns, Timothy
1994 Ambivalence to the Palatability Factors in Wild Food Plants, In: Etkins (ed.) *Eating on the Wild Side: The Pharmacologic, Ecologic, and Social Implications of Using Noncultigens*, University of Arizona Press, Tucson, pp. 46-61.

Kaddour, S., M. Bouhache and D. Bouya
2005 Viability of crenate broomrape seeds (*O. crenata* Forsk.) when buried in a soil/olive pomace mixture: changes according to depth and duration of burial, *OLIVÆ* 103:42-47.

Kelm, George and Amihai Mazar
1995 *Timnah: A Biblical City in the Sorek Valley*, Eisenbrauns, Winona Lake.

Kelm, George and Amihai Mazar
1996 7th Century B.C. Oil Presses at Tel Batash, Biblical Timnah, In: Eitam and Heltzer (eds.) *Olive Oil in Antiquity: Israel and Neighbouring Countries from the Neolithic to the Early Arab Period*, History of the Ancient Near East/Studies – Vol. VII, Sargon, Padova, pp. 243-248.

Khammash, Ammar
1995 *Notes On Village Architecture In Jordan*, Arabesque Int., Amman.

Kiritsakis, Apostolos
1990 *Olive Oil*, American Oil Chemists Society, Champaign.

Kislev, Mordechai E.
1994-5 Wild Olive Stones at Submerged Chalcolithic Kfar Samir, Haifa, Israel, *Mitekufat_Haeven, Journal of the Israel Prehistoric Society* 26:134-145.

Kislev, Mordechai E.
1996 The Domestication of the Olive Tree, In: Eitam and Heltzer (eds.) *Olive Oil in Antiquity: Israel and*

Neighbouring Countries from the Neolithic to the Early Arab Period*, History of the Ancient Near East/Studies – Vol. VII, Sargon, Padova, pp. 3-6.

Klein, Maggie Blyth
1994 *The Feast of the Olive: cooking with olives and olive oil*, Chronicle Books, San Francisco.

Knickerbocker, Peggy
1997 *Olive Oil: From Tree to Table*, Chronicle Books, San Francisco.

Kramer, Carol (ed.)
1979 *Ethnoarchaeology: Implications of Ethnography for Archaeology*, Columbia University Press, New York.

Kumar, Atul, Pallav Purohit, Santosh Rana and Tara Chandra Kandpal
2001 An approach to the estimation of the value of agricultural residues used as biofuels, *Biomass and Bioenergy* 22(3):195-203.

LaBianca, Oystein S.
1984 Objectives, Procedures and Findings of the Ethnoarchaeological Research in the Vicinity of Hesban in Jordan, *Annual of the Department of Antiquities of Jordan* 28:269-282.

Lafi, Walid K.
2001 Production of activated charcoal from acorns and olive seeds, *Biomass and Bioenergy* 20(1):57-62.

Lazreg, Nejib Ben
2001 Addendum: A further note on the fuels used in this region, In: Stirling, Mattingly and Lazreg, Leptiminus (Lamta) Report No. 2, The East Baths, Cemeteries, Kilns, Venus Mosaic, Site Museum, and Other Studies, *Journal of Roman Archaeology* Supplement 41, pp. 436.

Lesko, Leonard H.
1996 Egyptian Wine Production During the New Kingdom, In: McGovern *et al* (eds.) *The Origins and Ancient History of Wine*, Gordon and Breach, Canada, pp. 215-230.

Leonard, Albert Jr.
1996 "Canaanite Jars" and the Late Bronze Age Aegeo-Levantine Wine Trade, In: McGovern *et al* (eds.) *The Origins and Ancient History of Wine*, Gordon and Breach, Canada, pp. 233-254.

Levy, Thomas, David Alon, Patricia Smith, Yuval Yekutieli, Yorke Rowan, Paul Goldberg, Naomi Porat, Edwin van den Brink, Alan Witten, Jonathan Golden, Caroline Grigson, Eric Kansa, Lelsie Dawson, Augustin Holl, John Moreno, and Morag Kersel
1997 Egyptian-Canaanite Interaction at Nahal Tillah, Israel (ca. 4500-3000 B.C.E.): An Interim Report on the 1994-1995 Excavations, *BASOR* 307:1-51.

Liddell, Henry George and Robert Scott
1940 *A Greek-English Lexicon*, 9th Edition (1968 reprinting), Oxford at the Clarenden Press, Oxford.

Lines, Lee
1995 *Bronze Age Orchard Cultivation and Urbanization in the Jordan River Valley*, unpublished dissertation, Arizona State University.

Liphschitz, Nili
1996 Olives in Ancient Israel in View of Dendroarchaeological Investigations, In: Eitam and Heltzer (eds.) *Olive Oil in Antiquity: Israel and Neighbouring Countries from the Neolithic to the Early Arab Period*, History of the Ancient Near East/Studies – Vol. VII, Sargon, Padova, pp. 7-13.

Liphschitz, Nili, Ram Gophna, Moshe Hartman and Gideon Biger
1991 The Beginning of Olive (*Olea europaea*) Cultivation in the Old World: A Reassessment, *JAS* 18:441-453.

Litchfield, Carter
1984 Extracting Olive Oil with a Rotary Hand Quern, *Transactions of the Fifth Symposium: France, 1982, April 5-10*, International Molinological Society, Saint-Maurice, pp. 341-342.

London, Gloria
2000 Ethnoarchaeology and Interpretations of the Past, *NEA* 63(1):2-8.

Loubani, Mansour and Jaber Azraie
1994 *Project - TCP/JOR/4452 (T), Training in Management of Forest and Range Lands, Part II: Management Of Forests And Range Lands Of Irbid Agricultural District 1996-2005*, Jordanian Ministry of Agriculture and Forestry, Amman.

Mangafa, M. and K. Kotsakis
1996 A new method for the identification of wild and cultivated charred grape seeds, *JAS* 23:409-418.

Martin, Gary J.
1995 *Ethnobotany: A Methods Manual*, Chapman & Hall, New York.

Martin, Susan Taylor
2001 Symbol of peace hit hard in time of war: Palestinian olive growers in the West Bank harvest their crop but find it nearly impossible to sell it, *St. Petersburg Times Online Floridian*, November 20, 2001.

Mason, James R.B. and Khairieh ᶜAmr
1993 Nabataean bowl production: interim summary of developments, *Levant* XXV:207.

Mason, James R.B. and Khairieh ᶜAmr
1995 An Investigation into the Firing of Nabataean Pottery, *Studies in the History and Archaeology of Jordan (SHAJ)*, Vol. 5, pp. 629-636.

Matthews, Wendy, Christine Hastorf and Begumsen Ergenekon
2000 Ethnoarchaeology: Studies in Local Villages Aimed at Understanding Aspects of the Neolithic Site, In: Hodder (ed.) *Towards reflexive method in archaeology: the example at Çatalhöyük*, British Institute of Archaeology at Ankara Monograph No. 28, McDonald Institute for Archaeological Research, Cambridge, pp. 177-188.

Matson, Frederick R.
1966 Power and Fuel Resources in the Ancient Near East, *Advancement of Science* 23(109):146-153.

Matson, Frederick R.
1972 Ceramic Studies, In: McDonald and Rapp (eds.) *The Minnesota Messenia Expedition:*

Reconstructing a Bronze Age Regional Environment, University of Minnesota Press, Minneapolis, pp. 200-224.

Mattingly, David
1988a Megalithic Madness and Measurement. Or How Many Olives Could an Olive Press Press? *OJA* 7(2):177-195.

Mattingly, David
1988b Oil for export? A comparision of Libyan, Spanish and Tunisian olive oil production in the Roman empire, *Journal of Roman Archaeology* 1:33-56.

Mattingly, David
1996 First Fruit? The olive in the Roman world, In: Shipley and Salmon (eds.) *Human Landscapes In Classical Antiquity*, Routledge, New York, pp. 213-253.

Mazar, Amihai
1990 *Archaeology of the Land of the Bible 10,000-586 BCE*, Doubleday, New York.

McGovern, Patrick E., Stuart J. Fleming and Solomon H. Katz (eds.)
1996 *The Origins and Ancient History of Wine*, Gordon and Breach, Canada.

Melena, J. L.
1983 Olive Oil and Other Sorts of Oil in the Mycenaean Tablets, *Minos* ns XVIII:89-123.

Melkawi, Ansam Ousama
1995 Pottery Kilns in Jordan: an Ethnoarchaeological Study. Unpublished Masters Thesis, Yarmouk University, Irbid (Jordan).

Miller, Naomi
1984 The use of dung as fuel: an ethnographic example and an archaeological application, *Paléorient* 10:71-79.

Miller, Naomi
1988 Ratios in Paleoethnobotanical Analysis, In: Hastorf and Popper (eds.) *Current Paleoethnobotany*, University of Chicago Press, Chicago, pp. 72-85.

Miller, Naomi
1991 The Near East, In: Van Zeist, Wasylikowa & Behre (eds.) *Progress in Old World Palaeoethnobotany*, Balkema, Rotterdam, pp. 133-160.

Miller, Naomi
1995 Archaeobotany: Macroremains, *AJA* 99(1):91-93.

Miller, Naomi and Tristine L. Smart
1984 Intentional Burning of Dung as Fuel: A Mechanism for the Incorporation of Charred Seeds into the Archaeological Record, *Journal of Ethnobiology* 4(1):15-28.

Miroschedji, Pierre de
1999 Yarmouth: The Dawn of City-States in Southern Canaan, *NEA* 62(1):2-19.

Moore, Andrew M., Gordon C. Hillman and Anthony J. Legge
2000 *Village on the Euphrates: from foraging to farming at Abu Hureyra*, Oxford, New York.

Murray, Mary Anne
1999 Wine Production and Consumption in Pharaonic Egypt, in: Van der Veen (ed.) *The Exploitation*

of Plant Resources in Ancient Africa, Kluwer Academic/Plenum Publishers, New York, pp. 149-169.

Murray, Mary Anne
2000 Viticulture and wine production, In: Nicholson and Shaw (eds.) *Ancient Egyptian Materials and Technology,* Cambridge University Press, Cambridge, pp 577-608.

Musselman, Lytton John and Abdel Baset Al-Mouslem
2001 *Triticum durum* in Northern Syria - Parched Corn (*Frikeh*) of the Bible?, *Economic Botany* 55(2):187-189.

Neef, Reinder
1990 Introduction, development and environmental implications of olive culture: The evidence from Jordan, in: Bottema, Entjes-Nieborg and Van Zeist (eds.), *Man's Role in the Shaping of the Eastern Mediterranean Landscape,* Balkema, Rotterdam, pp. 295-306.

Ochsenschalger, Edward L.
1974 Modern Potters at Al-Hiba, With Some Reflections on the Excavated Early Dynastic Pottery, In: Donnan, Christopher B. and C. William Clewlow, Jr. (eds.) *Ethnoarchaeology,* Monograph IV, Archaeological Survey, Institute of Archaeology, University of California, Los Angeles, pp. 149-157.

Okla, Fathi and Jaber Azraie
1994 *Project - TCP/JOR/4452 (T), Training in Management of Forest and Range Lands, Part II: Management Of Forests And Range Lands Of Bani Kenaneh Agricultural District 1996-2005,* Jordanian Ministry of Agriculture and Forestry, Amman.

Olive Oil Source, the
2001 http://www.oliveoilsource.com/olive_waste.htm, April 06, 2001.

Olives Australia Newletter
1997 Olive By-Product Uses – Waste Cake, *Olives Australia Newletter* 11: 1, 16.

Ollero, P., A. Serrera, R. Arjona and S. Alcantarilla
2002 The CO_2 gasification kinetics of olive residue, *Biomass and Bioenergy* 24(2):151-161.

Omari, Ghazi Bader and Jaber Azraie
1994 *Project - TCP/JOR/4452 (T), Training in Management of Forest and Range Lands, Part II: Management Of Forests And Range Lands Of Ajloun Agricultural District 1996-2005,* Jordanian Ministry of Agriculture and Forestry, Amman.

Palmer, Carol
1998a 'Followingthe Plough': the Agricultural Environment of Northern Jordan, *Levant* XXX:129-165.

Palmer, Carol
1998b The Role of Fodder in the Farming System:a Case Study from Northern Jordan, *Environmental Archaeology* 1:1-10.

Peacock, D. P. S.
1982 *Pottery in the Roman world: an ethnoarchaeological approach,* Longman, New York.

Pearsall, Deborah
1995 Domestication and Agriculture in the New World Tropics, In: Price and Gebaur (eds.) *Last Hunters-First Farmers: New Perspectives on the Prehistoric Transition to Agriculture,* School of American Research Press, Santa Fe, pp. 157-192.

Pilcer, Mitch
1996 A taste of heaven comes in the earthly form of freshly pressed olive oil, Fast Forward: Out There, *Jerusalem Post Magazine,* Nov. 15th, pp. 4.

Pliny
Natural History, Translation by H. Rackham, Loeb Classical Library, Harvard University Press, Cambridge. (first print 1945, reprint, 1960).

Rast, Walter
1988 *Preliminary Reports of ASOR-Sponsored Excavations 1982-85, BASOR Supplement No. 25,* ASOR, Baltimore.

Rast, Walter
1990 *Preliminary Reports of ASOR-Sponsored Excavations 1983-87, BASOR Supplement No. 26,* ASOR, Baltimore.

Rast, Walter
1991 *Preliminary Reports of ASOR-Sponsored Excavations 1982-89, BASOR Supplement No. 27,* ASOR, Baltimore.

Renfrew, Jane M.
1973 *Palaeoethnobotany: The prehistoric food plants of the Near East and Europe,* Columbia University Press, New York.

Ridgeway, Judy
1996 *The Olive Oil Companion: The Authoritative Connoisseur's Guide,* Knickerbocker Press, New York.

Rindos, David
1980 Symbiosis, Instability, and the Origins and Spread of Agriculture: A New Model. *Current Anthropology* 21:751-772.

Rindos, David
1984 *The Origins of Agriculture: an Evolutionary Perspective,* Academic Press, New York.

Rogers, Ford
1995 *Olives: Cooking with Olives and Their Oils,* Ten Speed Press, Berkeley.

Roldán, M.T. Carmona, J. Úbeda Iranzo and A. Briones Pérez
2000 Biotechnological Utilisation of the By-Products of Olive Oil Processing, *OLIVÆ* 83:32-36.

Romero, Luis Rallo
1998 Olive Farming in the Age of Science and Innovation, *OLIVÆ* 72: 42-51.

Rosen, Arlene Miller
1999 Phytolith analysis in Near Eastern archaeology, In: Pike and Gitin (eds.) *The Practical Impact of Science on Near Eastern and Aegean Archaeology,* Wiener Laboratory Monograph 3, Archetype, Athens, pp. 9-15.

Rosenblum, Mort
1996 *Olives: The Life and Lore of a Noble Fruit*, North Point Press, New York.

Runnels, Curtis and Julie Hansen
1986 The Olive in the Prehistoric Aegean: The Evidence for Domestication in the Early Bronze Age. *Oxford Journal of Archaeology* 5(3):299-308.

Rye, Owen S.
1981 *Pottery Technology: Principles and Reconstruction*, Manual on Archaeology No. 4, Taraxacum, Washington.

Salt of the Earth: Palestinian Christians in the Northern West Bank. Documentary Film (unfinished), elizabeth@saltfilm.net

Samuel, Delwen
1993 Ancient Egyptian Cereal Processing: Beyond the Artistic Record, *Cambridge Archaeological Journal* 3(2):276-283.

Sandy, D. Brent
1989 *The Production and Use of Vegetable Oils in Ptolemaic Egypt*, Bulletin of the American Society of Papyrologists Supplement No. 6, Scholars Press, Atlanta.

Sansoucy, René
1985 *Olive by-products for animal feed*, Food and Agriculture Organization (FAO) Animal Production and Health Paper 43, FAO of the United Nations, Rome.

Sarpaki, Anaya
1999 The Archaeobotanical Study of Tzambakas House, Rethymnon, Crete, In: Tzedakis and Martlew (eds.) *Minoans and Mycenaeans: Flavours of Their Time*, Greek Ministry of Culture, National Archaeology Museum, Athens, pp. 40-41.

Scarre, Christopher and Brian M. Fagan
1997 *Ancient Civilizations*, Longman, New York.

Serpico, Margaret and Raymond White
2000 Oil, fat and wax, In: Nicholson and Shaw (eds.) *Ancient Egyptian Materials and Technology*, Cambridge University Press, Cambridge, pp 390-429.

Sethom, H.
1964 Les artisans potiers de Moknine, *Revue Tunisienne de Sciences Sociales* 1:53-70.

Simmonds, N.W. (ed.)
1976 *Evolution of Crop Plants*, Longman, Inc., New York.

Simpson, B.B. and M.C. Ogorzaly
1986 *Economic Botany: Plants in Our World*, McGraw-Hill, New York.

Singer, Avraham
1996 The Traditional Cultivation of the Olive Tree, In: Eitam and Heltzer (eds.) *Olive Oil in Antiquity: Israel and Neighbouring Countries from the Neolithic to the Early Arab Period*, History of the Ancient Near East/Studies - Vol. VII, Sargon, Padova, pp. 29-39.

Smith, Wendy
1998 Fuel for Thought: Archaeobotanical Evidence for the Use of Alternatives to Wood Fuel in Late

Antique North Africa, *Journal of Mediterranean Archaeology* 11.2: 191-205.

Smith, Wendy
2001 A Environmental Sampling, In: Lazreg, Mattingly and Stirling (eds.), Leptiminus (Lamta) Report No. 2, The East Baths, Cemeteries, Kilns, Venus Mosaic, Site Museum, and Other Studies, *Journal of Roman Archaeology* Supplement 41, pp. 420-439.

Smith, Wendy
in press Alternatives to Wood Fires: Traditional Fuels from Vandal/Late Antique Leptiminus, Tunisia and Late Antique Kom el-Nana, Middle Egypt, In: van der Veen (ed.) *Plants and People in Africa: Recent Archaeobotanical Evidence*, Plenum, New York.

Snedecor, George and William Cochran
1989 *Statistical Methods, 8th Edition*, Iowa State University Press, Ames.

Spradley, James P.
1979 *The Ethnographic Interview*, Harcourt Brace Jovanovich, Inc., Orlando.

Stager, Larry E.
1983 The Finest Olive Oil in Samaria, *Journal of Semitic Studies*, 28(1): 241-245.

Stager, Larry E.
1985 The first fruits of civilization, In: Tubb (ed.) *Palestine in the Bronze and Iron Ages: Papers in Honour of Olga Tufnell*, Institute of Archaeology, London, pp. 172-188.

Stager, Larry E. and Samuel Wolff
1981 Production and Commerce in Temple Courtyards: An Olive Press in the Sacred Precinct at Tel Dan, *BASOR* 243:95-102.

Stahl, Ann B.
1989 Plant-food processing: implications for dietary quality, in: Harris and Hillman (eds.), *Foraging and Farming: The evolution of plant exploitation*, Unwin Hyman, London, pp. 171-194.

Stanislawski, Michael B.
1974 The Relationships of Ethnoarchaeology, Traditional, and Systems Archaeology, In: Donnan, Christopher B. and C. William Clewlow, Jr. (eds.), *Ethnoarchaeology*, Monograph IV, Archaeological Survey, Institute of Archaeology, University of California, Los Angeles, pp. 15-26.

Stern, E. Marianne
1999 Roman Glassblowing in a Cultural Context, *AJA* 103:441-484.

Stewart, R.
1984 Carbonized seeds, In: H.R. Hurst and S.P. Roskams (eds.) *Excavations at Carthage, The British Mission I.1. The Avenue du President Habib Bourguiba, Salmmbo: The Site and Finds Other than Pottery*, Department of Archaeology and Prehistory, University of Sheffield, Sheffield, pp. 257.

Stirling, Lea and Nejib Ben Lazreg
2001 A Roman kiln complex (Site 290): preliminary results of excavations 1995-98, In: Stirling, Mattingly and Lazreg, Leptiminus (Lamta) Report No. 2, The

East Baths, Cemeteries, Kilns, Venus Mosaic, Site Museum, and Other Studies, *Journal of Roman Archaeology* Supplement 41, pp. 220-235.

Stirling, Lea, Nejib Ben Lazreg and D. Stone
1996 Leptiminus Archaeological Project: Reports of the 1996 Season, unpublished report.

Tamburino, Vincenzo, Santo Marcello Zimbone and Paolo Quattrone
1999 Storage and Land Application of Olive-oil Wastewater, *OLIVÆ* 76:36-45.

Tannahill, Reay
1988 *Food in History*, Crown Publishers, Inc., New York.

Tekkök-Biçken, Billur
2000 Pottery Production in the Troad: Ancient and Modern Akköy, *NEA* 63(2):94-101.

Terrel, Jean-Frédéric
2000 Exploitation and Management of the Olive Tree During Prehistoric Times in Mediterranean France and Spain, *JAS* 27(2):127-133.

Toussaint-Samat, Maguelonne
1992 *History of Food*, English translation, Blackwell, Malden, Mass.

Tyree, E. Loeta
1999 Using Phytoliths to Identify Plant Remains from Archaeological Sites: A Phytolith Analysis of Modern Olive Oil and Wine Sediment, In Vaughan and Coulson (eds.) *Palaeodiet in the Aegean*, Wiener Laboratory Monograph 1, Oxbow Books, Oxford, pp. 29-36.

Tyree, E. Loeta and Evangelia Stefanoudaki
1996 The Olive Pit and Roman Oil Making, *BA* 59(3):171-178.

Tzedakis, Yannis and Holley Martlew (eds.)
1999 *Minoans and Mycenaeans: Flavours of Their Time*, Greek Ministry of Culture, National Archaeology Museum, Athens, pp. 37.

Varro, Marcus Terentius
Rerum Rusticarum, in: *Cato and Varro*, Translation by W.D. Hooper, Loeb Classical Library, Harvard University Press, Cambridge.

Van der Veen, M. and W. van Zeist
1982 Note complémentaire 2: analyses paléobotaniques, In: S. Lancel (ed.) *Byrsa II: Rapports préliminaires sur les fouilles 1977-1978: minéraux et vestiges puniques*, École Française de Rome, Rome, pp. 389.

Van Zeist, W.
1994 Botanical Remains, In: Hurst (ed.) *Excavations at Carthage The British Mission: Volume II, 1 The Circular Harbour, North Side: The Site and Finds other than Pottery*, Oxford Univ. Press, Oxford, pp. 325.

Van Zeist, W. and S. Bottema
1983 Palaeobotanical studies of Carthage, *Centre d'Études et Documentation Archéologique de la conservation de Carthage Bulletin* 5:18-22.

Vickery, Kenton F.
1936 Food in Early Greece. *Studies in the Social Sciences*, University of Illinois Press vol. 20, Urbana.

Vitruvius
De Architectura, Translation by Frank Granger, Loeb Classical Library, Harvard University Press, Cambridge.

Vitto, Fanny
1986 Potters and Pottery Manufacture in Roman Palestine, *Institute of Archaeology Bulletin* (University of London) 23:47-64.

Vogelsang-Eastwood, Gillian
2000 Textiles, In: Nicholson and Shaw (eds.) *Ancient Egyptian Materials and Technology*, Cambridge University Press, Cambridge, pp 268-298.

Warnock, Peter and Pendleton, Michael
1994 Appendix B: Amurca, In: Kanellopoulos, *The Great Temple of Amman: The Architecture*, American Center of Oriental Research, Amman, pp. 104-105.

Warnock, Peter
1998 From Plant Domestication to Phytolith Interpretation: The History of Paleoethnobotany in the Near East, *NEA* 61(4):238-252.

Warren, P.
1972 *Myrtos: An Early Bronze Age Settlement in Crete*, British School of Archaeology, suppl. vol. 7, Thames and Hudson, London.

Watson, Patty Jo
1995 Explaining the Transition to Agriculture, In: Price and Gebaur (eds.) *Last Hunters – First Farmers: New Perspectives on the Prehistoric Transition to Agriculture*, School of American Research Press, Santa Fe, pp. 21-37

Weinfeld, Moshe
1996 The Use of Oil in the Cult of Ancient Israel, In: Eitam and Heltzer (eds.) *Olive Oil in Antiquity: Israel and Neighbouring Countries from the Neolithic to the Early Arab Period*, History of the Ancient Near East/Studies - Vol. VII, Sargon, Padova, pp. 125-128.

Werner, Louis
2001 Zillij in Fez, *Saudi Aramco World* 52(3):18-31

White, K.D.
1970 *Roman Farming*, Cornell University Press, Ithaca.

White, K.D.
1984 *Greek and Roman Technology*, Cornell University Press, Ithica.

Wilson, D.G.
1983 The carbonization of weed seeds and their representation in macrofossil assemblages. In: *Plants and Ancient Man: Studies in paleoethnobotany*, Van Zeist and Casparie (eds.), Balkema, Boston, pp. 201-206.

Wolf, Eric
1966 *Peasants*, Prentice Hall, Englewood Cliffs.

Wolff, Samuel R.
1976 Ancient Wine and Olive Oil Industries in Palestine, unpublished Master's paper, Department of Near Eastern Languages and Civilizations, University of Chicago.

103

Wolff, Samuel R.
1996　Oleoculture and Olive Oil Presses in Phoenician North Africa, In: Eitam and Heltzer (eds.) *Olive Oil in Antiquity: Israel and Neighbouring Countries from the Neolithic to the Early Arab Period*, History of the Ancient Near East/Studies - Vol. VII, Sargon, Padova, pp. 129-136.

Wright, Patti
2003　Preservation or destruction of plant remains by carbonization? *JAS* 30(5):577-583.

Zayadine, Fawzi
1982　Recent Excavations at Petra (1979-81), *Annual of the Department of Antiquities XXVI*, Royal Jordanian Department of Antiquities, Amman, pp. 365-393.

Zemer, Avshalom
1978　*Storage Jars in Ancient Sea Trade, Second Printing Revised*, The National Maritime Museum Foundation, Haifa.

Zisling, Yael
2000　Introduction, *Gems in Israel* (www.GemsinIsrael.com), Oct.-Nov. 2000.

Zisling, Yael
2000　Israel Oil Industry Museum, *Gems in Israel* (www.GemsinIsrael.com), Oct.-Nov. 2000.

Zohary, Michael
1982a　*Plants of the Bible*, Cambridge University Press, New York.

Zohary, Michael
1982b　*Vegetation of Israel and Adjacent Areas*, Reichert, Wiesbaden.

Zohary, Daniel
1986　The Origin and Early Spread of Agriculture in the Old World, In: Barigozzi (ed.), *The Origin and Domestication of Cultivated Plants*, Amsterdam, pp.3-20.

Zohary, Daniel and Maria Hopf
2000　*Domestication of Plants in the Old World, Third Edition*, Oxford University Press, Oxford.

Zohary, Daniel and Pinhas Spiegel-Roy
1975　Beginnings of Fruit Growing in the Old World, *Science* 187:319-327.

Zuckerman, Daphna
2000　Experimental Archaeology at Sha'ar Hagolan: A Reconstruction of Neolithic Pottery Production in the Jordan Valley, *NEA* 63(1):45-50.

www.ingramcontent.com/pod-product-compliance
Lightning Source LLC
Chambersburg PA
CBHW061007030426

42334CB00033B/3399

9781407300498